The New Online Investor

The New Online Investor

The Revolution Continues

2nd edition

Peter Temple

www.new-online-investor.co.uk

JOHN WILEY & SONS, LTD

CHICHESTER • NEW YORK • WEINHEIM • BRISBANE • SINGAPORE • TORONTO

Copyright © 2000 by John Wiley & Sons Ltd,
Baffins Lane, Chichester,
West Sussex PO19 1UD, England

National   01243 779777
International   (+44) 1243 779777
e-mail (for orders and customer service enquiries): cs-books@wiley.co.uk
Visit our Home Page on http://www.wiley.co.uk
         or http://www.wiley.com

Other Wiley Editorial Offices

John Wiley & Sons, Inc., 605 Third Avenue,
New York, NY 10158-0012, USA

WILEY-VCH Verlag GmbH, Pappelallee 3,
D-69469 Weinheim, Germany

Jacaranda Wiley Ltd, 33 Park Road, Milton,
Queensland 4064, Australia

John Wiley & Sons (Asia) Pte Ltd, 2 Clementi Loop #02-01,
Jin Xing Distripark, Singapore 129809

John Wiley & Sons (Canada) Ltd, 22 Worcester Road,
Rexdale, Ontario M9W 1L1, Canada

British Library Cataloguing in Publication Data

A catalogue record for this book is available from the British Library

ISBN 0-471-99877-X

Typeset in 11/13 Palatino by Dorwyn Ltd, Rowlands Castle, Hants.
Printed and bound in Great Britain by Bookcraft (Bath) Ltd, Midsomer Norton.
This book is printed on acid-free paper responsibly manufactured from sustainable forestry, in
which at least two trees are planted for each one used for paper production.

Contents

Acknowledgements

This book was written in Microsoft Word, for the most part on a Dell desktop PC, with tables produced using Microsoft Access and Microsoft Excel.

Web page and software images used as illustrations throughout the book were captured using Nildram Software's screen capture package Screen Thief for Windows and were accessed via an Internet connection from U-Net. The New Online Investor web site (www.new-online-investor.co.uk) was created using Microsoft Publisher and is hosted by CIX.

Illustrations are reproduced by kind permission of the owners and operators of the relevant web sites and/or software products, as follows (in order of appearance in the book):

Winsite.com; San Jose Mercury News; Charles Stanley and Co.; Securities & Exchange Commission; U-Net; PKWare; Northern Light; FIND; MoneyWorld; Qualisteam; DejaNews; The Motley Fool; Liszt; Newsnow; Euromoney Publications; Datastream/ICV; DBC; Ionic Information; ICB; Hemmington Scott; Strathclyde University and Sheila Webber; CIX; WPP Group plc; Microsoft; Investor AB; Logica plc; Richard Holway Ltd; Euro Sales Finance plc; GE Inc.; Datek; Xolia.com; ESI/E*Trade (UK); Charles Schwab Europe; Stocktrade; AAA Investment Guide; iii, Trustnet; Equitable Life; Nationwide plc; LIFFE; OM Group; Union CAL; The Underground Software Group; Kauders; JP Morgan; Dr Ed Yardeni and Deutsche Bank Securities New York; Lombard Street Research; Sarasin Investment Management; and HM Treasury.

Preface

The net can set you free: free to control your own personal finances and make investment decisions on the basis of high-quality information. More to the point, perhaps, not only can it set you free, but a lot of the net (as the Internet has become known) *is* free.

I did not foresee, when I wrote the original *Online Investor* in 1997, the phenomenal success of services such as Freeserve, Hotmail and others that operate without visible means of financial support. There are successful businesses on the world wide web (the Internet's 'library' of linked online information) that take money from subscribers, and there are those that have tried to. But net users resist paying for content. So the most common model is a free service supported by advertising you can choose to ignore.

The drawback to the web, though, is that there is *so much* content. Though free, much of the content is irrelevant or trivial or out of date. You need to know how to look for what is up to date and important to you. We hope this book will show you how.

Readers of this book who also read *The Online Investor* will find some major differences between the two. One is that I have focused to a much greater extent and, I hope, in a more systematic way on the provision of information by companies: which companies have web sites, and how good, bad or indifferent they are.

In doing this, I have tried to look at the sites dispassionately, scoring each one out of 10 on the basis of their specific features and on their ease of use. The main results of this research is presented in Chapter 6. The sizeable corporate web site database that contains the research information—called CoWeS—is available on diskette for £100 plus VAT. Email cowes@ptassoc.u-net.com for further details.

I have used the same approach in a number of other areas, assessing the characteristics of online press sites, brokers, exchanges and personal finance providers, among others. In each category I have tried to focus on the key characteristics that are important for online investors. The approach sometimes produces surprising results, with some well-known names scoring less well than perhaps they should.

However, web sites are constantly changing and inspecting all the sites included in our database on a regular basis is a full-time task. There is an inevitable time lag between the approval of final proofs and the book appearing on the shelf. Most of the initial research on the sites was conducted in late 1998 and from January to May 1999, with the sites revisited in September 1999.

As was the case with the original *Online Investor*, I have had to assume that the reader will have some knowledge of the basics of computing and investment. However, the appendix contains some notes on the history of the Internet and how it works, written in non-technical language. For those who consider themselves novice investors, my book *Getting Started in Shares*, also published by John Wiley, provides some essential background. Experienced net users can skip Chapter 2, Chapter 3 and the Appendix on page 257.

A short directory of sites mentioned is provided at the end of the book. But as the web changes so rapidly, I have created a web site specifically devoted to the book, with links to all the sites included in the database mentioned earlier and those others mentioned in these pages. The site can be found at www.new-online-investor.co.uk (click on 'linksite').

Finally, a few words of thanks. As noted in the preface to the first *Online Investor*, Nick Wallwork provided the original encouragement for a book of this type. Nick now works for John Wiley in Singapore. For *The New Online Investor*, the mantle was taken up by Sally Smith, who has offered constant support for this new version. I should also like to thank all of those companies who responded to my periodic requests for details of their plans for corporate web sites. Their responses have enabled the book to be as up to date as it is possible to be with subject matter of this type.

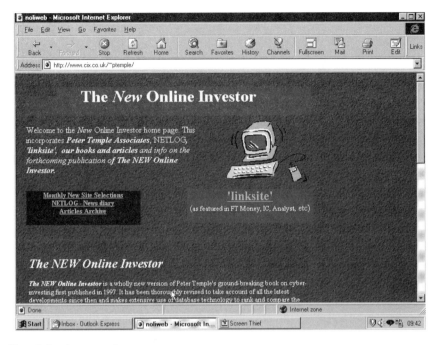

The New Online Investor site

Simon London at the *Financial Times* and Jeremy Utton at *Analyst* have given me the opportunity to test out in print some of the ideas in this book and their help is gratefully acknowledged.

My wife Lynn has worked as a more or less full-time researcher for this book, doing much of the work in designing, compiling and maintaining the underlying web site database. Without her help, this book would have taken much longer to complete.

Peter Temple
September 1999

CHAPTER 1

Why Online Investing?

When the first version of this book was written two to three years ago, the idea of using computers to retrieve information related to investment was a novel idea. Now it is less so, but online investors, though there are more of them, still remain in a minority even in the USA.

Yet the advantages of using online sources of information are even more apparent now than they were then. There are more web sites devoted to business and financial news and share prices, and more company web sites containing financial information than ever before. Web-based dealing services have become increasingly available. Information on life and pensions products is widely disseminated on the web. Even the staidest of insurance companies have a web presence

As I remarked at the beginning of the first version of this book, in the definitive history of the twentieth century the invention of the microprocessor and the advent of affordable computing power will rank alongside jet air travel and splitting the atom as the most revolutionary events of the era.

Computers are everywhere. We use them unconsciously—in cars, TVs, electronic calculators, personal organisers and CD players. Desktop computing power and sophisticated software is prevalent in offices and increasingly in ordinary homes.

A secondary aspect of the computer revolution, and what this book is largely about, relates to the invention of the modem and the ability it brings to transmit information between computers. For the uninitiated, a modem (short for MOdulator/DEModulator) transmits data from one computer to another by turning it into a form that can be sent down a telephone line to be received by another modem. It is then decoded and accessed by the user of the receiving computer.

Thanks to the modem we can now connect networks of computers, which has led to the Internet, email and the world wide web.

If you live in the developed world you would have had to have been remarkably reclusive not to have heard about the Internet and the world wide web. In the UK at the moment it is estimated that one in four households has a computer and one in four of those has two or more. But, even now, a good five years or more after the first stirrings of the Internet revolution in popular consciousness, I still find myself being surprised by pockets of ignorance about the medium, even among those seeking to market their products through it.

Some comments have been made about this revolution's potential significance for investors, but much of what has been written has been limited in scope. This book focuses on using free information from online sources to aid investment decision making. But it also tries to highlight differences in quality between the different sources.

I said in the first version of this book that using the web could 'level the investment playing field'. If used systematically, online and especially web-based information can allow investors to make decisions on the basis of information that approaches the same quality and timeliness as that used by professional investors. It is perfectly possible to assemble a detailed dossier on a company in which you might want to invest quickly, easily and free of charge using online sources.

I shall try to avoid wherever possible the use of computer jargon (but see the Glossary at the back of the book) and to describe what can be done, the information sources and services available, how to reach them and how good or bad they are, in as simple terms as possible.

Investors Need Online Information

The periodic turbulence of financial markets may from time to time put off previously enthusiastic stock market punters. But even in Europe, where stock market investing in shares is a much less important part of life than it is in the USA, many individuals have a good part of their wealth invested in financial assets of one sort or another.

In the UK, the PEP (personal equity plan) revolution has left many investors with sizeable tax free capital still invested, typically through collective investments such as unit trusts. ISAs (individual savings accounts)—PEP's successor—will doubtless continue the trend. Many individuals benefit from pension schemes, either through their employers or, increasingly, via personal pension schemes, which in turn are invested in the securities markets through unit trusts and other forms of investment. And for those who prefer more predictable investments, it is perhaps worth pointing out that the online information revolution also encompasses the bond markets

In the UK, as elsewhere in the world, the privatisation story is a well-known one. But though the flow of privatisations has now dried up, its effect has been to leave many individuals with small parcels of shares tucked away in the bottom drawer. The result has been at least a partial removing of the traditional uncertainty that many individuals may have had about the idea of owning shares. With some exceptions, profits on privatisation shares held over the long term have been significant. Yet there have been few perceived incentives for these embryonic investors to find out more about the general investment scene or about the possibility of investing in other companies. Volatility in global financial markets hardly alters that perception.

The popular and partly correct view is that investment professionals always have the upper hand, not only in terms of their financial fire-power but also in their access to information. But events have often proved that this does not necessarily mean that they always get it right: while having access to information is important, it is how that information is interpreted that is the crucial point. Not being able to react in a split second to the latest news can sometimes be a positive advantage.

In the past, the average individual may have felt that his or her nest-egg was better off invested by a professional through the medium of a unit trust or some such other collective vehicle rather than through a do-it-yourself approach to investing. Recent market volatility and the successes chalked up by so-called 'tracker' funds, which simply mimic the movement of the index, have thoroughly debunked the idea that fund managers have the edge. And if you, like many others, have collective investments such as unit trusts, the web is a great place to check discreetly on how your unit trust manager is doing relative to his or her peers, and what new investment products are on offer.

In *The Online Investor* I roundly castigated the Stock Exchange and the City in general for ignoring the interests of the small investor. I am pleased to say that over the past two years there have been signs—born largely out of self-interest, it has to be said—that have shown that some quarters of the broking community have taken to the web. The reason is the obvious one that it is a cheap and easy way of connecting with their clients and attracting new ones, whether or not the broker goes the whole way and launches an online dealing service. The Stock Exchange, after some years of trying to ignore the web, decided to use the new medium as a means of promoting greater awareness in shares, through its 'Share Aware' campaign and related web site, ironically launched at almost exactly the same time as a market peak in mid 1998.

Whether or not the initiative goes on, in calmer times, to attract new investors into the market, the fact remains that there are plenty of existing 'low-key' investors around, dating either from the privatisation era or from earlier involvement in new issues (when their participation was encouraged, rather than the opposite). They are 'one-time' investors who may not have thought of using their personal computer (PC) as a means of accessing information on shares and putting those languishing share certificates to work.

Equally, there are many long-standing and experienced investors who remain to be fully converted to the merits of using computers to further their investment habit and to access information on the shares they hold, or might be interested in buying. Having said that, surveys of Internet use do point to a category of affluent elderly users, so-called 'silver surfers', who are technologically aware and have the time to spend longer on the web than most.

It is to these three categories of investor or potential investor that this book is primarily addressed. In other words, it seeks to kindle the interest of the normal computer-literate person in the process of investment, whether in stocks, bonds, or unit trusts, through using a PC to access online information and services. And it seeks to explain to the already serious and experienced private investors how using a computer and online services can improve their own investment performance.

There may be a fourth category, too: the young computer-literate person, already tuned in to the online world, who is tempted to view the investment process simply as akin to another video game, all the more interesting because it is played with real money. Such investors will doubtless have had an interesting time of it in the markets in the last couple of years. To this category of reader, I must stress that there is more to the investment process than this, and it is essential to take time to read up on investment techniques before embarking on investment decisions with real money. John Wiley & Sons publishes a number of texts on the subject, including my own book *Getting Started in Shares* (1996).

Reading that book in conjunction with this one would be a good way for the computer buff-cum-first-time investor to get a grounding in investment techniques and in the way in which online information and services can be used to practise the art of investment and make better decisions.

Online Investing Defined

Before going any further, let's define precisely what we mean by online investing. This is not, for example, a book about using computers to chart share prices and make decisions using the various types of investment-oriented software available. (Having said that, there is software available to do this, free of charge on the web, and Chapter 5 will tell you where to find it. Nor is this book solely about using the Internet and world wide web for accessing investment information, although that is perhaps its most important aspect.

To qualify for inclusion in the book, an information source or service has to be available online. That is, it has to be accessible by modem, or by some other electronic or broadcast means. This could be via the Internet and world wide web, but also via a CD-ROM, through a private network, or through satellite, TV, pager, or other mobile technology.

This book is written primarily for readers in the UK and Europe. In the USA, using electronic means to access data on shares and to trade them is much further advanced. When the first version of this book was published in 1997, Internet and world wide web content was still heavily orientated towards US investors, although non-US content was growing quickly. Now there is a much greater availability of content of relevance to online investors in Europe, whether they are the corporate web sites of UK and European companies, UK-based investment bulletin boards (where interested parties can post messages), UK and European news sources, and so on. However, this book includes some examples of the ways in which online information is available from US sources, as well as ones that are more important to international and UK-based investors. And it is relatively easy for investors based in the UK to get online the information needed to make investment decisions on US companies.

Private investors should, I think, welcome this globalisation of investment, provided they stick to developed markets like the USA and continental Europe and deal with a broker that can offer a dealing service in these markets and the ancillary facilities to go with it. Investors do, however, need to be aware that the currency factor produces an added dimension to international investing. Stock market profits (and losses) can be eroded by a depreciating currency or enhanced by one that is increasing in value.

Having said that, this aspect of the online investing revolution does not yet appear to have caught on to any degree. Particularly in times of market turbulence, investors seem to prefer to stick to the companies with which they are most familiar. And of course there is nothing wrong with that, particularly if those companies are increasingly getting more investor-friendly by using the web to disseminate investor information.

The Advantages of Online Investing

Even though the mechanics of online investing are scarcely forbidding to anyone with an average degree of computer literacy, why is it worth pursuing the concept in the first place? The answer is that online investing has certain distinct advantages. We'll look later at exactly what capturing these advantages costs, but for the moment let's focus on the benefits.

The advantages of online investing can be grouped into five broad areas: speed, comprehensiveness, cost, convenience, and enlarged investment horizons.

Speed

Few new users are really prepared for the sheer speed with which data can be transferred from or to a remote computer using a modem. Downloading—transmitting information from the web onto my own computer—price data for all the shares listed in London and updating my database of share prices takes only a few seconds every evening.

Depending on the capabilities of your modem, downloading a basic software program might take five minutes or less. A good rule of thumb is that a standard 56K modem will download 100,000 bytes of data in around 30 seconds. Note that it is mainly the performance characteristics of the modem that governs the speed of the data download, rather than the speed of the receiving computer's processor or the size of its memory. So buy the fastest modem you can afford.

The advantages of using online information sources are already obvious. Taking the capturing of share price data as an example, compare my five-second download by modem to the time it would take you to manually enter 2000 share prices into separate datafiles in your PC, and the boredom involved in doing so day after day.

Similarly, acquiring a software program through conventional means might involve scanning through several different catalogues, choosing the right program for the purpose, sending for a demo disk, installing it in your PC, and then deciding whether or not to buy the full version. The online investor is able to view details of a program on screen, download a demo version in the time it takes to have a short coffee break, install it, check out how it works, and if necessary order the full working version online and download that, all within hours.

And in the future, technological advances offer the opportunity of even faster download speeds via new generations of modems and other technological advances, and even the option of accessing the web through the humble TV or handheld devices such as mobile phones and electronic organisers.

Comprehensiveness

It is no exaggeration to say that online information and services, particularly world wide web sites, are expanding at an exponential rate. A recent survey counted 56 million host computers linked to the Internet, any one of which could be home to thousands of files and hundreds of web sites. It is often said, for instance that there is roughly one web site per Internet user. A reasonably definitive estimate in October 1998 was that there were 150 million Internet users worldwide. What's the figure now?

Think of a number. One sober source has suggested that the 150 million could double to 300 million by 2002, but this could easily be overtaken by events. Some estimates suggest there are now 400 million web pages.

As an example of comprehensiveness, the popular Winsite (www. winsite.com) web site (by no means the largest) contains hundreds of thousands of different pieces of free software. No more hit and miss program buying on the basis of vague newspaper advertisements.

Another example is the London International Financial Futures Exchange (LIFFE) web site (www.liffe.com), which offers closing price and volatility data on every single equity and index option series traded on the exchange. Over 90% of the FTSE 100 constituent companies, 29 out of 30 Dow Jones index companies, and many other listed companies around the world have web sites providing financial data and other information including online annual reports, press releases, statistics and so on. Sites which have price data available during market hours (normally slightly delayed from real time) have multiplied in number over the past couple of years.

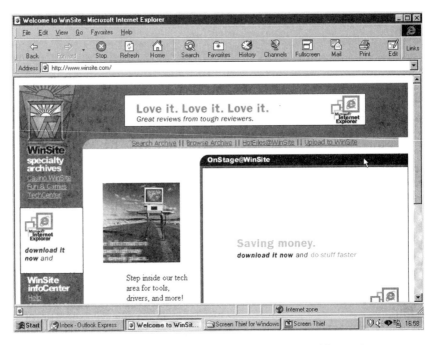

Figure 1.1   The popular Winsite web site contains a vast amount of free software

Assembling and storing this information in the conventional paper-based form is a huge task. But online, all you need do is access the web site of your favourite company and get the latest information delivered straight to your PC.

Cost

Online investing is a low-cost activity. The Internet and world wide web offer huge information resources at little or no cost. An online connection for unlimited use may cost in the region of £10–£15 per month plus telephone charges at local call rates. The past year has seen a dramatic upsurge in free Internet connection services, although some of these have their drawbacks (which we will look at later). And although there are services—for instance, access to some news sites—on the web that require subscriptions, very often a restricted (through still useful) version is available free of charge. In any case, charges made for online services tend to be low and the services offered are ones that would normally be out of reach of the average UK private investor.

Some of the best examples of free information are online newspapers and magazines. Most successful investors are avid readers, studying several newspapers each day, and several investment magazines and newsletters. Many of these are now available online free of charge. For instance, the UK online investor can read the City pages of *The Times*, the *Daily Telegraph*, the *Financial Times* and the *Daily Mail* and *Evening Standard* for free. If you have broader horizons you can browse the *LA Times* or Silicon Valley's own *San Jose Mercury News*. On the Continent, *Le Monde*, *Die Welt* and many other papers have online editions.

Many US magazines—*Forbes*, for instance—keep archives of past articles that are available free, even though getting an up-to-date online copy of the publication may necessitate a subscription. But online newspapers are—for the moment, at least—predominantly funded by advertising. They enable you to avoid an excessive paper bill and yet still be well informed.

Convenience

It should be obvious from the above examples that one of the really compelling aspects of online investing is that data, news, software programs,

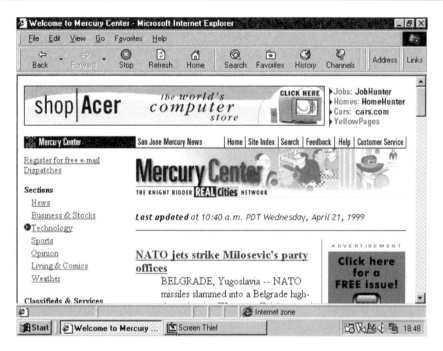

Figure 1.2   The San Jose Mercury News web site

and other information can be gathered electronically without the need for much physical effort. The information is stored online and can be retrieved as necessary. The updating is done for you.

Information downloaded from the Internet and other online sources can also quickly be incorporated into existing software with the minimum of effort and technical knowledge. If you wish to spend more time researching stocks and less time tramping the streets to the paper shop, the library, or the local software supplier, this is a compelling advantage. On a personal level, I have worked from home for over 11 years. As I have become more familiar with the online world, the time I have saved in visits of this nature has been astonishing. I have also been able to gain access to information sources I might never have thought of before. My productivity both as a writer and as a practising private investor has been improved immeasurably as a result of getting connected to the online world.

Broader Horizons

This brings me to another advantage of online investing. As well as enabling you to obtain information about the domestic stock market, it is an inevitable part of using online sources that you will also gain access to information on other markets, different types of securities, and new investment ideas and techniques that might otherwise have gone unnoticed.

This can be at the simple level of being exposed to information about, say, US companies, or the ability to access information about shares, bonds, software, investment books, newsletters, and other publications on a much wider scale than that simply encompassed by national boundaries.

National boundaries mean little in the online world and, as the habit of online investing spreads, this is likely to spill over into the stocks that private investors deal in, the brokers they deal with, what their software and data costs, the nature and price of the information they use, and in many other ways.

This should not be a source of concern provided that you follow sound investment disciplines. This can, of course, be easier said than done. But sticking to good disciplines is important whether or not you use online information or traditional paper-based ones. Online information is just more convenient and cheaper.

Private versus Professional Investor

It is no exaggeration to say that the UK private investor has had a raw deal from the City and the corporate sector over many years. This is true despite the strides that have been made in the past two or three years in the provision of information via the web.

The exception is the advent of cheap execution-only dealing, which even before the web had genuinely cut costs for the small investors. The web has continued to put downward pressure on commission levels to the benefit of pretty well all investors. This example aside, the City has often been a pretty unfriendly and unhelpful place to private investors, particularly those with comparatively modest sums to invest.

On the one hand the small investor has been seen as a convenient target for the flood of privatisation issues and other large-scale flotations emanating from the Square Mile. On the other, despite official lip-service being paid to wider share ownership, in most other respects the private investor has remained at a significant disadvantage to the professional. This has been especially true in terms of access to the technology to help value shares. Prompt access to the flow of news and information that move share prices day by day has often been out of the reach of many small investors.

Online investing presents an opportunity to private investors—at relatively low cost—to remove some of these disadvantages. The online revolution is very definitely well under way, but it still has some distance to go. And it arguably needs greater co-operation from the corporate sector to benefit the private investor fully. Some organisations and companies, such as the Treasury, Kingfisher, Severn-Trent, WPP and others, are showing the way, but a lot remains be done, especially among medium-sized and smaller listed companies. As usual, US companies lead the way in providing information online to private shareholders.

Many UK companies have a web site, although some do not seem to have been designed with communicating with investors in mind. We will point out some of the worst offenders later.

That said, times are changing. Some companies now offer the facility for broadcast email of press releases and other company announcements. Internet-broadcast analyst briefings are technically feasible and will be increasingly adopted. It is now commonplace for some companies to make available via the company web site copies of the slides presented at analyst meetings.

For those who are still not convinced about the virtues of the online revolution, we'll look briefly at a number of ways in which the facilities and information open to private investors differs from those available to the professionals and how the online revolution is helping to level the playing field for the small investor.

The differences can be isolated in a number of different categories, including: software, share prices, fundamental data, economic and company news, dealing, and relationships with companies.

Software

The *professional investor* has access to the latest versions of highly sophisticated technical analysis software and vast computing power to help analyse share prices and make investment decisions. This does not stop traders making mistakes, of course, but it arguably gives them an edge.

The *private investor* has the choice of a few packages, usually advertised each week in investor magazines such as the *Investors' Chronicle*. Few of these magazines are available through high street retailers. Comparative information about them is difficult to obtain and the investor ends up making the decision on the basis of imperfect information, perhaps buying a package that is unsuitable for his or her needs.

As an *online investor*, with software packages available on the Internet and world wide web, you have easy access to a wider range of programs. You can download demo versions and can tap into software that previously may only have been sold to US investors (care must obviously be taken to make sure that software packages like this can use data downloaded from non-US sources). The availability of online software makes it more likely that, as an online investor, you will be able to choose a package closer to that used by the professional, or at the very least one that is precisely tailored to your needs, at an affordable price.

Share Prices

The *professional investor* has the advantage of price display systems that relay price changes as they happen. These real-time services are often integrated with sophisticated technical analysis packages. The ability to view share price changes as they happen is something of a two-edged sword. While this facility is essential for 'day-trading', for longer-term investors it can be a distraction. Professionals and private investors alike have to try and ignore the short-term volatility of the market and focus on underlying trends and values.

Real-time price feeds are expensive, too, so much so that they are beyond the reach of all but a few private investors. In the past this has given the professional an information advantage in the market, particularly when shares react to price-sensitive information.

The *private investor* faces two problems. One is getting hold of up-to-date daily price information on which to make trading decisions and gauge the underlying state of the market. The second is obtaining cheap price data that can be fed into whichever technical analysis package is being used.

The wish to keep in touch with prices during the day can be solved in part by simply using the normal teletext services—which each have their roster of share prices updated several times daily. These can be supplemented if necessary by the telephone services such as FT Cityline, which give up-to-date share price quotes.

Investment decisions made by individual investors are in any case rarely improved by having access to real-time prices. It is difficult enough for the average investor to act in a way that is contrary to the 'crowd'—as is often necessary—if he or she is bombarded by a stream of prices suggesting that doing the opposite may be best.

So the major problem the private investor faces is obtaining comprehensive share price and trading volume data to download at a price that is cost-effective. Downloading prices from teletext is both free and more reliable than it once was, but its absence of volume data makes it less than satisfactory for many investors.

The *online investor* has some extra options available. Due to a change in charging policy by the London Stock Exchange shortly after *The Online Investor* was first published in 1997, basic end-of-day data is now freely available either at no cost or at a very nominal price. Some services bundle together price data and fundamental data in the same package. Data can be delivered either over the web or via email.

Online investors in the USA have long had the benefit of cheap data to feed into technical analysis packages, and exchanges there have been rewarded by increased trading by private investors as a result. This lesson is now being learnt in the UK, and electronic dissemination of share price data is beginning to make its presence felt as a cost-effective solution for the ordinary private investor.

Things have also changed for day-to-day prices. Free services now exist where continually updated 20-minute delayed prices are available which, for the reasons stated above, are probably as good as most private investors will ever usually need. Services such as Yahoo! Finance, Market Eye, Moneyworld and others make it easy for investors to check the price of leading stocks, or any that they might have an interest in, as little or as often they want to during the trading day at no charge. Some web-based brokers (Charles Stanley's Xest service is an example) offer their clients free access to real-time prices and news.

Fundamental Data

The *professional investor* has a variety of means available by which to obtain and analyse fundamental information, especially company accounts data.

Figure 1.3 Charles Stanley's Xest web site provides real-time prices and news

These include large online databases of accounts information and share price data maintained by organisations such as Reuters and DataStream, electronic Extel Cards analysing company accounts data, electronic access to reports from brokers' analysts, and a variety of other sources.

The *private investor* traditionally has had to rely on newspapers and magazines to get hold of fundamental information, supplemented by tips from friends or a stockbroker. Few private investors even go so far as buying reference publications, or telephone a company to obtain copies of the annual report.

The *online investor* can make this process relatively painless and more systematic. Reference publications such as the *The Company Guide*, published by Hemmington Scott, are increasingly being published in CD-ROM and online forms and, for those interested in investment trusts and unit trusts, there are web sites which enable large databases of fund performance data to be searched free of charge for those precisely matching particular requirements. Those wanting detailed analysis can find a pay-per-view version of the Company REFS financial statistics service also available at the Hemmington Scott web site (www.hemscott.com).

One possibility for the future—although seemingly still as far away as it was at the time *The Online Investor* was first published—is that the UK will be able to follow the lead of the USA in making the data contained in statutory company filings available online free of charge. The EDGAR database of the US Securities & Exchange Commission (SEC) is an online equivalent of the UK's Companies House. US listed companies now have to file their accounts information and other statutory documents electronically.

EDGAR (www.sec.gov/edgarhp/htm) is a searchable electronic resource that enables an online investor anywhere in the world to access up-to-date information on any listed company in the USA.

Will the UK's Companies House follow suit and simplify and cheapen the means by which ordinary investors can access company information, at least for listed companies and their subsidiaries, without a physical visit to its Bloomsbury premises? It looks as though it may.

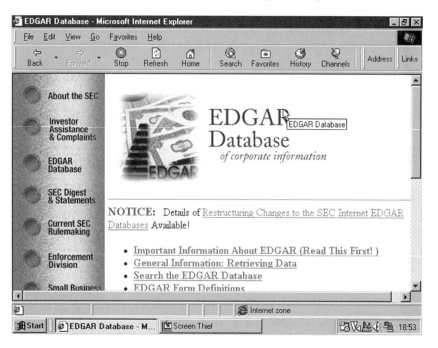

Figure 1.4   Use EDGAR to find information on US listed companies

The Companies House site (www.companies-house.gov.uk) now includes the ability to search by company name, with the database returning brief details, including the company number, after which the full details can be ordered by telephone. This ordering process is set to move onto the web in due course, although information is unlikely to be made available free of charge.

Economic and Company News

The *professional investor* has access to instantaneous company news on-screen from services such as Reuters, Bridge and Bloomberg, as well as the regulatory service relating to company announcements emanating from the Stock Exchange. This gives professional investors a significant edge. The cost of services of this type in the form in which they are used by the professionals is prohibitive for the average private investor.

The *private investor* has traditionally relied on daily newspapers, supplemented during the day by teletext and TV news bulletins, to obtain information of this type. However, these services are somewhat selective in their coverage, and slower to distribute time-sensitive information. Services like Datastream/ICV's real-time Market Eye service provide rapid and accurate coverage of economic and company news, but they are expensive and out of reach of many private investors.

The *online investor* can meet this problem half way. Internet editions of various quality newspapers enable the rival City pages to be scanned for titbits of news each day, while several web sites provide free access to major news stories relating to business and finance and of interest to investors. For instance, Yahoo! Finance (http://finance.yahoo.co.uk) contains regularly updated wire service stories. These services are evolving rapidly as time goes by. One particularly interesting development is an electronic mailing list operated by the Treasury, which distributes Treasury announcements by email to those who request it.

Dealing

The *professional investor* has the advantage of direct electronic access to large securities houses and electronic order books such as the UK's SETS

(Stock exchange Electronic Trading System) and Tradepoint, offering the ability to transact orders instantaneously, invariably electronically.

The *private investor* has traditionally had a telephone-based service from a broker. This relies on the broker answering the telephone promptly, providing accurate market prices on which to base dealing decisions, as well as producing valuations and other services.

The *online investor* still has to deal through a broker, but can do this via a PC without the need for human contact with a dealer. With the advent of the SETS order book and related improvements to the speed with which so-called 'retail' share orders can be transacted, several firms have launched Internet-based share dealing services, and more are in the pipeline.

This mirrors developments in the USA where services of this type are now reputed to handle approaching half of the orders placed by private investors. All services like this are secure and password protected and typically work in conjunction with a money market account to enable settlement to be effected quickly without the need for cheques and certificates passing back and forth.

Though commission charges for services of this type in the UK are comparable with those of conventional execution-only services, eventually—as has happened in the USA—competition will drive commission rates down further, reflecting the cost-saving convenience of the service for the broker. One online broking executive is on record as expecting commission rates in the UK to halve by 2002.

Relationships with Companies

The *professional investor* has traditionally had many advantages in dealing with companies. One big one takes the form of privileged access to management, at one time via one-on-one meetings but now almost exclusively through large-scale briefings for brokers and institutional investors.

Here price-sensitive information may be disclosed but it is considered to be disseminated sufficiently widely not to result in charges of insider dealing by those present who might act on it. On a more mundane level, press releases on company results and other announcements are distributed rapidly to City institutions.

The *private investor* has never been part of this process, except in the sense of being able to attend the company's annual shareholder meeting.

The private investor does not normally receive corporate press releases and is left to receive a printed copy of the appropriate announcement some time later or read the news in the City pages.

The *online investor* over the past few years has seen in the case of many companies a dramatic improvement over this unsatisfactory state of affairs. More and more companies now have web sites at which shareholders and other interested parties can view or download press releases and other company news and documents. Such a system is so easy to implement that it is worthwhile asking whether if companies do not provide such a service as a minimum they are really worth serious attention for investors.

A system like this, together with automatic email lists, which push out press releases simultaneously to those registered to receive them, goes a long way towards rectifying the problem keenly felt by many private investors: that the information 'playing field' is tilted too steeply in favour of the professional.

As noted previously, it is also possible for online investors to log on easily to a video or audio version of the meetings that companies hold with analysts. This will enable a much wider audience to hear management's response to the probing questions that are typically posed at these meetings. Such links are already technically feasible.

One important requirement to make these things happen is the goodwill of the listed company sector, which one hopes see that well-designed corporate web sites can promote its image very effectively and provide useful information for all classes of investor. There is also surely a case for arguing that the Stock Exchange or Companies Act should make it obligatory for companies to facilitate a broader electronic dissemination of shareholder information.

The Purpose of this Book

The previous pages should have given some indications as to how an online investor can gain cheap access to more information than a private investor operating in a more traditional way.

The following chapters cover how to get connected to the online world and how much it will cost. We look in more detail at the differing banks of information the online investor has at his or her fingertips. In most cases accessing the Internet and the online sources of information it offers is not expensive. Online sources can save time and substitute for more expensive 'hard-copy' forms of information.

The technicalities of getting connected and how to use the web effectively are not too forbidding and will be covered in the next two chapters. Thereafter I examine in turn the various facets of online information and the investment process, looking in detail at the online sites available, the information they contain, and how useful they are at helping an investor gain access to up-to-date information and services.

Throughout this book there are illustrations of world wide web sites, and there are many tables giving an objective comparison of several similar sites in order to provide an overview of the information in a standardised form. Online investors can then decide which sites to visit and which parts of the sites are relevant to their specific information needs. At the end of the book there is a list of Internet addresses mentioned in each chapter. These and many other web links are also available at the New Online Investor web site at www.new-online-investor.co.uk.

My aim is to help private investors gain access to cheap tools that can help improve their investment performance through better information and, in so doing, perhaps even beat the professionals at their own game.

As we said when the first *Online Investor* was published, this is an objective that accords with the laudable goal of widening and deepening share ownership. It is a concept to which many City worthies have paid homage over the years but which, by their action (or inaction) they have done little to advance. The online revolution is gradually taking the process out of their hands and has the power to make private investors in the UK and Europe the force they are in markets such as the USA.

It is a revolution which was long overdue. A start has been made, but there is a lot further to go down the route of levelling the information playing field.

CHAPTER 2

Getting Connected

For all the publicity there may have been about the Internet, taking that first step may still seem somewhat daunting. For the novice, the process of setting up a dial-up networking connection is not always straightforward, although it is somewhat easier in Windows 98 than it was in Windows 95. But it is worth the effort.

Choosing the right Internet service provider (ISP) is also becoming a more complex task. Since the *The Online Investor* was first published the number of ISPs first mushroomed and then subsequently coalesced has mushroomed again and may coalesce further as time goes by. It would be easy, for example, simply to sign up for AOL (America On Line) or CompuServe on the back of the free CDs that arrive periodically in the post or the offers bundled in with a new computer, but they are not necessarily the right providers for you. It needs some thought.

Also needing thought now is whether you sign up for a 'free' service or a paid-for one. 1999 has seen many new 'free' services. In the UK Dixons' Freeserve quickly garnered more than a million users (although not all of them are 'active') and spawned several imitators. At the end of 1999 there are reckoned to be in the region of 18 mainstream free ISPs, and a larger number (perhaps 200 in all) of other 'affinity'-style providers linked to football clubs, newspapers and the like.

The free nature of services like this is slightly misleading. Their economics derive from the presence of advertising which users have no choice but to view, from the call rebates that the provider earns from the telecoms companies who route the calls from users, and from charging heavily for helpdesk services, as well as avoiding the cost associated with billing. Conventional ISPs may cost £10 a month, but many have free helpdesks, the service is advertising-free, and so on.

However, there is little doubt that the advent of free ISP services have added to the UK's Internet-connected user base, and affected the economics of the ISP market. In short, they have made it harder for smaller ISPs to prosper.

Whoever you choose as your ISP, and whatever minor glitches there are in the process of getting connnected, the saving grace of the Internet and world wide web is that it quickly becomes apparent that the effort is well worthwhile. For the most part, other Internet users (with some exceptions) tend to be friendly and supportive to newcomers. This includes the support staff of many service providers (including those providing free help), especially the smaller ones, who respond quickly to queries and manage just the right amount of hand-holding.

This chapter is organised in sections covering:

❒ what you need to get started as an Internet user
❒ how to get connected—including an assessment of the relative merits of individual service providers and their charges
❒ what you get for your money, including a section on using web browsers
❒ some current issues relating to Internet service providers
❒ the profile (according to recent research) of a typical net user and his/her service preferences
❒ some dos and don'ts related to the Internet and how to use it.

What You Need

The very basic answer to the question of what equipment the online investor needs is simple:

❒ a computer
❒ a modem
❒ a telephone line
❒ an Internet service provider (ISP).

We'll deal first with the basic hardware. Computers come in all shape and sizes, so you need to be specific about precisely what is required. One or other service provider can normally offer software compatible with either the Windows (for IBM compatible computers) or Macintosh (for Apple computers) operating systems. But whether you are using an IBM-compatible PC or an Apple machine, there are some other essentials. The comments that follow relate primarily to my own experience using a Windows-based PC.

System memory is an obvious prerequisite. The general rule is probably the more the better. My current system is a Windows 95 PC with 64 Mb of system memory.

The speed of the computer's processor matters also to some degree. Although in theory it is the speed of the modem that governs how quickly web pages download, the computer has to process the images once they are downloaded, and having a low speed PC can slow up the process. My current, slightly ageing system has a 'clock speed' of 233 MHz, which works satisfactorily enough.

But remember, the Internet and world wide web work on the basis of downloading information over a phone line. It is the capacity of the device that does this, the modem, that is currently the potential bottleneck in the process, rather than necessarily the speed with which the information is processed once it has been received.

Hard drive space is another essential. Your system should have a hard drive with plenty of surplus storage space on it. The reason for this is that some of the activities the online investor might be expected to participate in (newsgroups and downloading software are examples) can use up significant quantities of hard drive capacity and it is as well not to be too worried about space. My current system has a 6.4 Gb hard drive which is now more than half full without my really trying consciously to fill it up.

Lastly, it is worth stressing that a full-size (or even outsize) colour monitor is also an essential. Although it is perfectly possible to connect to the Internet and download email from a remote location via a laptop computer, for everyday use a full-size screen makes everything much easier to view. Extra large monitors cost a little more, but can be worthwhile if you intend viewing (or indeed creating) a lot of web pages.

The short answer to most of the questions about basic hardware is that a reasonably up-to-date machine in either Mac or Windows format will do the job perfectly adequately.

Which Modem?

More attention needs to be given to the type of modem. The modem is the device by which the computer communicates with the outside world down a telephone line. Many computers are now being supplied with built-in modems, but also common are modems that are external add-ons to an existing PC.

The modem's function is to translate the information generated by a computer into a signal that can pass down a telephone line to be decoded (or demodulated) by the modem at the other end into the appropriate instructions or information.

Most modems also enable faxes to be received by a computer and transmitted from it, without the need for a stand-alone fax machine. Externally fitted ones usually come supplied with the communications and fax software required to perform these functions, and this is also built into some Windows operating systems such as Windows 95. If not, or if you prefer to use something else, it is perfectly easy to download a free fax driver from the web.

It is a moot point whether a modem and a normal household phone should share the same line. It is perfectly feasible to do this. Provided faxes are not expected to be received at all hours of the day and night (in which case the computer must be kept turned on and the fax software set to automatic for a fax to be received if the machine is unattended) each can coexist without much disturbance to the other, or to the user.

Internet sessions are initiated by the user, unlike faxes which may come in from outside at an unexpected time, so in this respect, too, sharing a line makes little difference. However, if your normal phone line is used for your Internet connection, when you are online the phone will give an engaged tone to a caller.

My own preference is to have a separate telephone line dedicated to fax and Internet use. That also helps keep a realistic check on telephone costs related to the telecommunications aspect of your Internet activities. A phone handset can also be attached and used if need be as an extra line for outgoing calls, or reserved for business use.

But the most important aspect of all is the speed of the modem. Internet users will inevitably experience frustration at the comparatively slow speed at which some web pages download, irrespective of their modem's speed. This is partly due to the level of Internet traffic. For European users, afternoons (when US use is at its peak) can be particularly slow. Nonetheless it is very definitely worth investing the modest extra amount to get the fastest modem possible.

Modem speeds are measured in bits per second (bps). The fastest generally available mass market modems currently run at 56,600 bps and are priced around the £90 mark or less. Although this price is perhaps a little more than the price of the slower 28,800 bps modems, it is a price worth paying.

The slower the modem speed the longer the time needed to stay online to download a specific piece of information, and therefore the higher the telephone charges incurred. Buying a slow modem is false economy if you are planning to use it to access the world wide web on a regular basis.

Credit card sized modems for use in laptop computers are significantly more expensive. You could, at the time of writing, expect to pay upwards of £200 for a 56 K card modem. Many newer laptops come with a built-in modem as part of the package. For true mobility, laptop modems can be upgraded to work with GSM (global system for mobile communications) mobile phones, but at the time of writing data transfer speeds can be slower and using them heavily in this way is costly.

Modem speeds may also increase significantly again in the near future. Modems with a speed of 128 K are a real possibility and modems linked directly to a cable network will be substantially faster than this. At least one UK electricity company is experimenting with the possibility that an Internet connection can be made via a normal domestic electricity circuit in the foreseeable future. Other, so-called 'broadband' services are being developed which will enlarge telecommunications capacity and make speed less of an issue in the future.

How long does it take to download data? In my own case, with a 56 K modem I can reckon on file downloading taking in the region of a minute per 200,000 bytes.

Modems are also a generic product and although there are some well-known brand names, a product from any well-known supplier is probably as good as any other. Well known manufacturers are US Robotics (now owned by 3Com), Pace and Psion Dacom. Modems are available for both Windows and Mac operating systems, but they are not interchangeable, so make sure you specify your system when you buy a modem.

ISDN and ADSL

A more costly but slightly faster alternative to two separate telephone lines is to have installed an ISDN (integrated services digital network) line.

You will need an ISDN card for your PC, or an external terminal adapter, which can cost between £75 and £250, instead of a modem. An ISDN line provides two channels, which means you can hold an ordinary telephone conversation on one while at the same time sending or receiving data down the other. The cost of calls is the same as with an ordinary (analogue) line, but the line rental is higher.

The two great advantages with ISDN, though, is the bandwidth of the link (you can send digital and voice information at speeds of 128 Kb—four to five times the speed of a normal modem) and the speed at which connections can be made and ended. It takes only milliseconds to establish a digital connection, compared to the tens of seconds it takes to set up a call with a modem and analogue line.

A compromise between analogue telephone lines and an ISDN line is to take advantage of BT's Homehighway, which gives you faster access than with a normal analogue line.

BT's new ADSL (asymmetric digital subscriber line) will turn an ordinary telephone line into a high speed digital connection capable of carrying information at between, BT claim, 10 and 40 times the speed of a conventional modem.

Choosing an Internet Service Provider

With computer and modem connected up, the new online investor is now ready to begin trips in cyberspace. What is needed to complete the picture is a connection to the Internet via an ISP.

It is at this point that the next big decision needs to be made. The problem is essentially one of choice. At the last count there were over 200 ISPs in the UK. These ranged from established suppliers with national coverage to those serving specific geographical areas.

Your choice of service provider really depends on what you feel you will require from the service. It is perhaps also worth bearing in mind that many experts expect the number of ISPs to contract due to competitive pressures over the next few years, especially since the advent of competition from free services. This contraction may mean, if you opt for a smaller

ISP, that the service provider you start off with may end up being absorbed by a larger entity.

Some observers even believe that to have a long-term future, an ISP needs to have at least 300,000 subscribers, which only the largest players do. This may be an exaggeration. Smaller ISPs often supplement their Internet access income by offering other activities, such as web design, web site hosting and other 'value-added' services. But there is no question that the advent of the free services referred to earlier has affected the viability of some smaller ISPs.

The choice boils down to making two basic decisions: whether you want your Internet connection supplied with lots of other services and facilities provided by, say, an established bulletin board operator (see below) such as CompuServe or AOL, or whether you want a simple no-frills service that simply gets you onto the net with the minimum of fuss and at low (or no) cost.

In times gone by, bulletin board operators used to offer the choice of an indirect, or 'shell', connection to the net, for those who primarily wished to use their account for accessing the bulletin board operator's conferencing facilities, and a direct Internet connection. These distinctions have all but disappeared, with the established bulletin board systems like CompuServe, AOL and CIX (Compulink Information Exchange) offering access to their conferencing forums and a direct net connection bundled together in the same account.

These direct connections are known as SLIP/PPP (Serial Line Internet Protocol/Point to Point Protocol) connections. PPP connections are now the most common. The reason they are preferable to anything else is that they allow the user to have the basic Internet communications software, known as a TCP/IP (transmission control protocol/Internet protocol) stack, on his or her own computer. In turn this supports a variety of Internet-related programs, including graphics-based web browsers such as Netscape Navigator or Microsoft Internet Explorer, email programs such as Eudora and Microsoft Outlook, and FTP (file transfer protocol) file selection and transfer programs.

Bulletin Board System or No-frills Operator

The evolution of the Internet resulted in three distinct strands of online connection gradually emerging.

One is the basic UNIX system that for years has been (and in some quarters still is) used by academics to communicate with each other, share files and collaborate on research. Many UNIX users continue to use it for basic email and file transfer because once learnt it is easy to use and avoids the frills and fripperies of the web.

The second strand of connection types stems from a newer group of ISPs which offer direct connections to the net and the world wide web but little else. Internet service provision has become a commodity activity and it is hard to distinguish between the services offered by many providers except by the slimmest of margins and nuances. We will examine some of these differences later in this chapter.

The third strand is represented online bulletin board services (BBS). These originally functioned as closed systems, albeit in some instances quite large ones. They allowed subscribers to communicate with each other and to tap into centralised databases of information but not to communicate with the outside world.

Things have changed. Now bulletin board members can log into their host system and tap into resident databases, but these systems have developed into hybrids which also offer these services plus direct net connections and hence the ability to send and receive Internet email and access to the world wide web.

From the standpoint of the online investor, as for any user, the choice is between signing up either with a 'no-frills' service provider, or with a BBS who will not only offer a net connection but other services and information as well. Leaving aside for a moment the question of cost, does it matter which you choose?

In a way it doesn't matter much at all. A no-frills PPP connection, either for around a tenner a month or completely free, may be all you need. On the other hand, UK-based bulletin board systems can be something of an antidote to the heavily US-oriented parts of the Internet that crop up elsewhere.

For example, my own Internet service provider is CIX. In addition to offering a direct Internet connection, CIX, because of its origins as an electronic bulletin board for computer buffs, also offers for the online investor a large number of its own newsgroups that are specifically orientated towards current affairs and to investment, personal finance and investment technology topics.

As the number of non-US users increases at CompuServe and AOL—both global BBS systems—the same is becoming true there too. Many other ISPs that originally started up as BBS systems to serve special interest groups can probably also claim the same.

The following section addresses in more detail the issue of who to choose, what it all costs, and what you get for your money—if indeed you pay for your service.

UK ISPs

UK Internet service providers fall into two categories: those who operate primary Internet capacity via fixed links to the Internet 'backbone', and secondary providers who lease capacity from them.

Primary providers include organisations such as BT, Cable & Wireless, Demon, GX Networks, and UUNet as well as several others. These large providers typically provide corporate access as well as accounts for individual subscribers. Other telecoms companies, for example Energis, also provide Internet backbone access for ISPs, even though they may not act in this capacity themselves.

In practice, for the average online investor there is little to choose between the two. Opting for a secondary supplier does not necessarily, for instance, affect the ability of that supplier to offer fast connections, and the average user is unlikely to notice any difference in service between primary and secondary providers.

Table 2.1 shows my own recent estimates for subscriber numbers for the UK's main ISPs. The list, which is partly derived from one compiled periodically by EMAP Online and *Internet* magazine, is best considered as a very rough guide to numbers. It does not include Internet users connecting through a company Internet facility or from a place of education. Nor does it factor up subscriber numbers to allow for the fact that often more than one person may access the net from a single account.

CompuServe and AOL are large bulletin board providers in addition to offering direct net connections, although despite their size they operate on the basis of leasing Internet 'backbone' capacity, rather than being a supplier of it.

In May 1998, Demon, now owned by Scottish Telecom, was the largest provider of normal non-bulletin board type dial-up services, with around 185,000 subscribers (now perhaps 250,000), but when BBS and Freeserve suppliers are brought into the equation, the company comes seventh after,

Table 2.1   UK Internet service providers—estimated subscriber numbers

ISP	Estimated number of 'live' subscribers
Freeserve	1200,000
AOL	600,000
CompuServe	400,000
BT Click	500,000
Demon	250,000
Global Internet	160,000
LineOne	400,000
MSN	200,000
Virgin Net	400,000
X-Stream	150,000

among others, CompuServe, AOL, Freeserve, Virgin and BT, all of which have significantly more UK subscribers. The growth in newer providers such as BT Click and LineOne (BT's equivalent of a BBS service) and Virgin Net, X-Stream and Freeserve is clearly evident from the table.

In addition to Freeserve, it is worth noting that BT, Virgin and Tesco, which all began as paid-for services, are now offering free connection, sometimes running these services alongside paid-for ones.

It is interesting to compare the figures in the table with the position when *The Online Investor* was published in 1997. Figures published in the *Financial Times* in late 1996, for example, put CompuServe's subscriber base at 200,000, AOL's at 90,000, MSN's at 85,000, and Demon's at 70,000.

While you might think that the straightforward decision would be to opt either for a free service or for one of the big players, it's not quite as simple as that. In the case of CompuServe and AOL it is worth remembering that, as BBS services, they do differ from the no-frills and free providers. AOL has recently launched a free service, Netscape Online (www.netscapeonline.co.uk).

Their operating costs per subscriber tend to be higher because of the administrative costs of running a BBS system, and hence their charges tend to be usage related.

It is hard to generalise, but while a typical no-frills paid-for supplier might charge a flat £10–£12 a month for unlimited access, a BBS would have a lower minimum threshold, but charge correspondingly more if the user logged, say, 25 hours a month of 'surfing'. If a user expected to be surfing three hours a day, day in day out, then a BBS cost could be several times the flat charge asked by other providers. Using a BBS service as a way of accessing the net can be an expensive proposition for a heavy user, although do bear in mind you are getting additional content not available to others.

Using a free service may also be an option, provided you are confident you are not likely to need much help from the chargeable helpdesk service. Some business users may also not want to be seen using a free service. Reliability of connection is also a key issue for some users, who are prepared to pay, or pay a premium, for a service which is guaranteed always to be easily accessible and which performs well. Internet magazines frequently publish league tables of the 'lab-tested' performance of ISPs.

How individual online investors reconcile this dilemma may differ in each case. In my time as an Internet user I have found my average monthly bill for using CIX as my ISP for both their bulletin boards and my web connection to be in the region of £15 plus VAT, with of course call charges on top. My wife has a net connection with U-Net which has

Figure 2.1   U-Net's home page

proved highly reliable and costs around £100 a year. Both ISPs have excellent free helpdesk facilities.

Before we go on to consider the other factors that might influence your decision, one very important point does need to be borne in mind. Getting the decision right first time is important. Once an account is set up, although in theory it is simple to move to another service provider, a change like this will involve changing your email address. This may be inconvenient if it has become the one with which friends and business contacts are familiar.

So it is worthwhile investigating the cost and benefits fully before committing yourself. Remember too that charging structures do change from time to time and the up-to-date position should always be checked out thoroughly. The mass market Internet magazines often contain useful data on this, sometimes in tabular form. It is best to investigate this first, rather than signing up for a service on impulse only to find a cheaper deal could have been had elsewhere.

There are a number of other points to bear in mind. One is whether or not the service provider offers software compatible for your operating system. Virtually all ISPs offer Windows-compatible services, but fewer offer the option of Mac-friendly software.

The response and reliability of helpdesks operated by the main providers is also worth checking. Try calling them to see how quickly they respond, or whether the numbers are permanently engaged. Tables given in Internet magazines usually show what hours they function.

Another important consideration, as previously indicated, is ease of access to the system, which essentially boils down to having a low ratio of subscribers to modem points at the host computer. Traffic tends to be heavy in the evening, for instance, and it is frustrating if your attempts to connect are likely to meet with an engaged tone at the other end. Again statistics are usually easily available on this point.

Another point to check is the 'bandwidth'—or Internet capacity—the ISP has at its disposal. Generally speaking the higher the better ought to be the norm, but the same point applies as for modems per subscriber: if an ISP has a relatively low amount of bandwidth per subscriber, then the service may slow down markedly at peak times. ISPs are wary of disclosing precise subscriber numbers, so this factor is hard to pin down.

Bandwidth will become less of a factor as telecommunications capacity rises and more efficient methods of utilising it are developed. But for the moment it needs to be borne in mind when choosing an ISP.

Increasingly important as individuals begin to design and promote their own personal web sites is the facility that is almost invariably offered by an ISP, that of hosting a subscriber's personal web site up to a certain size. Typically, ISPs will allow a web site or sites to be hosted up to around the 5 Mb or 10 Mb mark, enough for a fairly substantial presence. Charges may be levied on top if this size is exceeded, or if the site generates an undue amount of traffic. If launching your personal web site is part of the plan at some stage, then this is worth factoring into your decision on which ISP to choose.

Lastly, it is vital that the supplier you choose has a local point of presence (POP)—in other words, that your connection is made at local call rates. The larger providers have nationwide coverage. This simplifies logging on to collect email while on the road, otherwise the process can be an expensive one, involving long distance calls at expensive hotel telephone rates. A small local provider may be all right if you are not planning to 'surf' while on the move. But checking on telephone call charges and access points is always worthwhile before you subscribe.

Call charges do mount up, and the UK is reckoned to be significantly more expensive than the rest of Europe in this respect.

However, that some would-be net surfers will always want to sign up with a big organisation—and indeed for the reasons previously stated there is nothing wrong with that—Table 2.2 shows some salient statistics for the the current top 20 ISPs.

You are, however, strongly recommended to investigate the issue of charges and the level of service provision before signing up. The broad general rule is that pure paid-for ISPs may charge a signing-on fee and then a flat charge of £10–£15 per month irrespective of usage. However, some do not insist on a set-up charge. The list of ISPs (excluding free service providers) given in Table 2.3 represents those of the 200 or more to choose from who do not demand a set-up charge, have a monthly cost of less than £15 per month or a cost if paid annually of less than £150, offer national coverage, fewer than 20 users per modem and who will host at least 5 Mb of web space for each user (which you can use for your own web pages).

All of the statistics are subject to change at short notice but were correct at the time of writing.

Table 2.2   The top 20 ISPs

ISP Name	Maximum modem speed	Users per modum	Bandwidth	Number of POP3 emails	Amount of web space included	ISDN	Mac
AOL	33.6	n/a	n/a	5	10	No	No
BT Internet	33.6	n/a	n/a	5	5	Yes	Yes
Cable & Wireless	33.6	12	n/a	5	5	No	No
Cable Internet	56(X2)	10	45 Mbps	5	5	Yes	Yes
ClaraNET Ltd	56(Flex/X2)	15	100 Mbps	Unlimited	5	Yes	Yes
CompuServe	33.6	n/a	n/a	1	5	Yes	Yes
Demon Internet	33.6	n/a	n/a	Unlimited	5	Yes	Yes
Direct Connection	56(Flex)	10	n/a	Unlimited	5	Yes	Yes
Easynet Ltd	56(Flex)	20	n/a	1	2	Yes	Yes
Freeserve	56(Flex)	n/a	n/a	Unlimited	15	Yes	No
Global Internet Ltd	56(Flex/X2)	<20	10 Mbps	Unlimited	3	Yes	Yes
I-Way Limited	33.6	10	2 Mbps	1	0	Yes	Yes
LineOne	56(Flex/X2)	n/a	n/a	5	10	Yes	Yes
MSN	33.6	n/a	90 Mbps	1	1	Yes	No
Netcom	56(X2)	17	n/a	5	5	Yes	Yes
The X-Stream Network	56(Flex)	n/a	1 Mbps	Unlimited	0	No	No
U-Net Limited	56(Flex/X2)	19	17.5 Mbps	1	5	Yes	Yes
UUNET (Pipex Dial)	56(Flex/X2)	n/a	155 Mbps	5	2	Yes	Yes
Virgin Net	56(X2)	10	155 Mbps	1	10	Yes	Yes
Which? Online	56	10	2 Mbps	1	2	No	Yes

Table 2.3   ISPs not charging for set-up

ISP Name	Coverage	Cost per month	Cost per annum	Users per modem	Amount of web space included
Argonet	National 0645	£14.69	£141.00	18	5
Exconet	National 0845	£11.75	£141.00	<10	5
Pipemedia OnLine	National 0845	£11.75	£117.50	<10	5
Power Internet	National 0845	£14.10	£116.33	12	5
Prestel On-line	National 0845	£10.56	£117.48	<10	Unlimited
Telinco	National 0845	£5.00	£60.00	10	5

What You Get

What you get from your Internet service provider depends on whether or not you have opted for a BBS style system or a no-frills or free connection.

All types of connection should provide the following:

❒ an email address
❒ an email program such as Eudora (Outlook Express is part of Windows 95/98)
❒ a graphics-based web browser such as Netscape (Microsoft Internet Explorer is part of Windows 95/98)
❒ access to Internet newsgroups, normally via the web browser or possibly an offline reader
❒ a specific program to launch file transfer sessions (although one of these can be downloaded from the web easily enough if it isn't provided).

Most of this is self explanatory, but one or two items call for more detail.

The offline reader (OLR) allows the user, for example, to read messages from and compose messages to newsgroups while off-line. A connection can then be initiated, and the software acts as an auto pilot, accessing the appropriate software in the host computer, performing all the necessary tasks as efficiently and quickly as possible (for instance, downloading unread newsgroup messages and uploading fresh comments composed by the user) and then disconnecting. It allows messages to be composed and read off-line, which saves on connection charges.

File transfer protocol (FTP) for uploading and downloading files in this scenario does not normally entail using UNIX commands. FTP 'client' software allows connection to be automated and assuming the connection and login are successful, the program will simply show a file manager-style interface at the remote computer and the file can be selected and downloaded within a Windows or Macintosh 'point and click' environment, simply by selecting the file to be moved and clicking the appropriate 'arrow' in the program to either bring it from or send it to the remote computer.

As an aside, use of FTP in this way is part and parcel of maintaining a web site hosted on the ISP's computer, since a directory structure has to be created and certain additional files may need to be uploaded separately from those uploaded as part of the web site creation process. This may sound complicated, but it isn't and ISP helpdesk staff are usually able to offer advice if a subscriber finds the process too complex.

Internet service providers should normally also make copies of all relevant software available on disk, although there may sometimes be a nominal charge for this. Some net enthusiasts prefer the idea of downloading everything by modem, but in practice this can be time-consuming and less user-friendly than inserting a floppy disk or CD and using the normal *File Run* or *Start Run* command.

Another drawback is that while ISPs will provide bona fide versions of all the programs used, these are often not supported by full user manuals, but only by a basic instruction booklet. This provides information on the basic features of the programs but not much else. Although the programs themselves are usually easy to use intuitively, some trial and error may be involved in using them, and buying a manual or guide from a computer bookstore may be a good investment.

Browsers in Brief

Browser software (such as Netscape's Navigator or Microsoft's Internet Explorer) is also fairly easy to use. But for those new to the net, one or two practical pointers may be useful.

I have experience of using the two browsers mentioned above and these comments can be applied equally to both. Since Microsoft is, at the time of writing, still awaiting a judgement in its anti-trust court battles over its integration of browser and operating system in Windows 98, it is clearly inappropriate to comment on this aspect of how they work. The comments below are made in respect of how they work as mediums for navigating web sites, rather than in any other way.

Launching the browser by double clicking on its desktop icon will dial up the appropriate service provider number and establish the Internet connection that allows the browser to function. Occasionally a connection will not be made for a variety of reasons, usually an engaged tone at the ISP access point because of a heavier-than-normal number of users at that particular time.

By default, the first page shown on screen is likely to be the service provider's home page, which might contain a variety of background information. Sometimes the browser software will default to the software company's home page. Either way, these default settings can be changed easily. As an online investor you might, for instance, want this opening 'home' page to be one which displays various up-to-date market movements or news items. There are plenty to choose from, as we shall see later, and altering the 'preferences' built into the browser is a simple matter.

The basic browser screen may also provide direct one-button links to lists of new sites, which might be of general interest, upgrades of the browser program, basic Internet directories, newsgroups, and search engines. Using search engines will be covered in more detail in the next chapter.

Other facilities, contained in a toolbar at the top of the browser, allow for skipping forward and back to previously visited web pages—handy during a web browsing session—and for typing in known web page addresses (or uniform resource locators—URLs) from scratch. A stop button is there to halt unduly slow downloads. The reload button retries a previously aborted transfer of data from a web address.

The speed at which web pages download is mainly linked to the capacity of the modem you are using and traffic on the net, and to the amount of data on the page you happen to be trying to download. Web pages that contain a lot of images will take much longer to access than ones with a more basic design. In this case your computer's processing speed also assumes a degree of importance.

However, a toggle button on the browser can be used to turn off the images of downloading web pages. Pages are still displayed in colour with the appropriate hypertext links (which you can click on to move to the specified web site), only the pictures are absent. In some instances, however, the site's design may mean that picture displays are integral to navigating around the site, so turning off the images will make it harder to find your way around.

Another useful facility is the ability to 'bookmark' pages you are likely to return to, saving the URL for future use. In subsequent sessions the site is simply selected from the drag and drop menu in which it has automatically been stored. These 'bookmarks' or 'favourites' can be managed and edited easily, to save the list from becoming unwieldy or hard to understand.

It is also sometimes convenient to be able to save the contents of web pages for later use. This can be done either by saving the page to disk, or printing it out there and then. If you want to do the latter, you will need a good-quality colour inkjet or laser printer.

Browsers are intuitively very easy to use, once you grasp the essential point about using hypertext links.

Nonetheless, browsers are changing all the time and new versions of browser software are likely to contain fresh functions bundled into them.

Now, for instance, users can access email from within the browser and browsers routinely have a secure mode for conducting transactions over the web.

Although a lot has been made of the supposed lack of security inherent in web browsers, in reality they are rather more secure than reading a credit card number over the telephone line. However, for high-value transactions, using a browser in secure mode, as indicated by a solid 'key' icon in the bottom left corner of the screen, is only prudent.

'Netiquette'

There are a number of dos and don'ts related to activities on the net and it is as well to be aware of them in advance.

Some of these can be put in the category of avoiding wasting either time or Internet bandwidth capacity to the detriment of other users. But some are throwbacks to the non-commercial origins of the Internet. There are still purists out there who get offended at the solecisms unwittingly perpetrated by newer users.

A general point is that, for the moment, bandwidth (Internet capacity) is still a scarce resource. Some the general rules outlined below are only common sense ways of not being unduly profligate with it. Most of the comments below relate to the use of email, newsgroups and FTP, rather than the web, but they are issues which every net user and online investor will have to meet and deal with at some point.

Distant servers and web sites. It is obvious that you will get a quicker response from a web site predominently accessed by US users if you log onto it when they are asleep and when local traffic can be expected to be light. Most users get used to working with time differences in this way. This is practical as well as financially sensible: downloading files and web pages will be quicker if traffic is light, saving you money on telephone charges.

FTP. If you do this, when faced with the choice always log onto the server closest to you. It may be an attractive thought to log on to a server in Australia to download a file, but it is better to use the normal large UK net resources located in British universities such as Imperial College and the University of Kent.

Wasting bandwidth. If you encounter graphically heavy web sites and the graphics are not necessary for navigation, it makes sense to economise on bandwidth and speed up your download time by turning off the graphics section of your browser and downloading just text. Murphy's law applies here: the graphically light sites are often the only ones that are easy to navigate without images.

Signatures and repeat messages. Most email programs contain the option to append a personalised 'signature'—it may contain your address and phone number or be a (supposedly) witty quotation. Over-elaborate signatures are a needless waste of bandwidth. Other common practices that have the same wasteful effect are the attachment of the message to which you are replying to your new posting. Unless absolutely essential, avoid this.

Self-promotion. Internet purists frown on blatant attempts at self-promotion. I was once roundly chastised in an email from an American academic because I had answered a question posted in a newsgroup by suggesting that the enquirer buy a book on the subject I had just published. This is less of a problem now, but advertising your services in newsgroups is still probably best done in a discreet way via pointers to a relevant web site, or through encouraging those interested to email you for details.

Asking obvious questions. This tends to be frowned on. Many newsgroups and websites have FAQ (frequently asked questions) lists which can be downloaded to avoid posts that ask the obvious.

Spamming. Every newsgroup user gets very irritated by postings which are flagrantly off-topic, or which self-evidently promote money-making scams— of which there is no shortage. Unsolicited email is the curse of the Internet and posting to any newsgroup is likely to produce some unless you take steps to alter your return email address to eliminate it. This can be done comparatively easily in most off-line readers but many users, myself included, tend not to bother. Equally, cross-posting the same message to several related newsgroups is also intensely irritating and generally frowned on.

Libel. Be careful what you write, especially to newsgroups and to other sites in the public domain. The general rule is not to write anything you would be embarrassed to see published in a normal daily newspaper with your name attached to it. Journalists are normally asked not to quote from newsgroup postings without getting the permission of the original poster, but don't bank on it.

Keyboard style. Excessive use of upper case symbols, which sometimes do not translate well, is not encouraged. Brevity is encouraged. Use of block capitals is considered the equivalent of shouting to get attention, and is generally only to be done very sparingly, if at all. There are several standard abbreviations and acronyms that can be used: examples are IMHO (in my humble opinion), AIUI (as I understand it), FWIW (for what it's worth), and so on. In general, however, these are used to abbreviate redundant phrases that add nothing to the communication concerned. They also promote the image of the net as an organisation for insiders, which is counterproductive. Similarly, so-called emoticons or 'smileys' (normally viewed sideways—:-(or :-)), are naff and unnecessary.

The Typical User

As the Internet has grown in popularity, so increasingly serious attempts have been made to survey its users, with interesting results.

For the statistical purist, the Internet offers interesting challenges. Because there is no central registry of users, random sampling is difficult, and surveys have to rely on respondents selecting themselves for any survey, which introduce some bias into the results (that is, only the keenest users respond).

But whatever the arguments about methodology, it is becoming clear that the old stereotype of users being a mixture of crusty academics resentful of the incursion of commercial interests onto the online world, or spotty 'nerds' with nothing better to do, is giving way to a more rounded view of who uses the net and why.

The American university Georgia Tech has pioneered surveys into Internet demographics, looking at the subject not only from a US standpoint, but also including statistics relating to Europe and other areas of the world. Its latest (and tenth) annual survey, published in May 1999, shows a number of interesting trends. Detailed results of the survey can be found at www.cc.gatech.edu/gvu/user_surveys. The following comments are based on trends suggested by these surveys.

In terms of age, the average user is 35, but the tendency is for the number of over 40s to increase as a proportion. Younger users predominate in Europe. For instance 70% of all users in the USA are between 16 and 45, whereas in Europe 80% of users are between 16 and 35. Those with most online experience tend to be in the 21–30 age range.

The proportion of women on the net has stayed pretty constant at around 39%, although for the first time women make up a majority of users who have been online for less than a year.

In terms of educational attainment, the proportion represented by highly educated individuals has been declining as the net's mass market penetration has increased. Around half of all users are graduates and 80% have at least some experience of further education, although the figures are doubtless distorted because of the fact that a significant percentage of net users are current students.

In terms of the jobs that net users do, in Europe 22.6% of users are students, 2.5% self-employed, 11.9% are computer programmers, 2.6% writers and journalists, 3.6% engineers, and 1.9% work in marketing.

Around 41% of users in the USA are married and 39% are single, whereas in Europe, probably reflecting the younger base of users, 54% are single and 31% married. Household income among users reflects a similar pattern. In the USA houshold income of a majority of users falls in range of $30,000–$75,000 while in Europe the figure is $20,000–$40,000 although there is a significant core of more affluent users with income in the $50,000–$74,000 range.

Generally users access the web using a computer with a Windows operating system. Windows accounts for 75% of total users and 76% of European users. Mac users represent 12.5% overall and just 9% in Europe.

The Georgia Tech surveys have also found that users typically spend 10–20 hours a week on the web—around a third of users fall into this category although 40% use it for less time than this. There is tendency for those who have been connected for a greater period of time to use the net for longer periods.

Users surveyed continued to report that speed was still the main problem (for around two-thirds of respondents). This is despite nearly half of net users upgrading their modem in the past year—an indication that web pages are generally becoming 'heavier'. We'll explore this area later in this book, with particular reference to assessing the user-friendliness of web sites generally and corporate web sites in particular.

Online purchasing has become an increasingly topical issue. More users are buying online, and not just in the USA. The ninth Georgia survey, for example, showed that willingness to order goods online was not dissimilar between the US and Europe: around 78% of US users expressed willingness to do so, compared to 73% in Europe. The biggest turn-off to ordering online in both broad geographical areas is security, although as explained previously we believe that this is a problem that is more feared than real. The other big drawback is the inability to judge the quality of the goods. Users also often express a preference for ordering from a supplier within their legal jurisdiction in case action for redress needs to be taken for non-delivery or faulty goods.

Users surveyed were reasonably uniform in their views of what were the most important issues facing the Internet in coming years, with 15.4% of US users citing tax (that is, the web causing governments to lose tax revenue because of a trend to online purchasing). This was indicated as a concern by 11.6% of European users.

Navigation through the increasingly voluminous quantities of information is cited as an issue by 13% of US users but 24% of European ones, perhaps reflecting the relative inexperience of many European users. This concern may diminish as users get used to coping with net overload and use books such as this to learn how to use search tools, jumping off points and other techniques to get the best from the net.

Privacy and encryption are big issues for net users in the USA, cited by more than one-third of those surveyed, but less of a concern in Europe, where only a fifth mentioned it as an issue.

So there you have it. The balance between the sexes is evening up, and Europe is probably following the USA in making the net a medium more representative of society as a whole as the volume of users increases. But it's still the case, and likely to be so for some time, that net users tend to be younger than average, more affluent than average, and better educated than average. This also probably makes them more likely to be actual or potential investors.

The next steps . . .

This chapter has looked at how the Internet and world wide web can help the online investor, the tools that can be used to explore it, how to get connected and the pros and cons of different types of service, and who the typical user might be. The next task is to look at the investment-related information and investor services that can be gleaned from the online world and how to get at them.

Since news and information are what move share prices, we will look at newsgroups and email as sources of investment ideas and news, at online versions of print media such as newspapers and magazines, and at some other online news sources.

But first, in the next chapter, we'll examine specific issues that arise when using the web to assemble investment related information, and some short cuts to getting to the web sites that might be useful.

CHAPTER 3

Browsing and Searching

Whether or not you are an Internet enthusiast, it will have been difficult to avoid becoming aware of the world wide web over the last few years. The web is a big help to the online investor, but its sheer size can be daunting. One recent estimate suggests that around 1.5 million pages are added to the web every day. The web is now said to contain 800 million pages although as much as half of these may be duplicates.

Though there is a huge volume of commercial and educational content available at web sites, the medium of hypertext offers an easy way of moving quickly from one document to the next. And the web's sheer size can be tamed, if you know what you are looking for.

It can safely be assumed that the number of web sites will grow in tandem with numbers of users, as more and more commercial organisations become aware of the marketing possibilities offered by the web and as easy-to-use web publishing software enables anyone with an Internet connection to produce and publish their own web site. Tools such as Microsoft Publisher, now a standard part of the Microsoft Office suite, reduce the creation of web sites to a simple desktop publishing operation.

In the next chapter we will look also at Internet newsgroups. There are currently more than 80,000 Usenet newsgroups or online discussion forums, which in turn probably collectively contain upwards of 20 million recent articles and comments.

So though all of these figures should be treated with some reservations, it is clear that there is plenty of information out there. The task is how to track down exactly what you need. Indeed learning the techniques to locate quickly and effectively the information you require is vitally important.

Fortunately there are some easy ways of tackling this profuse content. The following points are worth remembering:

❐ Fewer than 900 key web sites account for 50% of the entire traffic on the web.
❐ Restricting one's attention to the finance and investment area reduces the number of relevant key sites considerably.
❐ There are both general and specialist directories and search tools that can help locate investment-related information.
❐ There are a number of key 'jumping off points', directories of investment-related links, that can be employed.
❐ Using your web browser's bookmark facility means that the sites of most use to you can be retrieved quickly and easily.

Before delving more deeply into these topics, for the benefit of Internet newcomers it is perhaps worth covering some basic points on the subject of browsers and issues that arise when browsing.

Basics of Browsing

The basic choice of browser is now between Netscape Navigator and Microsoft's Internet Explorer. Netscape became the de facto industry standard early in the game, but its market share has been gradually eroded by Microsoft's product. The long-running court action between the US Department of Justice and Microsoft in fact centres on whether or not Microsoft used its dominant position in the market for computer operating systems to help increase sales of its browser by effectively tying one to the other.

Be that as it may, for most users the choice of browser is not one to lose particular sleep over. Both contenders in the market have similar features and are sufficiently intuitive for users to switch between one and the other without the need to re-learn how to use the software.

To recap on the previous chapter, some key features of both browser 'brands' are:

❐ the ability to turn off the loading of graphical images if desired to speed up the downloading of particular web pages (although the design of many web sites is such that ease of navigation is impaired if this is done)

❑ the ability to 'bookmark' favourite sites, to enable their URLs to be retrieved quickly. Bookmarks are particularly useful for sites that have a registration and login structure, since they avoid the need to re-enter user names and passwords

❑ the ability to move quickly back and forth between sites that have been downloaded previously, and speedy return to the home page

❑ email integrated into the browser. Apart from convenience, this has the advantage that any web addresses quoted in emails are highlighted automatically as hypertext links, while email addresses quoted within web pages can be emailed directly from the web page

❑ the latest version of browsers should be Java enabled. This allows pages created in the Java programming language to be viewed. The presence of Java language is often used in financially oriented sites for features such as price 'tickers' and provided the Java 'applet' being used is not too complex, generally improves the speed at which pages are downloaded

❑ further integration of browser and hard drive navigation is a feature of Windows 98, but need not be used as such. It does not preclude using a Netscape browser if that is what you prefer.

If you browse web sites for any length of time you will soon become aware of huge differences in the way sites are designed and the speed at which they can be accessed. This a function of several different factors, including the time of day, the speed of the server distributing the pages at the host computer, the bandwidth constraints at the user's ISP, and most commonly the graphical content of the site being accessed.

This theme is explored in more detail in Chapter 6 on Corporate Information Online, since graphics-heavy company web sites are far from uncommon. Avoiding trying to access graphically heavy sites in the afteroon or evening in Europe (peak time for Internet use in the US) will minimise the frustrations. As mentioned previously the problems posed by bandwidth constraints may lessen as time goes by.

Downloads, Plug-ins, and other Accessories

One attraction of the web is that it enables files and data to be downloaded easily from the host computer and either displayed or stored on the hard drive of the user's computer. For investors, good examples of the use of this are downloading new investment software packages, in the form of either 'shareware' or demos, downloadable price data, and other statistical information, often in spreadsheet form.

We explore the options that investors have available in this area in later chapters. But it is worth pausing just to outline the mechanics of downloading files from web sites.

Downloading files is comparatively easy using a browser such as Netscape or Internet Explorer. Simply click on the appropriate hypertext. The browser will then prompt you to save the file to a particular directory, which can be selected using the normal Windows Explorer (or similar) file manager system.

It is worthwhile at this point having an empty directory already created in which to save the file, especially if it comes in zipped format. Zipped files are those in which the data is compressed to speed up the download process. They can be unzipped using a simple utility like Winzip or PKZIP. The latter is available from PKWare at www.pkware.com.

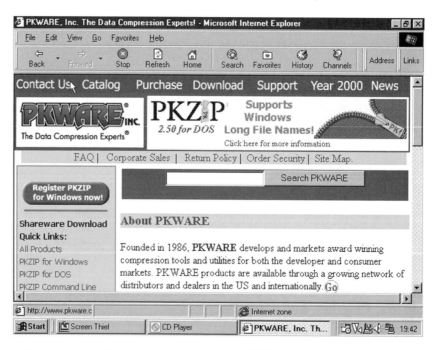

Figure 3.1   Download the decompression program PKZIP from the PKWare web site

The reason for creating a separate 'download' directory is that unzipping the file will probably release several new files. In a directory that already contains other items this can cause confusion. Once the download is unzipped, the normal procedure is followed to install the file. This will usually be by clicking on an *.exe* or *setup.ini* file.

The web site pages at which downloads are available will often contain instructions about how to install software once downloaded, and it is worthwhile printing these instructions to refer to once the file has been successfully downloaded. Installing software from a download requires a similar procedure to be followed as for installing from a disk or CD. No other Windows programs should be running during the installation— ignore this warning at your peril. Files not obtained from a recognised software company web site should also be checked for viruses before installation.

Documents downloaded from web sites often come in what is known as PDF (portable document file) format. This format presents downloaded text as an exact replica of the original document. For online investors this often crops up when viewing statistical tables available at stock exchanges, annual reports at company web sites, research from broker and investment bank web sites, and other sources.

Viewing PDF files requires a special piece of plug-in software called an Adobe Acrobat Reader. This is available free via downloading from the Adobe site at www.adobe.com, where you will find the latest version. The file is some 4.5 Mb in size and takes around 30–40 minutes to download via a 56 K modem. Users should take care to download a normal, rather than a 'beta' version. Installation is easy and the application is launched automatically whenever a PDF file is downloaded or opened.

Similar comments apply to the Microsoft PowerPoint program. Power-Point presentations, especially of slide presentations made by company managements to analysts, are increasingly becoming available at corporate web sites. If you do not have PowerPoint installed on your PC, a free PowerPoint viewer is available for download from the appropriate part of the Microsoft web site at www.microsoft.com. Those without Word or Excel can also download a similar reader for viewing downloaded Word documents or Excel spreadsheets.

Audio (and to a lesser extent video) is being used increasingly at investment related web sites, and also requires simple additional software, available free, to enable the broadcasts to be accessed via your web browser.

Microsoft's Media Player and the RealPlayer system offered by Real Networks are the two main options. The Microsoft Media Player may come as a standard part of the operating system of your computer. If not, it can be downloaded free of charge from the Microsoft web address stated above. The free RealPlayer system can be downloaded from www.realnetworks.com. A more sophisticated version is available at a cost, at the time of writing, of around $30.

Like the Acrobat Reader, these systems are easily installed and launch automatically when the system detects an audio or video file being downloaded. As well as allowing audio of analyst meetings and management presentations to be downloaded, these systems also allow users to access specialist financial news radio broadcasts such as Bloomberg News Radio (www.bloomberg.com) and others.

Commercial Realities of Web Sites

While the Internet may have begun as a co-operative and educational venture (see Appendix for the historical background), it is self-evident that the world wide web, best seen as the Internet's commercial offshoot, largely exists to pursue commercial, strategic, and above all profit-oriented goals and increasingly to facilitate the development of electronic commerce.

Financial services (including share dealing and other forms of investment) as well as books, music CDs, computers and several other goods and services, are examples of standardised products available in forms that make them naturals to buy and sell over the web, and trading in these items has taken off in the last year or so.

The power of the medium, and the access it gives commercial organisations to what may well be viewed as their ideal target market, has meant that the information that the web provides (often free of charge) that can be of use to investors—prices, software, data, access to news archives, company information—is frequently mixed in with a commercial agenda.

But brand owners need to take care. The frictionless nature of the web has meant that it has been notoriously difficult, for example, for web site operators to charge for content unless they have an exceptionally strong brand. Of the best known news organisation sites, for example, only the *Wall Street Journal* has no free content. Web users shy away from paying for content, quite simply because there are so many acceptable alternatives which are free. Similarly, for the web site operator setting up a secure micro-payments system is costly. Hence the 'advertising' rather than the 'charging for access' model tends to work better in many instances.

In short, information may be free, for which investors should be grateful, but the web site operators often use the traffic that free information generates to advertise and to sell other products and services. Price and news services aimed at US investors often contain advertisements for and links to online stockbroking services, to cite just one example. This generates advertising revenue for site operators, and new customers or extra business for the advertisers.

The upshot is that a typical commercial web site may well contain items for sale, and it will often contain advertisements and links to advertisers' own web pages, where goods and services may be offered for sale. But equally the sheer number of web sites means that each has to offer some unique content to attract visitors and therefore to be able to command good rates for advertising on it.

Popular web sites will contain banner advertising at the top or the bottom of the page, and smaller online ads know as 'buttons'. The number of 'hits' (times it is looked at) each page attracts can be measured, as can the percentage of those hits (the 'click', or 'click-through' rate) which result in users accessing the advertisers' pages via the hot links provided.

Because web sites contain multiple numbers of pages, what has become more important than the hit rate is the number of different pages (or impressions) that are viewed on the site during the course of typical visit. The most popular pages may then command premium advertising rates, much as would the inside cover or centre-spread of a magazine.

The web is a medium in which it is easy to flick back or forward to another page with more interesting content, so useful information is vitally important to the successful promotion of a web site.

Quality of content does not mean heavy graphics. Indeed most regular web users would probably argue the reverse. A picture may be worth a thousand words, but a thousand words will download more quickly. So if a picture takes several minutes to download, the user may get bored waiting and move on, diluting a site's appeal to an advertiser.

A web page that has simple graphics, downloads quickly and is well laid out with good content, will attract a bigger audience than web pages that have been over-designed and are hard to get through. That does not mean, though, that poorly designed sites do not have interesting information to offer.

Web site operators are learning as they go along and many sites get substantially upgraded and improved. So even a poorly designed site that might potentially have interesting information may be worth a repeat visit.

The cost of creating a simple web site is negligible, but if the site is to be a credible one and to attract significant numbers of hits, then its design and layout needs to be good. This means that the costs can escalate alarmingly. Although some advertisements suggest that a secure e-commerce site can be created for as little as £3000, according to Darryll Mattocks, who founded The Internet Bookshop (www.bookshop.co.uk, now part of WH Smith), the minimum cost for a serious commercial web site of this sort might be in the region of £1.5 million. And this estimate was made some years ago, since which time costs have probably risen.

Mattocks' experience may be an exception. But consultants who design web sites charge hefty fees, and though server prices have probably fallen (or become much more powerful for the same price) those with secure features do not come cheap.

Large organisations with big IT departments may find that the process of setting up a web site is easier and the marginal cost of maintaining it relatively low. For these organisations the issues are different: control of access, security, integration with existing systems and so on.

Image is important and attention needs to be paid to it. Rather like magazines, all web sites need periodic redesign and this can add to the cost. Similarly, attention must be paid, particularly by those companies offering products likely to be bought by 'net users, to portraying the right image of warmth and efficiency combined.

If, for instance, email addresses are given at the site and users invited to send messages and queries, then these need to be replied to quickly and efficiently. A poor and inefficient web site can have a negative impact on corporate image.

Many web sites have pages containing hypertext links to related sites. But remember that in the case of commercial organisations some of these links may have been paid for, rather than selected on their own merits. This is especially true if they are activated from a high-traffic page. Some established sites charge for links at advertising rates comparable to conventional media.

The diligent online investor can keep aware, through conventional media and other sources, of the launch of new web sites that may potentially be of interest. Newspapers such as the *Financial Times* and investor publications such as *Analyst* and the *Investors' Chronicle* contain information about investment related web sites in their print editions.

Most of the broadsheet dailies have supplements each week specifically devoted to computing and the web, and these often contain information on new sites. Corporate advertisements increasingly quote URLs and the sites may well contain useful financial information about the company. We explore this whole issue of corporate web sites in Chapter 6.

However, the sheer volume of new sites and the fact that some companies with web sites choose to adopt a low profile means that sites may be launched without their existence immediately seeping into the collective mind of the private investor community. The fact is, though, the number of investment related sites, and especially corporate web sites, has grown dramatically since the first edition of this book was published. The task now, even more than before, is identifying the sites you need to use, or which can be of help in your quest for information.

Guesswork and deduction are worth a try at the outset. Almost all web addresses begin with the standard *http://www* prefix. A very few omit the www part.

What comes next is where the guesswork comes in. Let's say you are keen to find out if a particular company has a corporate web site. As explained in the Appendix and elsewhere in this book, the domain suffix will narrow the field somewhat. If the company is a US corporation or an international organisation, then it is likely that its domain will be *.com*; if it is a UK company the suffix will probably be *.co.uk*. Hence it is a reasonable deduction that the Microsoft web site is at http://www.microsoft.com and that Netscape is at http://www.netscape.com and so on. BPAmoco's site is www.bpamoco.com, but the sites of smaller UK companies are more likely, though not certain, to have a *.co.uk* designation. There is no rhyme or reason to this, however. Sporting goods retailer JJB Sports has a web site at www.jjb.co.uk whereas the site of Britax, which sells children's car safety seats and aircraft lavatories, is www.britax.com. Sage Group's web address is www.sage.com, while Misys (another large UK-based IT group) is on the web at www.misys.co.uk.

This can make the search, particularly for UK corporate web addresses, a frustrating business. The system is unforgiving and if the address is not 'opened' absolutely correctly the user will simply receive an error message.

Trying a few slightly different alternatives may produce the right answer but, if these deductions fail, the obvious next step is to use one of the several Internet 'search engines' or directories.

How these work, the merits of different alternatives, and how to get the best out of them is covered in the next section.

Search Engines and How to Use Them

Search engines are sophisticated computer programs accessed via a web site and used to find web pages that deal with specific topics. For the online investor they are useful for these purposes and especially for finding information which relates to, for example, a specific company or organisation.

The term 'search engine' is a catch-all for different types of tool. It is probably worth identifying three different types of search tool.

The first, arguably typified by Yahoo! (www.yahoo.com), is essentially a large directory organised along a conventional hierarchical structure of an index and several sub-indices. These are sometimes also called meta-lists. Many have become so large that they are also searchable. The advantage of them is that information can be pinpointed reasonably accurately and quickly, without wading through a lot of irrelevant search engine 'hits' to get to the appropriate item.

The other advantage is that locating information on particular topics this way can produce unexpected benefits in the form of sources of which the user may have been unaware yet which contain relevant information.

In my experience, however, meta-lists such as Yahoo!—even though it now has separate country specific sites such as www.yahoo.co.uk and separate sites specifically devoted to finance such as http://finance.yahoo.co.uk—are not particularly good at locating company web sites. For this, and for information on specific and out of the ordinary topics, you would need to go to the second category, that of so-called 'true' search engines.

True search engines, for example AltaVista (www.altavista.com) operate on the principle that by typing in a word or phrase and initiating the search, all the web sites that contain that word or phrase can be retrieved and displayed—complete with the relevant hypertext links. This sounds good, but the problem is that the proliferation of web-based content has meant that even the most seemingly unusual search term can produce an unmanageable number of hits. The process is a haphazard one, and fine-tuning a search to produce a manageable number of correct hits is something of an art.

The whole subject of search engines is a huge one in itself, both in terms of understanding how they work and indeed in the sheer number of tools that are available (well over 200 commonly used ones at the last count).

There are those who have made serious academic studies of classifying and assessing the performance of different search tools and the way they work, and those who have made a business out of it. For an example of this, the site of Search Engine Showdown at www.notess.com is worth a visit. As an online investor, however, you will be more interested in getting results to a specific search for information, rather than in knowing how the search is performed.

It is worth bearing in mind one or two important points about the way search engines work and the limits to their powers. The analogy most often used, appropriately enough for the web, is that of a spider or 'crawler' which automatically tracks the appearance of new sites, revisits previously logged ones, and indexes their content on the basis of certain parameters, perhaps the title of the site and the first few words on the home page, in some cases all of the text in the site, and so on.

However, the web spider will only detect sites that appear on the radar screen (to mix the metaphor slightly) either because there are links to them in sites that are already indexed, if they attract significant amounts of web traffic or publicity (such as newsgroup mentions) in their own right, or if the site operator takes the specific step of submitting the URL to the search engine itself. Web sites exist where, for the payment of a fee, a new site can be submitted to all of the main search engines simultaneously.

The point about this is that in, say, searching for a company site, if it does not crop up as a result of an AltaVista search this does not *necessarily* mean that the site does not exist, merely that this search engine has not detected it or that it has not been submitted. For this reason, when searching for a specific company site you are probably advised to use the previously described 'trial and error' method, then resort to a search engine. If neither technique works, a phone call to the company should elicit the definitive answer.

Search engines also differ in their ease of defining a search. Some offer, for instance a 'quick and dirty' search as an initial foray, which can then be further refined. Others allow search terms to be easily specified with a greater degree of accuracy at the outset, for example by restricting the search to a particular subject area or geographical region. Some rank hits on the basis of relevance, although what appears relevant to a search engine in statistical terms may not represent the same degree of relevance to the user. Another frustrating aspect of some search engines is that a hit on a site with multiple pages will result in multiple hits.

Reducing the number of hits to a manageable number of, say, 50 or fewer relies on accurate specification of search terms to identify precisely the subject of the search. The key to specifying search criteria lies in the ease with which search 'operators' can be defined. This is not as straightforward as it might seem. It is perhaps simplest to explain why with an example.

Let's say you want to search for any web sites that mention 'traded endowment policies'. To those not familiar with the term, these are a tax-efficient investment medium offering attractive long-term investment returns. Policies that would be surrendered to the insurance company for a variety of reasons are instead sold to investors through market-makers: the seller receives an uplift over the surrender value, and the buyer keeps up the premium payments but reaps the investment returns that accrue at the end of the policy's life.

Simply typing in the words 'traded endowment policies' may retrieve a large number of spurious sites. These could mention, for example, methods of financing further education (another use of the word endowment), mentions of corporate or economic policies (rather than insurance policies), or sites to do with trading stocks and shares (rather than trade-able policies).

What is required is to be able to specify a particular phrase. And there are a number of conventional ways of going about this.

Putting plus signs between the words may work (words to be excluded from the search can be prefixed with a minus sign). Or a specific phrase may be sought by putting it between quotation marks. As an aside, these tricks often work when using search engines at specific sites with archived contents, such as those of newspapers and the like.

Rather than plus and minus signs, some search engines work via specific words (known as Boolean operators) such as AND and NOT. Specifying, for example, traded AND endowment AND policies NOT college, may exclude sites that deal with university endowments. Similarly you might expect that the search would also contain the words 'surrender value', or simply 'surrender', somewhere in the text. So adding 'NEAR surrender' might refine the search even more precisely.

Though not all search engines allow Boolean logic to be applied fully, some search engines not only do allow it to be used but give easily selected alternatives explained in plain English. They might, for instance, use pull-down menus to allow you to select words separated by AND, by OR, or to select THIS PHRASE. This will allow the correct Boolean logic to be specified accurately yet easily.

Specifying the search criteria is not the end of the story, however. As noted previously another common problem is that a search may retrieve a list of sites that contains large numbers of duplications. Some search engines do remove duplicate sites to some degree, but more often the elimination process needs to be done intuitively simply by looking at the information thrown up in the hit list.

Some search engines perform their searches on the text contained in a particular site, and some merely on the words contained in the title of the site. The former may take a little longer to complete their search, but the results are likely to be better.

There is one big advantage when using a search engine to search for a specific company web site. This is that because it is very rare indeed for two listed company names to be identical, specifying the company name as a search phrase (even down to the Inc., plc, SA, or AG suffix) will normally yield only a few hits, with the official company site at the head or near the top of the list.

Spurious hits in this context can include, however, hits which include the company name as part of a web-based database of listed company information. Those searching for UK company web sites, may often find, for instance, that prominent in the list of hits is the Hemmington Scott UK Equities Direct site (www.hemscott.com), a useful site in itself but not one which would offer the complete range of information available at the average corporate site.

Accessing popular search engines is easy. A button on the browser will direct you to some (although not all) of the most popular ones. But a better route can be to access them through a directory such as Yahoo!, to get an up-to-date list of search engines rather than ones which the provider of the browser software chooses, for whatever reason, to provide as defaults.

The home page of your ISP may also have links to search engines. For UK online investors this should contain one or more specific UK sources. There is also a very good web site at the University of Strathclyde—Business Information Sources on the Internet—(www.dis.strath.ac.uk/business)—which also contains a very useful list of popular single search engines and indexes, with a brief review of each, lists of search engines, and meta-search tools (sites which search several search engines simultaneously). The latter are discussed in more detail in the next section.

Since each user's use of the web is different, and each search tool operates in a slightly different way, the best way to approach the question of choice is to try several and opt for the one you find easiest to use. As a personal preference I have tended to use Northern Light, although FAST (www.alltheweb.com) also has an increasing number of adherents. Northern Light has in the past claimed it indexes more web pages (120 million at the last count) than AltaVista. AltaVista is, however, reckoned by some independent sources to have 140–150 million pages indexed. However, Northern Light does have some interesting features, including the

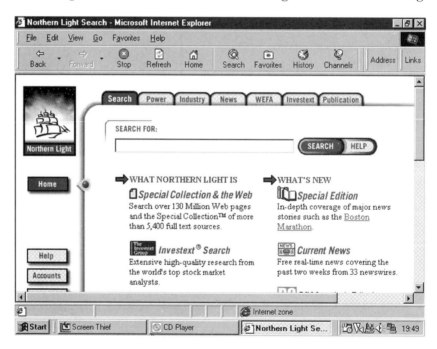

Figure 3.2   The Northern Light search tool has some interesting features

automatic classification of multiple hits into a smaller number of categories which can then be viewed separately, an easily configurable 'power search' facility, and the ability to search both the web and other databases, including news-related sites. FAST claims to have indexed over 200 million pages, although search results are not categorised.

Although there are a number of UK specific search engines, for the purposes of finding investment-related information, there is little to be gained from using them that cannot be achieved by using a broader-based search tool and configuring a search to a tighter geographical area. In other words, a recognised large-scale search engine will often produce a better result than a smaller one restricted to a single geographical area.

Internet search technology primarily originated in and has been extensively developed in the USA, and in my opinion US-originated search tools are the best instruments to use. In any case many now have a range of non-US versions which often simply appear by default depending on the country from which the user is accessing. If, for instance, I choose to access Lycos (www.lycos.com) from the UK, the Lycos UK home page (www.lycos.co.uk) will load instead. Ironically, FAST is Norwegian in origin.

Table 3.1 gives a brief summary of the characteristics of some of the main search engines. Since each individual's use of the web differs, and different search tools may be appropriate in different situations, we have not attempted to rank them in terms of their relative usefulness.

Longer lists of search tools can be found at the following URLs:

❒ All-in-one (www.albany.net/allinone/) allows the simultaneous searching of several search engines.
❒ Beaucoup (www.beaucoup.com/engines.html) has a list of 800 different search engines and directories including many outside the USA.
❒ eDirectory (www.edirectory.com) is a specific country-by-country list of search tools originating in that country.
❒ the VirtualSearch Engine site (www.dreamscape.com/frankvad/search.htm) has links to 1000 search engines and directories.

Finally, it is worth making a mental note of a newer trend: that of specialist search tools related to finance and investment. The USA has had these for some time, but two sites which have appeared since the first edition of *The Online Investor* was published are Financewise (www.financewise.com) which is a searchable list of worldwide finance-related

Table 3.1 Popular search engines and their characteristcs

Name	Web address	Type	Search universe	Pages indexed (m)	Advanced search	Search method	Non-US localised	Personal- isation
FAST	www.alltheweb.com	Spider	Web pages	235	Yes	text, Boolean	No	No
AltaVista	www.altavista.com	Spider	Web pages	150	Yes	text, Boolean	No	No
Deja	www.deja.com	Archive	Usenet	n/a	Yes	text, Boolean	No	No
Excite	www.excite.com	Spider	Web sites	60	No	text, Boolean	Yes	Yes
Hotbot	www.hotbot.com	Spider	Web pages	110	Yes	text, Boolean	No	No
Infoseek	www.infoseek.com	Spider	Web sites	n/a	Yes	text of unique pages	No	No
Lycos	www.lycos.com	Samples	Web + directories	50	Yes	text, first 20 lines	Yes	No
Northern Light	www.northernlight.com	Spider	Web + directories	120	Yes	text	Yes	No
Webcrawler	www.webcrawler.com	Spider	Sample www	n/a	Yes	text, Boolean	No	No
Yahoo!	search.yahoo.com	Directory	web, usenet	n/a	Yes	browse, keywords	Yes	Yes

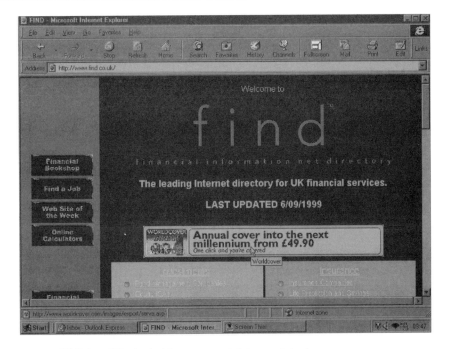

Figure 3.3   FIND is a UK-oriented finance-specialist search tool

sites grouped into broad categories, and FIND (Financial Information Net Directory) (www.find.co.uk), which is a similar concept but arguably more orientated towards the UK personal finance market. This site is a particularly good one for UK-based private investors.

Both sites are best considered in the category of 'jumping-off points' and are examined in a later section of this chapter.

Meta-search Engines

Since different search tools each have slightly different characteristics and conventions, some web users believe that the best type of search engine is the one that searches several search tools simultaneously and produces a consolidated list of hits, with—as far as possible—duplications removed. These are collectively know as meta-search engines. Table 3.2 shows the half dozen or so that are the most popular, and some of their characteristics.

Table 3.2 Meta-search tools and their characteristics

Name	Web address	Number searched	Con-figure	Results format	Boolean allowed
Cyber411	www.cyber411.com	14	Yes	Sequential	Yes
Dogpile	www.dogpile.com	13	Yes	Sequential	Yes
Inference Find	www.infind.com	6	No	Clustered	Some
Metacrawler	www.metacrawler.com	7	Yes	Ranked by relevance	Yes
Metafind	www.metafind.com	5	No	Clustered, A–Z	Yes
Savvysearch	www.savvysearch.com	7	No	Sequential	No

It is very important to bear in mind that meta-search engines work at their best if you are already familiar with the best ways of using search engines generally. The meta-search tools also differ themselves, as the table makes clear, in the scope of what they do, what they will allow, and how they work. They are also only as good as the underlying search engines from which they are drawing their results. Few, if any, of the meta-search tools mentioned in the table search either Northern Light or HotBot, another popular search engine as FAST.

Common features, however, are that a list of hits obtained from all the leading search engines are collated into a single list with either duplications removed, hits categorised, or ranked for relevance, and then displayed (as far as is practicable) on a single page. There is also usually the option to choose between a quick and comprehensive search and in most cases the option to use, or automatic use of, Boolean operators.

However, some of the underlying search tools used may not support Boolean format and the number of hits may be reduced accordingly. Another drawback is that the meta-searchers will only pull in a restricted list (perhaps the top 10 or top 50) hits from each search engine, and therefore from the standpoint of thoroughness there may be no substitute for performing individual searches.

There are also hybrids available which operate both as meta-search engines and also collections of interfaces to different search tools, organised in directory format. One of the best of these is The Big Hub, located at www.thebighub.com. Formerly called Internet Sleuth, this site claims to have over 1000 different searchable databases. There are separate categories related to search engines to do with business, finance and investment. These databases tend, however, often to have a US orientation. The home page of The Big Hub allows users to perform a meta-search on six main search engines and has a variety of other features.

Jumping-off Points and 'Portals'

In a slightly different category are what can perhaps be termed 'jumping-off points'. These are not really necessarily primarily search engines (although they may be searchable), but rather sites that represent a good point to begin a search for information because of the large numbers of related links assembled in one place.

Some well-known indexes, such as Yahoo!, fall into this category. But there are also a number of sites that are of specific interest to UK online investors and which have good links to a range of investment-related information. Some of these are considered below.

Business Information on the Internet. A good starting point is the University of Strathclyde site (www.dis.strath.ac.uk/business). This is organised into a number of broad categories including, for instance, search tools and lists of business information sources, directories and lists of commercial sites, company profiles and financial information, country information, statistics and economic information, news sources and so on.

BUBL. Another academic source that has none of the trivia, clumsy design and advertising that many commercial sites have is BUBL (www.bubl.ac.uk/link). This is a site categorised by reference to different academic disciplines, but users can cut through to business and finance links fairly easily, and the site contains a number of links not normally found elsewhere and is assiduously updated for new useful links.

Financewise. This site, at www.financewise.com, is comparatively new and attempts to categorise the increasingly large number of financially-oriented sites. Users can either search the entire site or browse categories which include capital markets, personal finance, services, government, commercial and retail banking and so on. Moreover, the site claims that those web sites included are vetted before being added to the site. From the online investor standpoint, the site has a good mix of those sites of interest to professionals and those new to investing and the site makes a good starting point for this reason.

FIND. Located at www.find.co.uk, this newish site is strictly finance-related and UK-oriented. Since its launch it has built up an impressive quantity of well-categorised links with a minimum of text or other extraneous content. No attempt is made to differentiate the site, other than the fact that site sponsors are given priority billing within the category listings and a brief descriptive sentence describing their services. For UK investors this is probably the single best concentration of links to UK-based finance relevant web addresses.

iii. Interactive Investor (www.iii.co.uk) has an extensive range of information of use to UK investors. It includes in particular a searchable database of unit and investment trusts including performance figures from Micropal and background data on investment trusts from leading specialists in the area, and data from leading personal finance and investment management product providers such as M&G, Gartmore and Fidelity. It also has a searchable index of articles from specific personal finance publications, links to an online dealing service, and the facility to create personal portfolios which are regularly updated for changes in market price.

Investorama. This site (www.investorama.com) has a well-ordered directory of links to a variety of different resources as well as a section specifically devoted to investment-related jumping-off points. The content is particularly slanted to the USA.

Investormap: The Investormap site (http://investormap.com) claims to have more than 8000 specifically finance and investment-related links, and does differentiate between US and non-US sources of information. The categorisation of sites is good, but the non-US content has some obvious gaps, particularly of more recently launched sites.

Lenape Investment Corporation. Richard Sauers of Lenape Investment Corporation, a US firm, has in the past compiled an exhaustive list of sites of interest to investors (www.enter.net/~rsauers/) where an abbreviated edition of his regularly published sourcebook is available in both text and hypertext mark-up format. The links displayed in the site are indexed by the first letter of the second part of the URL (i.e. after the *http://www.* prefix), and a brief description is given. A more detailed classified list is available by subscription in a downloadable or in hard copy format. At the time of writing, however, the Sauers site had not been updated for some time, but the site is a useful one nonetheless.

MoneyWorld. This site (www.moneyworld.co.uk) is another excellent source of personal finance information, share prices and news for the UK online investor. Sections include financial contacts, newsbriefs, a daily business report, comprehensive share prices avilable throughout the trading day, easy-to-understand guides, a UK personal finance directory, mortgages, savings products, rates and performance, and a glossary. The site is an excellent starting point for newcomers to the finance and investing scene. Of particular note is the 'directory' section (now called Start!), which is a conveniently indexed collection of links to various sites of relevance to UK investors, including links to accountants, cash card services, commodities,

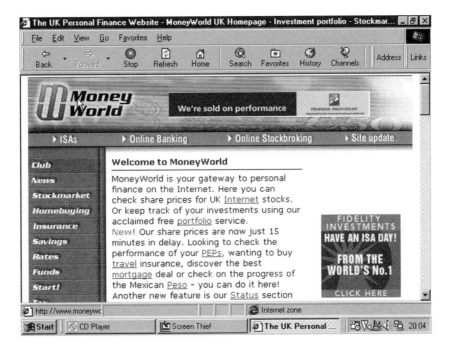

Figure 3.4   MoneyWorld is an excellent source of personal finance information

derivatives, financial publications, offshore centres, brokers and funds managers, venture capital, and world stock markets.

Qualisteam. A useful jumping-off point with a European rather than US orientation is Qualisteam. This is a French site (www.qualisteam.com) which has specific and comprehensive links to a range of banks, brokers, and exchanges around Europe and elsewhere. Qualisteam claims to have links to 95% of banking web sites worldwide, more than 6000 in all, and to the stockmarkets and derivatives exchanges of over 100 countries. The site also includes calculators, downloadable software and various other features. Banking dominates the site and makes it an excellent starting point for those working in or interested in this area.

UK Directory. This site, located at http://www.ukdirectory.com, is a comprehensive collection of web sites. Its earlier claim to list all UK web sites was quite naturally suspect, but the site is a good index of all the conceivable interests it thinks UK surfers might have (it is not just business and

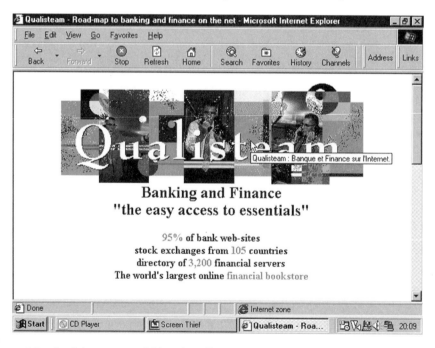

Figure 3.5 Qualisteam—a useful jumping-off point

finance-related). It has specific links to business and finance topics as well as to government-related pages and others that online investors might find interesting. Following the finance and investment related link brings up a list of sites broadly grouped into banks, finance, insurance, the stock market and so on. Although the site might be considered a reasonable starting point, it is by no means as comprehensive as some other sites that are more tightly focused on the financial area.

UK Invest. This site, at www.ukinvest.com, is a magazine style site which provides finance-related content aimed at Freeserve users, who are able to access real time short prices. The site contains news stories, index information and columns written by financial and investing pundits.

It can probably be seen from this brief résumé that there are a number of ways in which the web's mass of content can be tamed: by intelligent searching of either single search engines, multiple searches or meta-search tools, and by bookmarking a specific number of jumping-off sites that contain material that may be used regularly.

This brings us to the question of so-called 'portal' sites. These are sites which, as their name suggests, are often configured as home pages on browsers and represent the first point of contact for newcomers surfing the net. They are popular because they include easy links to every conceivable interest a net user might require. Yahoo! probably represents the original and best single example of a portal site that doubles as a search tool. However, Netscape's Netcenter site (www.netscape.com), AOL's home page (www.aol.com), Go.com (www.go.com) the product of links between Infoseek and Disney, Lycos (www.lycos.com), Excite (www.excite.com) and several others, fulfil much the same function.

The numbers of users at these sites are huge. AOL (which merged with Netscape in 1998) now has probably around 30 million visitors a week, as does Yahoo!. MSN (www.msn.com), another portal site run by Microsoft, claims 21 million visitors, Go.com has 21 million, Lycos 17 million and Excite 17 million. In their role as search tools some of these numbers are less impressive. Compare the 100 million plus pages indexed by Northern Light and AltaVista and FAST's 235 million with similar figures for Go.com of 48 million, MSN's 43 million, Excite's 33 million and Lycos's 20 million. These figures date from comparisons made during 1999 and are published in Search Engine Showdown, available at the web site www.notess.com/search/stats/size.html.

Impressive though these numbers are, and while I have nothing against portals per se, I would argue strongly that the budding online investor needs to be much more adventurous in the ways in which he or she approaches the quest for information. Good though they are, portals represent a lazy way out and learning to use search tools and bookmarking good financially orientated jumping-off points represents a better route to more rewarding information sources.

However, for convenience's sake, and as mentioned at the start of this book, I have created a site which contains all of the links mentioned in this chapter and those mentioned in later chapters. These are freely available at the URL www.cix.co.uk/~ptemple/linksite/ or via the New Online Investor web site at www.new-online-investor.co.uk.

One of the most precious commodities for the online investor is news, both past and present—to react to immediately or to browse for research purposes. The next chapter concentrates on where it is and how to get it.

CHAPTER 4

Online News and Opinion

Investors of all kinds thrive on information. But until comparatively recently the ability of ordinary investors to tap into market-moving news announcements more or less as they happened during the trading day was very limited.

Live price and news feeds were available for investors, but only at an annual subscription upwards of £1200. Though the price of live feeds has come down a little, now a subscription of a few pounds a month will guarantee access to company news announcements over the web, and there are plenty of Internet news resources offering company and other announcements delayed by, say, 20 minutes and which are totally free.

It is worth getting the issue of real time news in perspective. In practice it will be impossible for a private investor, even one glued to a screen for 12 hours a day, to beat the professional reaction to a news announcement such as a profit warning, a takeover announcement, or some other similar piece of news. With this in mind, the value of real-time news is in my view often overstated. In addition, it is often the case that the market's initial reaction to a piece of news is incorrect. Getting swayed by the reactions of the crowd is the antithesis of what makes a successful investor.

In short, it's the quality of the information that really matters. The veteran US fund manager turned author Peter Lynch, for example, makes much of the advantage the private investor possesses in being able to invest on the basis of his or her own experiences as a consumer or as a member of a local community. This experience, he argues, may very well include examples of successful, yet undervalued, businesses.

Let's apply this to the online investor. The physical community you inhabit and the experiences you have are still available and still valid, but they are supplemented by the 'virtual' community and experiences represented by the web in its various facets.

What the web allows the online investor to do is to access the opinions of other investors and to have web access to the normal TV-based news organisations such as the BBC and CNN. In the print media area, online investors can access with ease press comment on specific topics and companies from the archives of a wide variety of newspapers and magazines, and also in many cases to access news releases from companies as they are released into the market.

Corporate web sites (see Chapter 6) have grown in importance dramatically in recent years. The more enlightened companies make their news releases available by email as they are announced to anyone who registers at their site for this service. Amendments to the Companies Act are being considered to make dissemination in this way to those who request an optional alternative to posting announcements to shareholders.

So there are many ways in which the online investor can tap into both hard news and gossip about investment subjects. As elsewhere on the Internet and world wide web, much of the current content has a US flavour, but as time goes by an increasing proportion of it is about topics relevant to investors in the UK, Europe and elsewhere.

It falls into several categories. So I have divided this chapter into several sections, each of which has a newsy bias, but also points up the diversity of information available online.

These broad categories are as follows:

❏ bulletin board newsgroups
❏ usenet newsgroups
❏ web site bulletin boards
❏ email lists
❏ online newswires and broadcasters
❏ online newspapers and magazines.

The first four of these categories represent ways in which opinon can be exchanged with other investors. This is important for online investors because of the upsurge in the use of execution-only stockbroking services.

For those who wish to take advantage of them, using bulletin boards as a sounding board can act as a partial substitute for the role normally performed by the traditional private client advisory stockbroker.

This is with the proviso that opinions expressed in newsgroups and bulletin boards are often from those with an axe to grind, and additional independent research—perhaps via newspaper archives and the corporate website—is necessary before taking action. Put more strongly, there have also been instances where the medium has been used for the fraudulent manipulation of share prices, for instance by using heavily used bulletin boards to plant false stories about companies. Regulators are on the case and some small BBS operators have been shut down for not doing enough to eliminate abuses of this sort.

You have been warned. Treat newsgroups as the digital equivalent of picking up share tips in the pub or golf club bar.

Bulletin Board Newsgroups

Some Internet users tend to dismiss bulletin board systems, many of which pre-dated the rise of the Internet as a mass market medium, as rather old hat.

But for the UK online investor, bulletin board newsgroups (sometimes called conferences or forums) have the advantage that they can offer a source of comment and opinion that is specifically UK-oriented. The same is true of some of the newer web-based bulletin boards.

For those not familiar with the way they work, email is at the core of the way the groups function. Instead of sending email on a bilateral basis to a single correspondent, perhaps a friend or colleague whose email address you know, bulletin board newsgroups are simply a central point into which all the discussion and opinion can be posted and where it is seen by all the participants in the group.

The obvious analogy is that it is like pinning a card to a notice board in a public place like a library or a college. Someone (whom you may not know) can reply either by leaving a message on the board, or by communicating directly with you.

Another advantage of bulletin board conferences is that they are often 'moderated' or refereed. This means that posts to the group which are irrelevant or abusive can be removed by the bulletin board operator. This is in marked contrast to the unmoderated newsgroups in the Usenet system (discussed later). On occasion these contain a big proportion of irrelevant information.

By convention, information in conferences and newsgroups is connected together in 'threads'. This is a collection comprising the original message and the responses to it. A potential poster to a bulletin board can therefore either initiate a new thread, or reply to an existing one.

The norm is for messages to be composed off-line, using an off-line reader (OLR)—this is like an autopilot which batches all the messages to be uploaded and downloaded and completes the task in the minimum time possible before disconnecting. By employing it, users do not need to waste valuable connection time to read messages or compose replies while online.

However, the use of OLRs means that discussions can take some time to complete and the responses to an initial posting on a topic almost certainly will not be replied to immediately. This phenomenon is known as 'OLR lag'.

It happens because a post to a newsgroup may not be uploaded immediately, for example. It may then take some time for the potential replier to note the message and respond. Then his or her reply may also not be uploaded to the bulletin board or newsgroup immediately. Days and weeks can sometimes go by before a discussion is satisfactorily concluded.

Web-based bulletin boards, a newer innovation, have the advantage that all messages are composed online and therefore the timelags, though not eliminated, tend to be much shorter.

Most OLRs permit the configuration of messages in different ways. The reader can either move from one unread message to the next in chronological order, or from thread to thread. Most newsgroups also enable the user to identify which subscribers are joined up to that particular conference (i.e. receiving its messages) and therefore ready in the background to participate in discussions that interest them.

At the time of writing the leading bulletin board groups operating in the UK are CompuServe and AOL. Most ISPs offer access to Usenet newsgroups (of which more later) but only a few have internal investment conferences and forums. Since I am connected through CIX, which is a bulletin board operator, I will use their conferences as the main basis for the examples that follow, but other major bulletin boards offer an analogous service.

In CompuServe, for instance, a variety of forums exist for investors. These cover topics such as personal finance, tax, financial software, and so on. Each of these forums contain subdivisions on particular topics. CompuServe's investment forum, for example, deals variously with share trading, options, mutual funds and unit trusts, and a variety of other subjects.

But let's have a quick look at CIX and the various investment-related conferences it operates, as an illustration of the way the system works and some of the topics discussed.

Under the heading of 'money, investment and financial institutions' in the index of conferences operated in the CIX system are a range of conferences including, for example, Abbey National, banks in general, First Direct, handling debt, investment, money, tax and financial planning, options, money laundering, negative equity, and so on.

Let's take a couple of these and look at their structure:

Money. In CIX, the Money conference now has 250 plus participants (like everything else related to the net, this figure has doubled in the past couple of years) and is subdivided into a number of different topics variously entitled: making it; losing it; debt; general; contacts; enquiries; and practice. The 'enquiries' topic is the most active, with 130 plus messages in the month of writing, on topics including pension AVCs (additional voluntary contributions), transferring CGT (capital gains tax) between husband and wives, and several other issues.

Investment. The investment conference has 380 plus participants and rather more topics. These include sections for: beginners; files; a 'general' section; and separate topics on penny shares, options, pensions, PEPs, shares in general, software, and technical analysis. The 'general' topic is an active one, with several messages daily and around 200 messages a month.

At the time of writing, subjects covered have included: the debate about building societies floating and how best to take advantage of the trend; which shares are included in the FTSE 100 index; how financial advisers justify their fees; a list of the TESSAs (tax exempt special savings accounts) on offer; and information on a new finance-oriented world wide web site.

That said, many of the other topics are more or less dormant. There is, however, a reasonable amount of interesting cut and thrust between participants, who range from professionals and experienced private investors, to beginners to the investment scene and/or the Internet. As with many CIX conferences, the atmosphere is friendly, and helpful, with a touch of banter.

One general point about all bulletin board systems is that they often come with files available for members to download. In the case of the investment conference on CIX, for example, these files include demonstration disks for several different types of investment software, historic data on the FTSE 100 index, a list of suggested reading, and other useful snippets. In the money conference is a small file list which contains background briefing notes on various financial planning topics, and 'ten awkward question to ask your financial adviser'.

It is always open to the enthusiastic user to start up a conference if you feel that there is a topic that might be worthy of discussion. This is subject to obtaining the permission of the system operator to do this, and being prepared to spend time moderating the discussion. Off-line readers supplied as part of a bulletin board conferencing package often have a special add-in program that enables the moderator to do his or her job, removing off-topic messages if need be, and commenting on others.

Newsgroups operated by BBS operators tend to be smaller and more participative than the larger ones on Usenet (see below). It is more difficult, for example, to hide in a corner (known in Internet jargon as 'lurking') and not participate. It is also up to the individual participant, if a topic that he or she might want to know about is not being discussed, to post a provocative comment and try and get a discussion going.

It is also worth bearing in mind that some of the less obvious conferences may include discussion on financial topics. For instance, in the CIX system there are conferences related to all the major broadsheet newspapers, magazines such as *The Economist* and *Private Eye*, and all the main political parties. If these are of no other use, they often provide a thought-provoking and humorous insight into current events.

To reiterate one important point: it is self-evident in a national bulletin board system like CIX that all of those logged onto UK investment-related conferences will either be UK online investors or those with an interest in the UK finance scene. Most discussions do tend therefore to be of specific interest to UK online investors. This is not always the case with Usenet newsgroups, which we move on to look at next.

Usenet Newsgroups

History provides no definitive answer as to why Usenet is called what it is. However, by common consent it is reckoned to be a contraction of Users'

Network, or USENIX Network, reflecting its origin as a spin-off from a large UNIX user group. But don't panic at the mention of UNIX.

You can read Usenet newsgroups using UNIX commands if you want to. But most users view and contribute to them in plain text either online or using an OLR. In this respect they are similar to, and sit comfortably alongside, the conferences and forums operated by a BBS such as CIX or CompuServe.

There are, however, other differences between the conferences and forums of bulletin board systems and those of Usenet. These are manifested in several ways.

The first difference is in the sheer number of them. At the last count, for example, there were around 5000 individual conferences in the CIX system (the BBS with which I am most familiar), but there are reputed to be more than 80,000 Usenet newsgroups. Not all ISPs will offer access to all newsgroups.

The Usenet system is made slightly more manageable by the fact that the newsgroups operate in a broad hierarchical system which enables a specific field of interest to be identified more quickly. There are, for instance, sections of the hierarchy for newsgroups devoted to particular US states, particular countries, to computer topics, to scientific topics, to social topics, to news about Internet-related matters, and to recreations of various types. Everything else, and for the most part this includes anything to do with investment or finance, is lumped together in a *miscellaneous* (or *misc.*) category.

For UK online investors, the choice of relevant Usenet newsgroups is a surprisingly small one. There are, for example, *misc.invest* categories with suffixes such as *.technical* (technical analysis), *.stocks*, *.futures*, *.funds* (to do with bond, equity and derivatives funds), *.canada* (investment in Canadian markets), *.real-estate*, and so on. Newsgroups with specific UK content are confined to one, namely *uk.finance*.

Investment topics to do with other countries may be available, although some may well be conducted in the host language. Where no country prefix is displayed in the Usenet index it can safely be assumed that the newsgroup will have predominently US content.

Of course, US-oriented newsgroups need not be totally ignored. They may contain information (for instance about software or investment-related web sites) that is interesting to non-US investors.

Before we go on to look at a brief sampling of the type of messages from these various newsgroups, however, let's look further at some of the other differences between Usenet newsgroups and the typical bulletin board forum or conference.

One difference, for instance, is that as well as there being many more newsgroups to choose from (although only a handful of really relevant investment-oriented ones), there is a vastly larger pool of potential participants. If, for instance, CIX's 15,000 or so subscribers produce 300–400 people interested in an investment-related forum, the number potentially interested in an investment related Usenet newsgroup—open to all those with Usenet access in the US and the rest of the world—is multiplied many times over.

This could be viewed as an advantage. But having a large number of participants is a two-edged sword. Putting out a general request for information on a particular investment topic, for example, may be answered several times over. Or it may simply be buried in the welter of other information in the group, and therefore ignored. The trick is to give the posting a relevant and eye-catching lead-in and to make it succinct. This increases the chances that it will get read.

The second point is that most of the Usenet newsgroups are unmoderated. Hence they can contain a number of less desirable aspects of the Internet. These include blatant self-promotion, scams, irrelevant or abusive postings, stock pushing, and other nastiness which tends to be deterred or weeded out by BBS system operators.

All this is best summarised as a low 'signal to noise' ratio. In other words, a lot of irrelevant postings may have to be waded through in order to catch information that is relevant and useful. There are ways around this, however.

One is that most OLRs will contain a simple command that can weed out, mark as 'read' or 'to be ignored' threads that are irrelevant. The other is that, with practice, most users become used to scanning through newsgroups quickly and skilled at detecting which items are of interest.

One plus point for Usenet newsgroups on investment topics is that they are invaluable informal sounding boards for the twists and turns of investor sentiment, and a good way of applying contrary opinion theory.

A good example of this has been the rather chequered ride that high technology and Internet-related stocks have offered, especially in the US market, over the past couple of years. Using investment-related newsgroups it would, for instance, have been easy to spot these turning points by noting the opinion of the 'crowd' and taking the opposite tack when the clamour reached its height.

There have also, in my experience, been several instances where news-groups have highlighted stocks worthy of further research. But it needs stressing that the picking up of tips like this must be followed up by solid research, since newsgroups represent an ideal forum for investors who have shares in a particular company to 'talk them up' on pretty insubstantial grounds. Indeed stock market regulators in the USA in particular have become concerned at the sharp price movements that have sometimes accompanied the tipping of shares in influential investment newsgroups and web-based bulletin boards, as well as the planting of false information.

With these cautions in mind, let's have a look at the character of some of the finance and investment-related Usenet newsgroups mentioned earlier. These are shown in Table 4.1. The table demonstrates that logging on to Usenet newsgroups needs to be done sparingly. It is perfectly possible for some of the more popular newsgroups—such as *misc.invest.stocks* and *misc.invest*—to have well over 100, or in some cases over 200, messages a day. Wading through this quantity of messages does take some time.

From the standpoint of the UK online investor, logging onto the *uk.finance* group is essential, while the extent to which US-oriented groups are used is another matter. The *misc.invest.technical* group does tend to contain information that can be of use to a wider audience than just US investors. For instance, there is often information on new or existing software available for downloading.

As new web sites are launched that are relevant to investors, they do also tend to crop up in newsgroups. This gives Usenet groups another handy function: that of alerting the investor to new material that has become available elsewhere. It is not, however, necessary to log on to all of the half a dozen or so finance-related newsgroups to pick up these flags: many announcements of this type are cross-posted to all relevant ones.

The extent to which you make use of Usenet newsgroups will depend on the amount of time you are able to devote to the material, relative to the use you might get out of it. In my own case, I might spend up to half an hour most days participating in newsgroups, but part of my interest is professional rather than just to do with my personal investment activities.

Posting to newsgroups—rather than just passive reading—is obviously part of the process. You can reply to queries posted by other users, ask questions or make comments of your own. In *The New Internet Navigator* (John Wiley, 1995), Paul Gilster describes several 'rules of the road' that

Table 4.1 Investment-related Usenet groups

	misc.invest. technical	misc.invest. stocks	misc.invest	uk.finance	misc.invest. futures	misc.invest. funds
Main subject	Software; technical analysis	Stock picking/pushing	General investment topics	UK personal finance	Mainly US futures and options	US mutual funds
No. of posts	30–35	250–300	60–70	30–40	35–40	50–60
Typical posts	Bollinger bands Recurrence IV—any views A new derivatives mag Market technicians seminar Shock analysis System testing software	16 yo wants invest. advice Yahoo! Symantec—any followers? DDIM—what happened? Stocks to explode in 99 IOMEGA up 3 at $35!	Holt optional stock report New Internet IPO HK market technical pos'n Need prof. financial planner Canadian mining newsletter Rant at Charles Schwab	Inv. Chronicle—subscribe? Remaning mutuals Building Socs and Bristol & W Profit from British beef? Loophole in inheritance tax Traded endowments	Dec. Corn/Wheat spread? OptionVue software for sale Commodit-E Journal 99 live hogs French Franc/Lira? KL options market—new?	Warning about mutual funds Performance of S&P 500 Buying cash at a discount? Alberta SE Fidelity's new qtly statement Load funds—less panic if crash
Signal/noise ratio	Medium	Low	Medium	High	High	High
Relevance to UK online investors	Moderate	Low	Moderate	High	Moderate	Low
Comment	Can be source of information on software download sites	Opinionated pushing, especially of technology stocks	Some useful information on investment related Web sites	Emphasis on insurance, PEPs and so on rather than stocks	Some theory; good on futures-related Web sites	Almost exclusively US-oriented

are worth reiterating here. These echo the comments on 'netiquette' made elsewhere.

Gilster's rules for newsgroups are:

❐ Do you really need to post?
❐ Use email where you can.
❐ Know your destination.
❐ Use descriptive titles for your post.
❐ Avoid blatant advertising.
❐ Avoid abusive discussions.
❐ Keep your 'signature' short.
❐ Exercise care in quoting earlier messages at length.
❐ Remember that news to you isn't always news to everybody.

Readers familar with Usenet newsgroups will note that I have omitted any reference to those organised under the *clari.* heading in the Usenet hierarchy. *ClariNet* is an electronic publishing service that provides an edited feed of significant news stories taken from wire services such as AP and Reuters, and repackages them in newsgroup format on a 'read-only' basis. Not all ISPs offer *clari.* newsgroups as part of their package (since subscribing to it costs them money). Because it is more in the nature of a news feed than a participative newsgroup it is included in a later part of this chapter along with other news services.

Finally, tracking all the newsgroups that might have potential relevance to an investment query is clearly a time-consuming business. So it is worth knowing that there is a search tool, known as Deja (www.deja.com), available to give assistance for specific queries.

Using search engines was covered in some detail in the previous chapter. Deja is easy to use and, given the right search terms to work with, should come up with interesting recent news on a particular topic. As with most search tools, it has become more sophisticated as time has gone by and offers the facility to perform both a quick search, across all Usenet groups, or a more tailored search across a selected list filtered by group, by author, by date, by subject and so on.

The ease with which good search results are achieved clearly depends on how tightly you are able to define its terms, excluding common words that might crop up in normal conversation. For instance, a search performed on the small UK engineering company Thomas Locker produces a

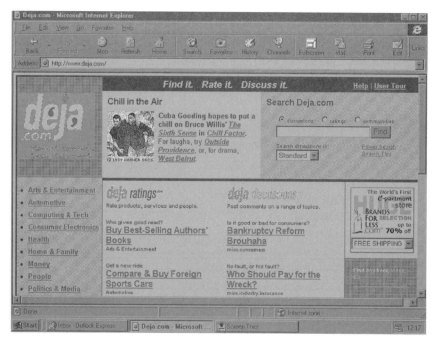

Figure 4.1   Deja gives assistance for specific queries

large number of hits with a sporting theme (locker rooms and so on). But near the top of the list were references to articles posted in the *uk.finance* newsgroup—closer to what I really had in mind.

Searching for companies by name can also throw up posts on other topics from employees at the company concerned. This is because email addresses are usually quoted in posts. For example, a recent search I performed for messages about Logica threw up a lot of messages (no doubt interesting to the posters and intended recipients, but not to me) from employees with 'logica.com' email addresses.

Searching is, nevertheless, accomplished very quickly even with a very broad enquiry, and the results display the hit rate (the extent to which some or all of the words crop up in the post), a headline or part of a headline, the newsgroup from which it is taken, and the author.

The quoting of the newsgroup is particularly important. Given the limited number of finance-oriented newsgroups, it is comparatively easy to spot from the search results which items are relevant to a particular investment related enquiry.

In addition, the use of a search tool sometimes leads to serendipity in the form of posts in newsgroups that it may not have been imagined contained relevant information. I once searched for news on an obscure (and now defunct) computer company and uncovered a post from a newsgroup I would not normally have frequented. This post contained a lengthy discussion of the relationship between the target company and one of its business partners, good background information unlikely to appear in the company's annual report or corporate brochure.

This is an example of the importance of quality information I referred to at the beginning of this chapter. It's not 'inside information' as such. But at the same time it's not easily available to everyone, and thus can have solid investment value.

So Usenet, though it is the repository of a lot of trite and ill-informed comment and speculation, can be made to work via intelligent searching. Deja is free to use, and is funded by advertising.

There is, though, a trade-off to be struck between minimising the number of relevant hits, while keeping the search wide enough to include some element of unearthing the unexpected and the interesting.

In the same way, a happy medium can be struck between the potentially parochial BBS newsgroups with comparatively few 'subscribers', and the anarchic and uncontrolled nature of the Usenet system. These come in the form of web-based bulletin boards and specialist email discussion lists, to which interested parties can subscribe. We look at both of these categories in the next two sections.

Web-site Based Bulletin Boards

One of the interesting developments since the *The Online Investor* was first published has been the growth in web sites offering bulletin board facilities. Several investment related sites for UK investors have launched these in the past couple of years.

They represent a useful compromise between the more basic content of some of the discussion on BBS bulletin boards, and the chaos of Usenet boards which remain dominated by US content even in sites intended to be about related investment topics. This is because the sites are accessed, by definition, by active investors who want news and views on stocks and are pretty well informed.

Arguably, the best of these web based services is the Eye to Eye bulletin board operated by Datastream ICV's Market Eye web site at www.market-eye.co.uk. Investors can now register for the free 'Investor' service and gain access to the Eye to Eye board. Here messages are posted while online at the site and responses often come quickly. The subject matter is all directly relevant to UK investors.

The UK Equities Direct web site at www.hemscott.com also has an 'information exchange', which is free to use and which contains postings from traders and investors. On the basis of a recent sampling the content appears less thoughtful than that at the Market Eye site, and rather more 'trader-driven' than the more considered views expressed on the Eye to Eye site. E*Trade UK—formerly Electronic Share Information (www.etrade.co.uk) also has a bulletin board run along similar lines to these two, but at the time of writing it was available only for paying subscribers. E*Trade has 150,000 bulletin board subscribers in the USA.

Another good site that chimes in well with a value investing philosophy is that of The Motley Fool. The UK Fool site (www.fool.co.uk) has a number of interconnected message boards, including one specifically devoted to 'all British shares', as well as articles on general investment topics.

For a look at the way forward for online investment forums it's worth looking at Yahoo! Finance (http://finance.yahoo.co.uk). Clicking on the 'stocks messages' part of the 'chat and message boards' subsection of the home page shows hundreds of message boards with a separate one devoted to many individual (US) stocks, indexed by sector. This is now starting to develop in a modest way in the UK.

Once again, treat the comments made on these message boards with a grain of salt. Remember that people will shamelessly 'talk their own book'. At the same time, it's good to talk to other investors and many of the messages contain hard information and news you can use. Stick to those and ignore the flagrant tipsters and you won't go too far wrong.

Email Lists

Email lists are rather different from newsgroups and more akin to the conferences encountered in a BBS. They may have a more limited number

Figure 4.2   Motley Fool has a number of interconnected message boards

of participants than may be the case in Usenet, a referee, and a tendency to stick to the topic in hand. The reason for this is obvious. You don't sign up to a list unless you are interested in participating in it.

The quirks of automatic mailing list management software meant that joining lists like this could be something of a trial. But many lists can now be joined more easily via web sites rather than, in the old way, through sending a specifically configured email to an email subscription address. The problem with many discussion lists of this type is that there are only a handful of them that have a direct relevance to issues of specific interest to a UK online investor.

The character of these lists is more like a private discussion group than the boisterous and anarchic exuberance of the Usenet newsgroups. Many of the lists grew out of scholarly conferences on particular topics and are still run and refereed by academics.

The software that runs a mailing list is usually automatic so it is important when sending messages that the correct address is specified in the email. This should be the address to access the list's recipients rather than the system administrator. Equally when subscribing to or leaving a list, exit using instructions at the website or send a message to the system administrator, not the address that accesses all of the list recipients. It sounds an obvious point, but it is sometimes forgotten.

When sending commands to so-called 'listserv' automatic software like this, the subject header line is left blank and the message is typed in the message area below. It is also important to turn off any signatures that are automatically added to email messages. These can be misinterpreted by list management software.

Messages posted to the list address pop into the email boxes of every participant of the list. Rather as in a newsgroup, the recipient can choose to reply or not.

Other types of email list—rather more common these days—are simply 'read-only'. This means they simply function as a means for an organisation to disseminate information to 'subscribers'. An increasingly large category of these are corporate or commercial web sites, which send out email bulletins or news releases periodically, to keep 'subscribers' up to date.

The real problem with mailing lists is actually finding out that they exist. Mailing list information is sometimes posted in newsgroups and given out in Internet-related magazines. However, an easier way to access some of the relevant information is via a number of world wide web sites specifically devoted to cataloguing them.

For a flavour of the topics on offer at the various scholarly e-conferences, Liszt, a searchable index of lists and newsgroups located at www.liszt.com, is worth a visit. It is probably the easiest of such sites to navigate and search, although there are others which aficionados regard as equally useful.

Another feature of Liszt is a link to commercial email lists that contain advertising, press releases and the like, rather than the scholarly discussion these forums have traditionally contained. This is just another way in which the net is adapting to changing times and a dramatically increased number of users.

For UK online investors, there are investment-related websites operating mailing lists to keep interested investors up to date with what is happening at their site.

One site that does publish information of this kind is the Interactive Investor (www.iii.co.uk), which emails out periodic newsletters to those

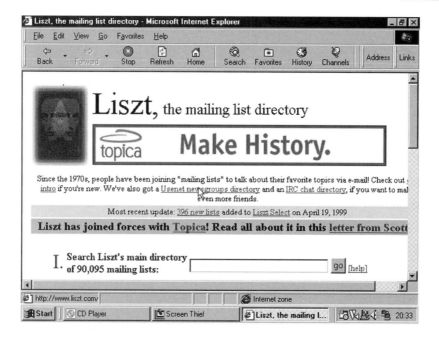

Figure 4.3 Check out scholarly e-conferences at Liszt

who are interested. Those keen to subscribe to this list, which has a distinct personal finance flavour, can do so by sending email to subscribe@iii.co.uk with the message 'subscribe interactive investoralert'. Interactive Investor also has a number of other discussion lists of interest to investors, which can be joined by visiting the iii web site.

Another passive mailing list of interest to investors is the one operated by HM Treasury. This list emails out news releases and other announcements to subscribers. To be added to the list simply send an email message to maillist@hmt.gov.uk with the message 'subscribe press' or 'subscribe whatsnew' in the body of the message, leaving the subject line blank—or follow the instructions at the Treasury site at www.hm-treasury.gov.uk.

Note that although we have used the word 'subscribe' and 'subscriber' throughout this section, this is simply shorthand to describe the process of signing up to the list. All of the lists are totally free to join.

One very obvious point is that automatic mailing lists represent an ideal way for companies to keep in touch with their shareholders and any other interested parties, and an ideal way of making sure that price sensitive information is disseminated as widely and as quickly as possible.

And as noted previously, following the interest shown in this by US companies, the more progressive UK companies are beginning to offer a broadcast email service as part of their web presence.

In the next section we look at the way in which online investors can access news via the Internet and world wide web from conventional sources similar to those used by professional investors, and at little or no cost.

Online News Feeds

Newsgroups, discussion lists and BBS conferences are not the only way for the online investor to gain access to news and opinion. In fact, what newsgroups and conferences offer is strictly a mixture of opinion, questions and fact. Hard news is an altogether more precious commodity.

In particular, stock-specific hard news, though easier than it was to obtain with the help of corporate web sites, can sometimes be elusive. Nonetheless, there are many other helpful sources that can save money and time for investors, and give them a window into the types of services viewed by the professionals.

We can subdivide them into three main categories: passive hard news related Usenet newsgroups, such as ClariNet; online news services such as Reuters, CNN, and Bloomberg; and online versions of daily newspapers and weekly or monthly magazines. These are covered in the remainder of this chapter.

ClariNet

Clari.net (www.clari.net) is an electronic publisher offering a series of newsgroups to which are posted (on a read-only basis) news stories from the main wire services such as Reuters, UPI and AP.

Among its coverage of a huge variety of topics ClariNet has over 100 newsgroups covering items of general interest to investors, including stock market reports and economic news, some of which is specific to the UK or to European markets. There is also news relevant to specific industry groups, but this is generally dominated by US content.

Posts tend to be occasional, although they are specific and relevant when they do appear, with none of the opinionated dross that clutters up the normal Usenet investment forums.

The following handful of recent headlines simply gives a flavour of the type of stories the groups contain (the newsgroup and source is quoted in brackets after the headline):

❏ Palladium price slumps on Russian exports (*.biz.economy*/AFP)
❏ New blitz of travel software (*.biz.features*/AFP)
❏ Deutsche Telekom confident on Italian merger (*.biz.mergers*/AFP)
❏ Philippine exports up 19% (*.biz.world_trade*/UPI).

Remember, however, that because ClariNet is a service to which your ISP must subscribe to be able to include it in its Usenet feed, not all ISPs will carry these newsgroups. So check that this service is available before signing up.

Online News Services

A number of large news agencies and similar organisations provide services that can be accessed either directly or indirectly via the web. These include Reuters, Bloomberg, CNN and others.

At the time the first edition of *The Online Investor* was published, many news-related websites adopted the ploy of using the web to tease those logging on into taking out a more expensive subscription (perhaps by displaying headlines but reserving the meat of the story for the subscription-based service). Since then, however, with some notable exceptions, most no longer take this tack and are essentially funded by online advertising or by wholesaling subscription revenue.

Reuters, for example, keeps a fairly low profile in terms of a direct web presence for its news stories, but wholesales them to banks and brokers, and to web sites such as Yahoo! for dissemination to the wider market.

The result is that a web portal, for example Yahoo!, make Reuters news stories available free of charge at its site (http://finance.yahoo.com) while brokers such as Charles Schwab and banks such as ABN Amro take Reuters services which they repackage and provide to their clients on either a free 'delayed' basis or in real time for a small monthly subscription.

In doing this Reuters has quite subtly kept separate its service provision for the private investor and for the professionals in trading rooms, who still demand the timeliness and comprehensiveness of the full Reuters service and are unable to access it in any other way but by subscribing as normal. But equally it has been able to generate substantial revenue from wholesaling news to other financial and business web site operators.

Bloomberg has been more upfront about providing news stories at its site (www.bloomberg.com), but though the service is interesting and impressive and has good slant towards the bond markets, it would clearly be inadequate for a professional trader, who would still want the highly necessary subscription to the infinitely more sophisticated Bloomberg terminal. Mike Bloomberg, the company's founder, was a trader first and media magnate second, and so is unlikely to ignore the needs of the professional user.

Another interesting feature of Bloomberg is the fact that its Bloomberg TV and News Radio features are available at its web site, where users can download free of charge the video and audio of past broadcasts or listen to the live feed. Reuters is also developing an Internet-based TV service.

Broadcasters such as the BBC (www.news.bbc.co.uk), Sky (www.skynews.co.uk) and CNN (www.cnn.com and www.cnnfn.com, CNN's financial news site) and others such as UPI and AFP each has a web presence with up-to-the-minute news stories available free of charge.

The Press Association also has a web site, located at the URL www.pa.press.net, containing stories updated hourly. These tend mainly to be general news stories rather than those with a business, finance or investment angle. The press release distributor PR Newswire also has a web site (www.twoten.press.net), where verbatim press releases from companies signed up by PRN are displayed on a minute-by-minute basis. Like the PA service, many of these stories do not have an investment or finance flavour.

One of the best resources for keeping track of stories from major newswires is the UK-based web site Newsnow (www.newsnow.co.uk). Launched in the past couple of years Newsnow has a number of categories (general news, sport, business and finance, IT and so on) and displays headlines from newswire stories and links to the relevant pages containing them. The stories are updated every few minutes, time-stamped and shown strictly in the order in which they have been received, with the most recent first. The service also has a link to a press release service specifically for IT-related news.

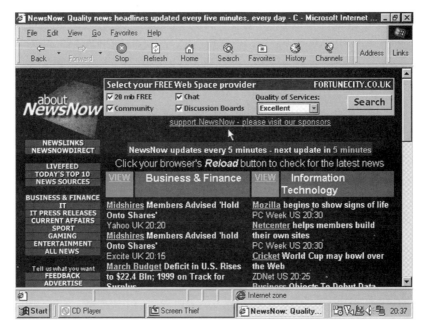

Figure 4.4 Newsnow—one of the best resources for keeping track of news stories

Newsnow not only includes newswire stories but also stories from broad-cast media and newspapers, making it a good all-round site of easily accessible news. Between this and Yahoo! Finance, investors can easily keep track of breaking business news stories as they happen.

News websites are developing quickly and it is worth investigating on a regular basis to see whether or not these and other news organisations have more extensive operations under development. For instance, the website News 365 (www.news365.com) is in effect a 'site of sites' of news-related market links including newswires, newspapers, comment on shares, and other resources. The only drawback to the site is that content is predominently US-oriented.

Online Newspapers

Online daily newspapers clearly do not quite have the immediacy of wire service news or even such 'steam age' devices as teletext which, though crude in technological terms, nonetheless represent as good a source as any for investors to use to keep up with company news and share prices.

However, it is important for investors to be catholic in their business reading and the online editions of certain daily newspapers provide a good way of going about this without racking up a huge paper bill.

However, the real value of newspaper and magazine web sites in my view lies elsewhere. As with corporate web sites, online newspapers can be an excellent source of information in the research process that diligent investors should carry out before investing in a company's shares.

An online investor can often use a corporate site to check on the latest annual report and news releases, but equally important are the views of the business press on a company. Researching an online newspaper archive for comments on a company is a way of doing the basic investment legwork without keeping files of press cuttings on every company under the sun. Web technology, with its search capabilities, is ideal for this task.

However, newpaper publishers being commercial animals, not all newspaper archives offer a free service, although generally searching is free and the cost of purchasing articles retrieved is low. The availablility of a searchable archive, preferably free of charge is therefore a key attribute of the online edition of a business newspaper.

Other features that are important include the ease with which the site can be entered. Does the site, for example, have a registration procedure (where the user, even at a free site, has to provide some details about himself or herself before being granted a user name and password). Free sites use this as a way of gathering data in order to provide demographic information to advertisers on the site. Once the initial registration procedure has been completed, however, returning to the site is usually easy. Either the post-registration home page can be bookmarked, or the operating system software can be configured to 'remember' the user name and password, making later access to the site an easy matter.

Other useful attributes are whether or not the site has detailed business news and share price information. Many US newspaper sites have links to conventional web 'quote servers' (see next chapter for more on this).

A good starting point for linking to newspaper and magazine sites worldwide is Newslink (www.newslink.org). Masterminded by the *American Journalism Review*, this site has links to more than 9000 newspapers, magazines, broadcast organisations and newswires around the world and is structured as a directory and is also searchable.

Some brief comments on the sites of online newspapers and magazines particularly relevant to investors, or the leading papers in their market, are given in the following paragraphs.

UK-based Publications

UK-based publications generally offer a reasonable level of information and searchability but with some sizeable variations. Table 4.2 shows those newspapers and magazines which might be consulted by the average investor. In other words, I have not included the more scurrilous tabloids, local papers and others which may have web sites but which have little or no investment-related news or comment.

This whittles the list down to around ten. The best site at the moment is actually the original pioneer of online newspapers in the UK, The Electronic Telegraph. This scores because it has a decent achive which is searchable and where stories can be accessed free of charge with no restrictions. The Telegraph has from time to time threatened to impose charges, but has so far refrained from doing so and the market appears to be moving away from this type of approach for now.

The *Financial Times* site, which might have been thought an obvious port of call for investors, has some limitations when it comes to accessing company information. Although the *FT* some time ago launched an archive service, and has periodically allowed totally free access to it, items of

Table 4.2 Web sites for UK-based publications

Publication	Web address	Business content	Useful co. news	Share price info.	Search archive	Country	Score
The Economist	www.economist.com	Yes	No	No	Yes	UK	4
Euromoney	www.euromoney.com	Yes	Yes	No	Yes	UK	7
Financial Times	www.ft.com	Yes	No	Yes	Yes	UK	5
Guardian	www.newsunlimited.co.uk	Yes	Yes	No	Yes	UK	8
Investors' Chronicle	www.investorschronicle.co.uk	No	No	No	No	UK	4
Observer	www.observer.co.uk	Yes	No	No	No	UK	7
Scotsman	www.scotsman.com	Yes	No	No	Yes	UK	7
Standard/Mail	www.thisismoney.co.uk	Yes	Yes	Yes	Yes	UK	9
Telegraph	www.telegraph.co.uk	Yes	Yes	Yes	Yes	UK	9
The Times	www.the-times.co.uk	Yes	No	No	No	UK	4

company news more than a month old are now being charged for, albeit at the relatively modest rate of $1.50 per story.

The reason for the *FT*'s coyness here is obvious. *FT* also sells FT Profile, an electronic database used by professionals, and the fear has always been that a too freely available web-based service would have a negative impact on this profitable service.

The Times Newspapers site is currently not searchable, which is something of a drawback, although there is a 'back numbers' service which allows the user to access company news comments on, for example, company results, provided that the date of the likely comment is known (i.e. the paper for the day following the announcement).

A site produced by London's *Evening Standard* and the previous Financial Mail Online sites have been replaced by an excellent new Associated Newspapers site This Is Money (www.thisismoney.co.uk), which aims to be as much a portal site as a newspaper one, but which offers news stories, search facilities and has a number of other attributes.

The disappointing one on the list is of the *Investors' Chronicle*, which has adopted the approach that it will make very little available to the casual surfer (presumably for fear of cannibalising its customer base). The *Guardian* has a useful searchable site (www.newsunlimited.co.uk) which contains stories from all the papers in the Guardian Media Group.

One of the best sites, especially for those interested in wider investment issues, used to be the Euromoney site (www.euromoney.com). Although this is devoted in large part to bonds, eurobonds and international equities, it has a superb user interface. However the site now restricts access to its search facility, which limits its usefulness to investors. *The Economist* archive is now free to those who subscribe to the print edition and well worth a visit.

US-based Publications

The sites displayed in Table 4.3 represent only a small fraction of those available, but I have tried to include those with national or major metro coverage and those which are sought out by investors. We would strongly counsel readers to visit the Newslink site to get a flavour for the sheer range of online news sites available in the USA.

There are obvious omissions in the list. I have adopted the criterion that

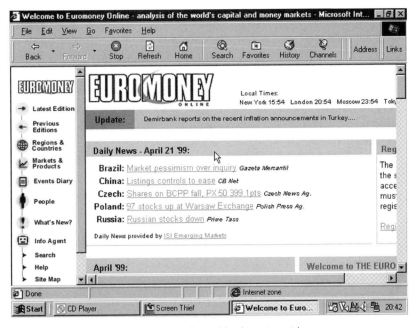

Figure 4.5 The free Euromoney site good on wider investment issues

Table 4.3 Web sites for US-based publications

Publication	Web address	Business content	Useful co. news	Share price info.	Search archive	Country	Score
Business Week	www.businessweek.com	Yes	No	No	Yes	USA	4
Chicago Sun-Times	www.suntimes.com	Yes	Yes	Yes	Yes	USA	9
Forbes	www.forbes.com	Yes	Yes	Yes	Yes	USA	10
Fortune	www.fortune.com	Yes	No	Yes	No	USA	5
Kiplingers	kiplinger.com	Yes	Yes	Yes	Yes	USA	8
Los Angeles Times	www.latimes.com	Yes	Yes	Yes	Yes	USA	9
Miami Herald	www.herald.com	Yes	Yes	Yes	Yes	USA	7
New York Times	www.nytimes.com	Yes	Yes	Yes	Yes	USA	8
San Jose Mercury News	www.sjmercury.com	Yes	Yes	Yes	Yes	USA	8
USA Today	www.usatoday.com	Yes	Yes	Yes	No	USA	6
Washington Post	www.washingtonpost.com	Yes	Yes	Yes	Yes	USA	8

a site must be free to enter to qualify for inclusion and this rules out *Investors Business Daily* and the *Wall Street Journal* which have, for the moment, taken the view that investors must pay even to access the most trivial of content. Interestingly enough, the *WSJ* site now claims to have some 250,000 subscribers with 68% not buying the print edition and therefore paying $49 per year to access the content. However, other leading US papers, including such heavyweights as the *Washington Post*, the *LA Times*, the *Miami Herald* and the *Chicago Sun-Times* all have sites which can be accessed free of charge.

All of the sites have searchable archives with the exception of *USA Today* and *Fortune*. The best site is Forbes Digital Tool, which has light graphics, a freely searchable archive and plenty of useful information. By contrast *Business Week*, rather like the *Investors' Chronicle*, is a little disappointing, requiring users to register and charging $2 per article for search retrieval from an archive which admittedly goes back to 1991. However, those subscribing to the print edition can access the archive free of charge.

Special mention should perhaps go to the San Jose Mercury News (www.sjmercury.com), which was a pioneer of the online medium, perhaps not surprisingly since it is the de facto business newspaper for Silicon Valley.

European-based Publications

Of non-UK publications based in Europe only two of ten, the *Irish Times* and *Handelsblatt*, have sites with an English version. The Handelsblatt site (www.handelsblatt.de) scores highly anyway, by far the best of the German papers with the *FAZ* (the Frankfurt business paper) particularly disappointing with little to commend it apart from some external links. Handelsblatt's site is flexible and easy to use. By and large, however, these sites are for linguists or native speakers only.

Table 4.4   Web sites for European-based publications

Publication	Web address	Business content	Useful co. news	Share price info.	Search archive	Country	Score
Corriera della Sera	www.globnet.rcs.it	No	Yes	No	No	Italy	4
Die Telegraaf	www.telegraaf.nl	Yes	No	No	Yes	Holland	5
Die Welt	www.welt.de	No	No	Yes	Yes	Germany	6
Die Zeit	www.zeit.de	Yes	No	No	Yes	Germany	7
FAZ	www.faz.de	No	No	No	No	Germany	1
Figaro	www.lefigaro.fr	No	No	No	No	France	3
Handelsblatt	www.handelsblatt.de	Yes	Yes	Yes	Yes	Germany	9
Irish Times	www.irish-times.ie	Yes	No	No	Yes	Eire	7
La Stampa	www.lastampa.it	Yes	No	No	No	Italy	4
Le Monde	www.lemonde.fr	Yes	Yes	Yes	No	France	6

Other Sites

Of the remaining publications, all coincidentally based in Commonwealth or former Commonwealth countries, the sites are mixed. The *South African Financial Mail* (www.fm.co.za) and the *Australian Financial Review* (www.afr.com.au) both score highly, but others are mixed, with the *Toronto Globe and Mail* let down by a complex search procedure including hard copy or fax dissemination of results and a high cost for search retrievals.

Summary

The best all-round newspaper and magazine sites can be scored on the basis of whether or not they are wholly free and without the need for registration, are in English or have an English version, and have business content, company information, share prices, a searchable archive and external links. They should also be easy to navigate.

On this basis we believe the Forbes site (www.forbes.com) is about the best, closely followed, depending on your location, by the Chicago Sun-Times (www.suntimes.com), Handelsblatt (www.handelsblatt.de), The South African Financial Mail (www.fm.co.za), The Australian Financial Review (www.afr.com.au), the Los Angeles Times (www.latimes.com), The Electronic Telegraph (www.telegraph.co.uk) and London's This is Money (www.thisismoney.co.uk).

However, newspaper web sites change constantly and it is worth exploring the Newslink site for other newspapers producing online editions and for improvements in the ones that currently offer less help to investors than perhaps they might.

CHAPTER 5

Share Prices, Company Data and Software Online

Value, rather than price, is what the investment process is all about. All the same, it's hard to make a judgement about whether or not to invest in a share without knowing its price. Equally, access to basic accounting numbers, or even a full annual report, is a prerequisite of any successful investment. The means to analyse this data is also valuable. Last of all, charting a share price over time is an important aid to making your purchase and sale at the right time.

Most of the information that falls into this category can be had for free on the net. You just have to know where to look for it.

Professional investors sometimes feel they have too much information on which to base decisions, making it difficult for them to arrive at a detached judgement. The near failure of the Long Term Capital Management hedge fund in Autumn 1998 resulted not from lack of information or the means to analyse it (the company had two Nobel mathematics laureates among its staff) but from incorrect judgements and the impact of external events.

Yet, in the past private investors often felt they lacked up-to-the-minute information. When markets are moving quickly, they are frustrated that they do not know what is happening to the market price of their shares.

About a month after the first edition of *The Online Investor* was published, the London Stock Exchange relaxed its earlier rule that effectively prevented private investors having cheap access even to delayed price information. Until that point, teletext services such as Ceefax were the only means of getting hold of price information during the trading day, and these were typically updated only a few times a day.

Now the choice is between free delayed (typically by 20 minutes) prices on the web, and real time data available (sometimes for a restricted but freely configurable group of shares) for a few pounds a month. For this few pounds a month you could, for instance, keep track of, in real time, half a dozen shares that you might hold, while checking others in which you were interested (but did not hold) on a 20-minute delayed basis. Once you acquired a new share, this could be added to the list of those watched in real time. Actually, some online dealing services now also allow full access to real-time prices and news.

Basic end-of-day data, for loading into a chart software package, has also come down in price dramatically and has improved out of all recognition in terms of delivery. If you want a more sophisticated array of data (for example, opening price, daily high–low and trading volume details) it will cost appreciably more. Accounts data is also available either free or in a reasonably economical form for the basics, and at a price if more detail is required.

This abundant choice means that it is important to be realistic about your data needs, and the methods you adopt (or rather should and should not adopt) when looking at companies as potential investments.

Assessing Your Price and Data Needs

In my view, the issues involved in selecting which combination of free or paid-for data to choose boil down to answering a few relatively simple questions:

Do I need real-time prices? In my view, real-time data is expensive for the advantages it gives the average private investor. For most 'retail' investors investment performance comes from careful selection of stocks, spotting value, and astute timing of major market moves. Trading on an intra-day basis is expensive for those not dealing in large amounts (by which I mean a £50,000 trade rather than a £1000 one) and is best left to the professionals. I have also personally found the presence of a real-time screen can have a disruptive effect on my trading decisions, pushing me into unwise moves. Up-to-the-minute prices are really only relevant when you need to deal.

Do I need intra-day prices at all? Personally I like to have an indication of which way the market is moving and, since this information is now available on the web free of charge, is it a separate service worth having anyway?

What kind of end-of-day price data do I require? There is no easy answer to this question. It will depend on whether or not you lean towards a chart-based or 'fundamentals'-based style of investing. If chart-based you will want to have the most comprehensive data you can afford. If you are oriented towards fundamentals, then a basic price service will be all that is required and may be available free of charge. Money thus saved can be spent on more sophisticated fundamental information.

What type of fundamental data do I require? This depends on the answer to the last question. Those oriented towards chart-based investment may feel they make do with the briefest of fundamental data, normally available free of charge on the web. Others want more detail, either by obtaining company accounts and doing the analysis work themselves if they have sufficient skill, or else through subscribing to online analysis services.

Intra-day Prices—Basic Services

We'll look first at the various methods of getting online price displays in the course of the trading day. We can start with basic services.

Teletext

This is a classic source of share prices during the day, and still used by many UK private investors. It is a generic term for the rival services offered by the BBC (Ceefax), Channel 4 (Teletext) and now other networks such as Sky and CNN. Each usually offers prices of the largest stocks and a (slightly different) selection of smaller ones updated regularly during the day.

Teletext services can be accessed from any TV equipped to receive them, and use what is known as the vertical blanking interval (VBI), the spare lines at the top of a TV picture, to transmit data.

The services differ between the two main providers. The BBC version, for example, includes the FTSE 100 index updated minute by minute, as well as its roster of share prices. Teletext, the Channel 4 offering, is a commercial service and therefore has advertising interspersed in its pages, but only updates the index every 15 minutes.

However, Teletext does have two pages dedicated to end-of-day prices for all the stocks listed in London. The result of these differences is that the two services combined add up to more than each of the services represents on its own.

The main advantage of teletext services is that they are free, other than the initial cost (perhaps) of buying a dedicated teletext TV set that can permanently be tuned to the service during the day.

Teletext services also have pages of risers and fallers, popular stocks, new issues, and a limited amount of news, including company results.

As mentioned previously, cable and satellite services, notably Sky News and CNN, also produce business-oriented teletext services with good menus of news, but CNN's teletext service has a minimal offering in terms of prices. Sky News's teletext service has UK equity and index option prices.

Teletext's advantage is that it can be run continuously in the background with none of the charges (such as telephone costs) that accompany web-based services used in this way. Teletext is not ideal in many respects, but to my mind it probably represents the optimum intra-day price service for most investors.

Web Price Displays

Market Eye's web-based service (www.market-eye.co.uk) is something of a boon for investors. Designed to approximate the look of the old style Market Eye screen it has a number of attractive attributes for active investors, notably a FTSE 100 'trigger page', with all the prices of the top 100 shares displayed simultaneously, detailed price quotes for individual stocks and a variety of other features, including charts of individual shares and built-in links to some companies' web sites.

In addition, and as discussed in a previous chapter, the site has the Eye-to-Eye bulletin board for investors to post messages on investment topics

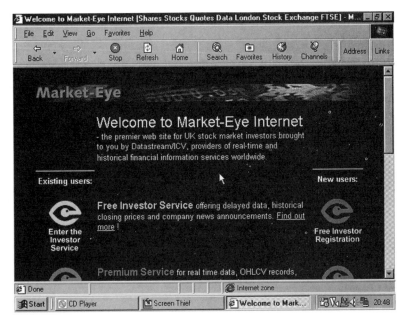

Figure 5.1 Market Eye has free share prices

and initiate discussion. Market Eye operates a two-tier version of its service: the free (Investor) service has 20-minute delayed prices, the Premium service offers real-time prices and enhanced news on UK stocks for a subscription of less than £7 a month.

There are several other web-based services that offer a similar deal. ESI (now part of E*Trade UK), one of the originators of this type of service, has a similar two-tier charging structure with the difference that its web-based message board is accessible only to paying subscribers. Interactive Investor (www.iii.co.uk) offers a real-time equity price service for as little as £5 per month. Moneyworld (www.moneyworld.co.uk) also offers a wholly free 15-minute delayed service, with price tables which offer a greater degree of manipulability than the Market Eye or ESI services.

Quote Servers

Typical of the services available in the USA are so-called quote servers, which dispense free time-delayed quotes upon the insertion of a company name or 'ticker' symbol (the short two-, three-, or four-letter code for the company's shares). Yahoo!'s finance page at http://finance.yahoo.co.uk has a built-in quote server in a page of news and general market information including minute-by-minute updated index figures for major world markets. You need probably go no further. Most sites like this have a ticker look-up facility whereby the the ticker symbol can be searched for by inputting the company name.

Elsewhere, Yahoo!'s 'markets and investments—stocks' index lists about 50 US sites offering quote information of some kind, many of which offer free snap quotes on a limited number of stocks a day, or a variety of prices on a 15–20-minute delayed basis. A similar UK offering is Freequotes (www.freequotes.co.uk).

These offerings are not entirely altruistic. Some will require you to register to be able to receive fuller information. Registration normally requires parting with basic contact details.

Some services, such as Track Data with MyTrack (www.mytrack.com) and Quote.com (www.my.quote.com) offer personalised services which display a limited number of 20-minute delayed quotes in a standard format. Personal finance-related web sites such as FTQuicken (www.ftquicken.com) and MoneyeXtra (www.moneyextra.com) and newspaper sites like This Is Money (www.thisismoney.co.uk) do the same.

The central point to bear in mind with services like this, as with other aspects of the web, is that free information is generally used either as a draw to a site to increase traffic and make the site more attractive to advertisers, or as a hook to sell subscriptions to more expensive services. But the private online investor does not necessarily need the level of detail that the professionals demand.

The lesson is that information for which existing professional subscribers pay heavily will not normally be available in a form that can easily be accessed. Commercial organisations—such as stock exchanges and data vendors—do not normally behave in an altruistic manner. If they appear to be doing so, there is invariably a catch.

There is an exception. Some brokers offering online dealing services are moving to offer real-time prices and news free of charge as part of the package. These services are discussed in more detail in Chapter 8, but the service I use, Xest, (www.xest.com) does this, and it works pretty well.

Real-time Prices

Having declared our bias that we believe real-time prices are not really worth the average investor paying for, let's nonetheless examine what's on offer.

Real-time Broadcast Services

Pretty popular with investors over the years has been ICV's Market Eye service, which also works off a TV signal. ICV has around 3000 subscribers for this service. It offers a real-time price feed from the Stock Exchange, and will enable you to get up-to-date price data in the form of the best bid and offer in the market at any one time for all listed stocks. These can be built into custom pages so that different portfolios can be carried on separate pages, for example, or a 'watch list' of stocks built up. In addition the service includes company and market news, a ticker of stock exchange trades as they happen, the biggest risers and fallers in the day, and a lot of other information.

At the time of its original launch more than a decade ago, Market Eye was available only via a dedicated terminal and decoder box, which the customer had to buy or rent at the outset. A few years ago ICV launched a PC version of Market Eye. Initially this had only comparatively limited impact, perhaps because users were reluctant to abandon the equipment they had paid for. More recently a greater proportion of users have begun to convert to the new system. Though this version will sit on any normal desktop PC, to make full use of the system may necessitate having a dedicated PC for the display, so there is a hardware cost involved.

The advantage of Market Eye in this form is that you have live prices at the touch of a button, and the ability to have a genuine feel for the market as it unfolds in the course of the trading day. I have mixed feelings about how useful this really is for many private investors. But one big plus point of Market Eye is that you can save on data download costs. End-of-day data and, for the real aficionado, real-time data can be downloaded into most popular software packages at no extra cost. This aspect is discussed in more detail later.

The disadvantage is that it is expensive. The basic services cost around £1000 a year, on top of which has to be added a near £200 exchange fee, and more if you choose also to take option prices from LIFFE. An optional licence fee for Market Eye for Windows software, which pretties up the display, is an extra £195 per annum, while you initially need to spend about £400 on the datacard to enable the service to be received and, if necessary, the PC hardware to slot it into.

Market Eye has had competition lately from Citifeed (details at www. citifeed.co.uk) service of late. Among its ploys to gain market share, the company has marketed this in conjunction with Updata Software, a leading investment software supplier, to produce a real-time service at a price substantially lower than Market Eye's.

Satellite Systems

Stock market data by satellite has been around for some time but has its drawbacks from the standpoint of private investors. One is that it is expensive and only a limited number of services offer information on UK Equities. The second drawback is that usual domestic satellite dishes will not normally receive this data and there is extra expense buying and installing suitable equipment.

Some companies offer a 'buyback' policy to take the risk out of the process, but a service such as Tenfore, the obvious choice for a UK online investor since it includes comprehensive UK coverage, still costs in the region of £170 a month, and you may receive a considerable amount of data that is not really required. DBC Signal, the other main satellite-based price feed, is similarly expensive.

Pager Products

Another way of keeping in touch with share prices is via pager-based products. At present there is a choice of products of this type, from Futures Pager (part of Reuters), the Pulse product from Hutchison Telecom, Share Sentry and Sprintel.

Pagers really come into their own for investors on the move, and especially if you simply want to check the progress of the index, futures prices, or a few selected shares. Technological advances have meant that

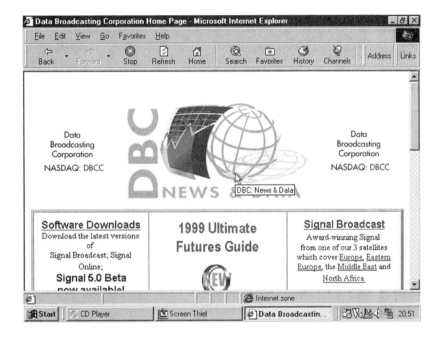

Figure 5.2 DBC's extensive menu

pagers now update much more frequently than they used to and to all intents and purposes can be considered real-time products.

The main problem is that the physical size of the pager means that there is a limit to the quantity of information that can be displayed in an intelligible form. Pagers also developed as a way of keeping dealers in touch with fast-moving futures and foreign exchange markets, and still concentrate in large measure on this type of information.

Futures Pager, Pulse and Share Sentry all fall into this category, although Share Sentry does have data on major risers and fallers and will display movements in a range of shares, but these are not updated on a real-time basis.

Experiments delivering information of this sort via mobile phone alerts have not really proved competitive with pagers, but in the future, mobile phone text message services, and other forms of hand-held devices, may be used to deliver information of this sort even to the point of allowing web-based dealing services to be hooked up to them as well.

Stock Exchanges as Data Sources

So far in this chapter we have looked at this issue mainly from the stand-point of a UK-based investor seeking information on UK companies. But online investors now abound in many countries and the frictionless nature of the web makes it natural that investors in any country will become more international in their outlook.

Local stock exchanges in some markets are increasingly a good source of price information about their listed shares. The services vary from country to country and from market to market. Some newer stock exchanges have extensive price information, partly because with a limited list of shares managing the data is a comparatively easy task. Table 5.1 shows the stock exchange web sites in Europe, the Americas and Asia which contain some form of intra-day free share price information about their listed securities.

As you can see, 15 exchanges have price displays which are delayed by 20 minutes or less, of which nine are real time. Of the five stock exchanges in North and South America that offer intra-day price displays, two are real time. Similarly, of the five stock exchanges in the Asian region that offer intra-day prices, four offer them on a real-time basis, with only Taiwan having a delay (and this is only five minutes).

Table 5.1   Stock exchange web sites in Europe, the Americas and Asia

Exchange	Web address	Prices	Minutes delay	Free prices	Country	Score
Bombay SE	www.bseindia.com	Yes	0	Yes	India	6
Chicago SE	www.chicagostockex.com	Yes	20	Yes	USA	6
Guayaquil SE	www.bvg.fin.ec	Yes	0	Yes	Ecuador	5
Luxembourg SE	www.bourse.lu	Yes	0	Yes	Luxembourg	6
Nasdaq-Amex	www.nasdaq.com	Yes	0	Yes	USA	9
National SE of Lithuania	www.nse.lt	Yes	0	Yes	Lithuania	6
New York SE	www.nyse.com	Yes	15	Yes	USA	8
New Zealand SE	www.nzse.co.nz	Yes	0	Yes	New Zealand	8
Singapore SE	www.ses.com.sg	Yes	0	Yes	Singapore	9
Stockholm SE	www.xsse.se	Yes	15	Yes	Sweden	7
Taiwan SE	www.tse.com.tw	Yes	5	Yes	Taiwan	5
Tallin SE	www.tse.ee	Yes	0	Yes	Estonia	8
Thai SE	www.set.or.th	Yes	0	Yes	Thailand	9
Tradepoint	www.tradepoint.co.uk	Yes	20	Yes	U.K.	6
Vancouver SE	www.vse.com	Yes	15	Yes	Canada	8

We'll now look at end-of-day data downloading. In the case of some worldwide exchanges data download facilities are also offered, although more common is the straightforward display of closing price data rather than its availability to download free of charge in zipped files.

End-of-day Downloads

While many investors are rightly ambivalent about their need for real-time quotes during the trading day, for the serious investor the ability to download share prices into a graphing package is a must.

Even if you do not perform sophisticated technical analysis on the price data, the ability to see a snapshot of the share's movement over an extended period has considerable value. Interpretation is still important, but even at its simplest level the information is of value.

The ability also to download 'open, high, low, close and volume' (OHLCV) data is important for those adopting a more sophisticated 'chartist' approach. The volume of trading in a stock is an important guide to the significance or otherwise of movement in the shares and to do without this is considered by some to be false economy, even if you do not wish to perform sophisticated technical analysis with the information. That said, many investors, myself included, seem to manage reasonably well without it.

Many intra-day price services, notably the web-based Market Eye and Yahoo!'s quote page mentioned earlier, include volume data as part of the display when a quote is called up, so if you notice a particularly sharp movement in a share on a particular day, the volume position can be checked.

A range of alternatives for downloading price data is available to the online investor, with varying costs, and these are examined next.

Teletext Downloads

Teletext downloading works in a comparatively simple way. You buy, for about £150, a normal PC expansion card which has a standard TV aerial socket. This allows a spur off your TV aerial to be connected to your PC. Then, other things being equal, the computer can be tuned to read the teletext signal on the prices pages. Teletext prices are closing mid-prices only.

Downloading from teletext services has in the past had a reputation for being less than wholly reliable, and can suffer in particular from poor TV reception and unusual atmospheric conditions. Coping with updating during absences from home can also be tricky.

An earlier drawback to teletext—that stocks were dropped from the list for no reason—has been circumvented by the fact that Channel 4's Teletext service now includes end-of-day prices for the whole market, while software programs have been developed which smarten up the display of this information and ease the process of downloading. Changes to price retrieval codes, another bugbear of the old system, can also now be logged automatically.

Dial-in Databases

Updating by modem has increasingly overtaken teletext as a means of getting end-of-day data into software packages, and enables more complex forms of data to be downloaded. In the past, this type of updating was considered an expensive luxury, but prices have fallen sharply following the Stock Exchange's deregulation of price data. Citifeed, for instance, offers a high-speed download of OHLCV data for all UK equities and gilts for only £125 a year, in a format compatible with popular software. Complete London Stock Exchange price histories are also available. Sharescope (www.sharescope.co.uk), a software package published by Ionic that incorporates fundamental data, has a dial-in database which can be accessed for around £10 a month.

Synergy Software's (www.synergy-software.co.uk) Portfolio Advantage offers a bundled package of price and fundamental data and software for an annual subscription of £395. This system also enables the checking of prices on an intra-day basis, and incorporates a sophisticated portfolio management module.

Downloading from Real-time Datafeeds

The various real-time feeds mentioned above offer the facility for downloading of OHLCV data at the end of every trading day. In the case of Market Eye, for instance, around 20 software packages, including all the

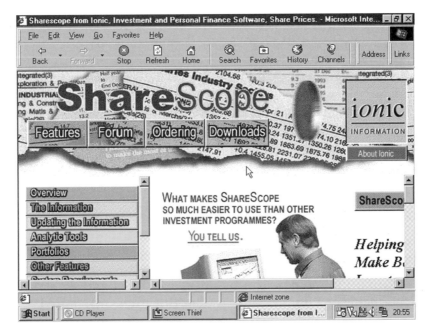

Figure 5.3 Sharescope has a dial-in database

popular ones, now offer an interface to the system, enabling price files to be updated at no extra charge.

Downloading is obviously also possible from DBC Signal, Tenfore and other real-time feeds. In most cases the process of importing the data is comparatively simple. Data download options usually allow data to be converted into ASCII (American Standard Code for Information Interchange) or CSV (comma separated values) formats, which most software packages will accept, and software manuals will give instructions on how this can be done.

Before signing up for a data package, however, it is vital to ensure that the software you use is compatible with the data you propose to download. Software suppliers can usually offer a range of options and will allow you to pick one that represents the right combination of detail and price.

Downloading from Web Sites

Some UK web sites offer the opportunity of downloading stock market data. More will undoubtedly develop as time goes by. The original and best known was ESI (www.esi.co.uk) now part of E*Trade UK. ESI data originally could be accessed for a minimum subscription of £5 a month plus VAT, which represented one of the best bargains around, but the service now costs £150 plus VAT for an annual subscription for OHLCV data.

The data is supplied in a wide variety of formats, including ASCII, CSV or Indexia (a commonly used chart package) and can be imported easily into most popular investment software. Previous days' data is cached for a month, allowing users to catch up on any prices that might have been missed. It can be supplied either in the form of a compressed *.zip* file, or in uncompressed form.

Another useful point to remember is that complete price histories for individual stocks can be downloaded from the Market Eye web site free of charge. In theory these could then be plugged into a software package. For those only needing a relatively unsophisticated view of the movement in a share price, the data can be opened in Excel and a chart created in the normal way with the data saved or discarded as required.

Downloads by Email

Downloading share price data is also possible by email. ESI offers you the option of receiving its data in this way on an overnight basis. Other organisations offer a similar service. Winstock Software's 'Analyst' package (www.winstock.co.uk) allows data to be accessed in this way at very low cost; conversion of the email message to a form that can be imported into the chart package is very simple and can be completed in less than a minute. Winstock provides the data by email for free, but to purchase the software package to enable you to receive data in this way costs an additional £40 on top of the normal £80 purchase price.

Online Fundamental Data

The distinction between downloading share price and trading volume data on the one hand and fundamental information on the other is an important one.

In this context fundamental information means earnings forecasts, directors' dealings and other sensitive information, and all the standard financial information to be found in company accounts.

As with price data, you get what you pay for. Some is free, but the more comprehensive the data and the more key ratios are calculated for you, the more expensive the product becomes. This is also true of brokers' research reports, some of which are now being made available for free. The site at www.ukonlineinvesting.com has links to some of these free services.

At the most basic level, the paper-based annual report of companies featured in the FT Annual Reports service (marked with a 'club' symbol on the prices pages) can be ordered online at www.icbinc.com. Users going to this site should select the FT option from the range of alternatives provided. Completing the order entails typing a mailing address into a standard form. Reports generally arrive in 2–3 working days.

Basic company information, including company contact details, names of directors and advisers, and five years of very abbreviated accounts data, has long been available in printed form as part of *The Company Guide*, published by Hemmington Scott. The same information can be accessed

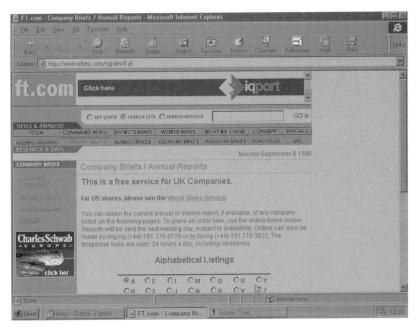

Figure 5.4 Order annual reports from FT Annual Reports service

free of charge (as opposed to a £100 plus annual subscription for the paper version) on the web at Hemmington Scott's UK Equities Direct site (www.hemscott.com). A monthly CD version of the service, which can be accessed without incurring online charges is currently being made available to professional users and subscribers to Hemmington Scott's other services, especially the well-known CD REFS product.

While not strictly an online product, REFS (which stands for Really Essential Financial Statistics) was devised by Jim Slater and is a distillation of the company's record and presentation of key ratios in more depth than many services provide. The CD version substitutes for the extremely bulky paper-based product, is searchable, and presents the pages in PDF format. Filtering criteria can also be constructed to screen for companies with particular financial characteristics.

The CD version in its monthly format costs around £675 a year plus VAT, but is, in my view, well worth the price. However, the Equities Direct web site offers the option of buying REFS pages on a pay-per-view basis at a cost of £10 per company, which may be a more economical way

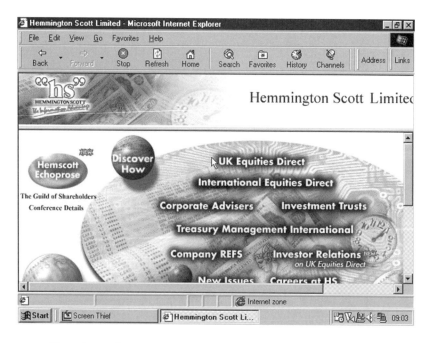

Figure 5.5 Hemmington Scott's comprehensive services

of getting hold of the data for those not expecting to look at a lot of companies each month. In addition, Hemmington Scott has recently launched a financial portal Hemscott.net (www.hemscott.net) which offers, among other information, free access to the REFS pages of companies in the news.

In recent years the distinctions between fundamentals-oriented services and technical analysis-oriented charting software has become somewhat blurred. Several services have been launched which blend the two, notably the Synergy Portfolio Advantage product and Ionic's Sharescope package, both of which were mentioned previously. In the case of the latter, basic accounts data can be tabulated either by company or in datasheet format capable of being sifted and ranked according to various criteria using the usual database conventions. The resulting tables can also be output in spreadsheet format for further manipulation.

Another interesting service is CAROL (Company Annual Reports On Line—www.carol.co.uk) which has expanded to cover not just UK companies but those in Europe and Asia too.

As always, the USA leads the way in the provision of raw fundamental data with the well-known EDGAR site (www.sec.gov/edgarhp.htm) operated by the SEC. This is a searchable index of official SEC filings, including annual and quarterly financial statements and other data. Electronic filing of company information has now been extended to cover virtually the whole gamut of publicly listed securities in the USA. Although the index is slightly quirky to use, the availability of what in UK terms is tantamount to an electronic Companies House for listed stocks is a superb resource for the investor and one that is widely used.

It remains to be seen if such an initiative would get off the ground in the UK. With Companies House now an executive agency and talk of its privatisation, the notion of it providing even part of the information filed there free to online users may not be commercially acceptable. It is now possible (for a set-up fee of £50 and a monthly subscription of £7) to download documents direct from the the Companies House database.

A web-based version of the service is expected to be launched at the end of 1999. Brief company details can now be searched freely via the web. Even as a pay-as-you-go electronic service it is expected there will be considerable demand from those who do not relish the expense (and tedium) of a trip to its Bloomsbury premises.

The Problem of Choice

Keeping the supply of information to a relevant and manageable size—which has long been a problem for the professional investor—is a task demanding some skill.

As the preceding pages indicate, there is a complex pattern of services available online through which you can access real-time price data, delayed price data, and end-of-day data through a variety of channels. Sometimes it is provided on a stand-alone basis, and sometimes in conjunction with other services which may not be needed.

Corporate financial information is also available in both free and paid-for services, again often bundled in with other services.

Working out what is worth paying for and what isn't depends on you. However, do bear in mind the following:

❐ The cost of micro-billed services tends to add up, and although the data provided can be convenient to access from one source in this way, in many cases it is available online elsewhere for free. Seek out free services wherever you can.

❐ Real-time price data is an expensive luxury for all but the keenest investor or those committed to active trading on a minute-by-minute basis. Teletext services provide adequate intra-day information for most investors.

❐ Up-to-the-minute news is comforting to have, but in practice even the most assiduous investor will be unable to beat the market reaction to price-sensitive announcements.

❐ Potentially more useful are services such as the Hemmington Scott's UK Equities Direct, which gives access to useful information on every listed company, and also services such as CAROL (and, for that matter, company web sites—see next chapter).

❐ Depending on their investment style, investors should therefore concentrate their spending, if they are 'chartists', on paying for quality data for end-of-day downloading, paying particular attention to getting OHLCV data and loading this into a good quality charting package. The cost of this data is coming down rapidly. If they are 'fundamentalists', a service like CD REFS is probably a 'must'.

❐ An increasing number of budget priced chart packages are offering a combination of bundled price and fundamental data in an easy-to-use-format that many investors will find perfectly adequate.

❐ Costs have been falling, although whether they will fall further from now on is a moot point. But the real key is only to pay for data that cannot be duplicated by a web-based source.

The next section looks at how to get hold of tools to analyse your data. Many of these software packages are available either in shareware or demo form via the web.

Software and Data Analysis Tools Online

One of the main features of the Internet is the ability it offers to transfer files from remote computers.

And as even the most complex computer programs are simply collections of files, computer software can be downloaded via FTP (file transfer protocol) from a remote computer to the user's own machine, and installed with the minimum of fuss.

This is a very important attribute. The majority of computer software originates in the USA. This goes for investment software as much as for any other type. So (in theory) an online investor can get access to software online at US prices and, with only a little adaptation, use it with UK data.

In reality most software users will probably opt for buying a package from a UK supplier—if only because of its familiarity, and the more certain knowledge that the data generally available in the UK can be used to drive it.

But investment software does not just mean chart packages. There are several spreadsheet-based programs that perform useful functions for the investor. These can be downloaded from the sites in the US and easily used with UK figures.

A lot of software on the net is 'freeware' or 'shareware'. The shareware concept allows you to download software 'for evaluation' and, if you like it and find it useful, places a moral obligation on you to buy a registered version and thereby get a manual, news on upgrades, and access to user support. This moral obligation may be more honoured in the breach than anything else, however, and one result is that, for investment software at least, the downloads available often take the form of demo disks, i.e. versions of the program that can be used a fixed number of times, or versions that have their functions crippled so as to hamper normal use.

The sheer volume of choice available can be gauged by looking at the Yahoo! software index, which lists about 65 different categories, each with multiple numbers of entries. Many of these are not relevant for the online investor, but they show nonetheless the degree to which the Internet is becoming a recognised major distribution channel for software. Yahoo! lists about 300 shareware sites, some of which will be worth exploring. A search option is also available.

There are several other ways in which online investors tend to come across useful software programs.

Publications. Mentions in publications are a less attractive option on the grounds of cost. Internet-oriented magazines can be interesting but, from the standpoint of the online investor, their content is normally of limited use. Until specialist investment-related Internet magazines begin to appear, a development still some way away, the online investor is probably better advised to seek information elsewhere.

Newsgroup mentions. These can be a good source of information. But the problem with using recommendations from newsgroups is that, although the posts concerned usually give some details of the program, they may be posted by people with an axe to grind. They could be the program developers themselves, friends, and other related parties. And many posts often omit to say whether or not the software comes with a price attached, or whether the advertised download is a full version of the program, or one that has restricted functionality.

Software download sites. In the period since the first edition of *The Online Investor* was published, sites like this have consolidated and coalesced into a few key ones, most of which are listed at the Yahoo! 'shareware' page. Obvious ports of call are Download.com (www.download.com), Shareware.com (www.shareware.com), Winsite (www.winsite.com), File Pile (www.filepile.com) and Filez (www.filez.com). Most of these sites are searchable, with pull-down menus that enable the user to specify the search more accurately and so increase the chances of finding the right item. However, many of them will also contain similar or duplicated items.

With the possible exception of Wall Street Directory (www.wsdinc.com) and Investorsoftware (www.investorsoftware.com), there are few download sites specifically devoted to financial software. These sites' primary purpose is the commercial one of selling fully featured packages, although some demos are available.

Some software download sites offer links to sites where the software can be downloaded; some simply give reviews of software; some list products produced by different software developers (essentially searchable indexes that will cross reference products and/or producers). Most of the sites are free to use. Those that aren't will allow a search to be conducted, but may not permit a download to be performed unless a fee has been paid and a user name and password entered.

With all this in mind, let's have a look at a few packages that can help investors get to grips with the fundamentals of a particular share. I have selected three that I use on a regular basis. You may well be able to find other equally useful ones.

Mathwiz

This is a financial calculator produced by Informatik. Inc and download-able from several sites, typically in the 'calculators' directory.

The product includes a number of features including the calculation of days from dates (useful for determining bond interest payments), amor-tisation schedules, which can be used to calculate loan repayments, and a financial calculator that provides the functions associated with discount-ing back a future stream of income to produce figures such as net present value and internal rate of return.

The package can be used for both steady and irregular flows of cash and is cheaper and more flexible than hand-held financial calculators which typically cost upwards of £30. If ordered online this package costs about $7.50 and a fully functioning 30-day trial version can be downloaded from the company's site (www.informatik.com).

StockQuest

This is also downloadable from various sites (try, for example, at www.shareware.com); at the time of writing the filename was *stckwz22.zip*.

The program is a deceptively simple tool for working out the correct value for a security. The model assumes that the investor knows the total return he or she wishes to derive from an investment over a specified time period. For a given stock, the investor will also know the historic earnings per share and dividends. An assumption needs to be made about the likely growth potential for the company.

The basic questions the investor must ask are: How fast will earnings grow? For how many years (i.e. over what term) is it expected or required for this growth to continue? And, what return (or total yield) is required from the investment?

The real value of this software is that the user is able to see how the three parameters—growth, term and total return (yield)—interact. The three combine to produce a per share value for the security. This can then be compared with the share price to determine whether the stock is cheap or dear if the assumptions being made are correct. The impact of changing any of the assumptions while leaving the others unchanged can also be seen instantly.

How does it work? Earnings are compounded at the growth rate specified for the term of the investment to produce the estimated annual earnings at the end of the projected period. These earnings are then capitalised at the specified rate of return to arrive at the expected future stock value at the end of the term.

This future stock value is then discounted back at the yield rate to produce the net price for the shares. Dividends are assumed to grow at the same rate as earnings and the stream of dividends over the term of the shares is discounted back to arrive at their present value. This is added to the net price of the shares to produce the indicated total value.

The advantage of this model and ones like it is that if assumptions are changed—either new profit figures are disclosed, the assumed growth rate changes, bond yields (say) rise and therefore the return demanded from an equity investment also increases—then the impact on the share price can be seen easily.

Equally the required change in one variable needed to compensate for a change in another can also be determined. What improvement in the growth rate for instance might be needed to offset a half-point rise in yields?

StockQuest uses a simple form of discounting to arrive at its conclusion. A more sophisticated, yet still easy to use, version of the same concept is the Warren Buffett Way Spreadsheet.

Warren Buffett Way Spreadsheet

In his book *The Warren Buffett Way* (John Wiley, 1994), Robert Hagstrom describes the well-known American investor's penchant for investing on the basis of 'owner earnings'. This really means assessing a company on the basis of the long-term cash flow it is capable of generating under a comparatively frugal management regime.

Bob Costa, the operator of a web site known as Investorweb (now at www.financialweb.com) took this one stage further and devised a spreadsheet which works with Microsoft Excel Version 5 and upwards. It can be used to value shares with the entry of a minimum of data. At the time of writing the Investorweb site is under reconstruction but I have posted a downloadable copy of the spreadsheet, including some worked examples, at the New Online Investor site in the 'software' page.

The screenshot reproduces part of the spreadsheet display, with the items shown in italic the only ones that require entering. This can be done

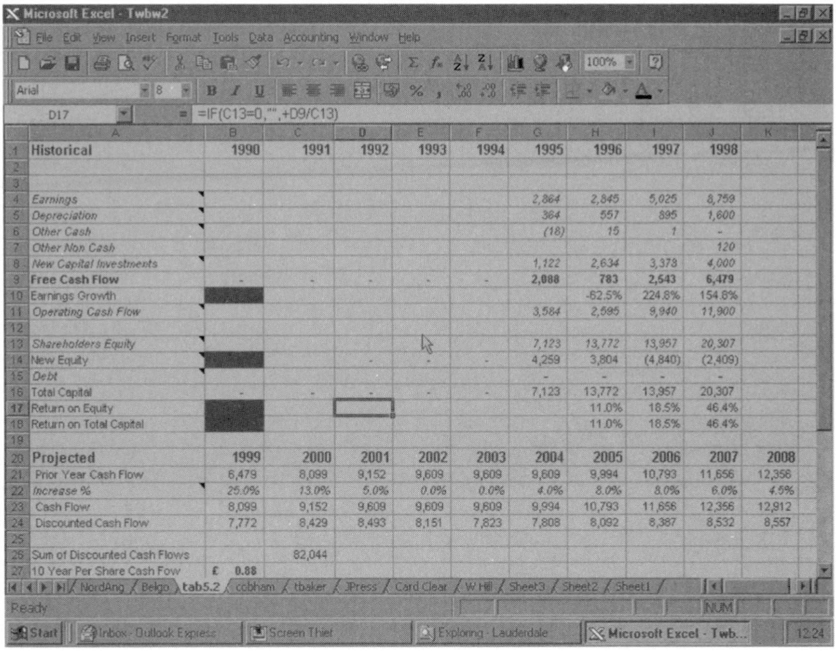

	A	B	C	D	E	F	G	H	I	J	K
1	**Historical**	**1990**	**1991**	**1992**	**1993**	**1994**	**1995**	**1996**	**1997**	**1998**	
2											
3											
4	*Earnings*						*2,864*	*2,845*	*5,025*	*8,759*	
5	*Depreciation*						*364*	*557*	*895*	*1,600*	
6	*Other Cash*						*(18)*	*15*	*1*	*-*	
7	*Other Non Cash*									*120*	
8	*New Capital Investments*						*1,122*	*2,634*	*3,378*	*4,000*	
9	**Free Cash Flow**	-	-	-	-	-	**2,088**	**783**	**2,543**	**6,479**	
10	Earnings Growth							-62.5%	224.8%	154.8%	
11	*Operating Cash Flow*						*3,584*	*2,595*	*9,940*	*11,900*	
12											
13	*Shareholders Equity*						*7,123*	*13,772*	*13,957*	*20,307*	
14	New Equity			-	-	-	4,259	3,804	(4,840)	(2,409)	
15	*Debt*						-	-	-	-	
16	Total Capital	-	-	-	-	-	7,123	13,772	13,957	20,307	
17	Return on Equity							11.0%	18.5%	46.4%	
18	Return on Total Capital							11.0%	18.5%	46.4%	
19											
20	**Projected**	**1999**	**2000**	**2001**	**2002**	**2003**	**2004**	**2005**	**2006**	**2007**	**2008**
21	Prior Year Cash Flow	6,479	8,099	9,152	9,609	9,609	9,609	9,994	10,793	11,656	12,356
22	*Increase %*	*25.0%*	*13.0%*	*5.0%*	*0.0%*	*0.0%*	*4.0%*	*8.0%*	*8.0%*	*6.0%*	*4.5%*
23	Cash Flow	8,099	9,152	9,609	9,609	9,609	9,994	10,793	11,656	12,356	12,912
24	Discounted Cash Flow	7,772	8,429	8,493	8,151	7,823	7,808	8,092	8,387	8,532	8,557
25											
26	Sum of Discounted Cash Flows		82,044								
27	10 Year Per Share Cash Fow	£ **0.88**									

Figure 5.6 Using the Warren Buffett Way spreadsheet to value shares

quite quickly from an annual report or press releases that normally accompany a company's preliminary results announcement and which normally now give cash flow and balance sheet data.

The most important aspect of the spreadsheet, however, are the assumptions entered in the lower part of the table, which determine how cash flow is likely to pan out in the future. The difference between this spreadsheet and the more basic calculating tool represented by StockQuest is that a much more subtle pattern of future cash flow growth can be assumed.

This can take in ups and downs in the economy, or peculiarities specific to the company involved. The example shows that the assumptions entered produce much the same result as was achieved by the simpler model.

Mathwiz, StockQuest and the Warren Buffett Way Spreadsheet are just three examples of the types of software on offer on the net. The Warren Buffett Way Spreadsheet is free but requires you to have a relatively recent version of Excel (version 5 or later), while the other two products are low-cost shareware that function on a stand-alone basis.

Table 5.2   UK and European-oriented investment software

Company	Package	Telepone	Web/email address
AIQ	AIQ Trading Expert	0181 367 8808	www.trendsoft.com/win/aiq
Equis International	Metastock	001 800 8823040	www.metastock.com
Fairshares	Fairshares	01703 660111	www.fairshares.com
Gannsoft	Ganntrader	01737 845231	www.adest.com.au/gannsoft.htm
Indexia	Indexia	01442 878015	www.indexia.co.uk
Intuit	Quicken	01932 578502	www.intuit.co.uk
Investment Data Services	Gann Management	0161 474 0080	www.gannmanagement.co.uk
InvestorEase	InvestorEase	0181 402 9224	www.investorease.com
Ionic Information	Sharescope	0500 321456	www.ionic.co.uk
Meridian Software	Stockmarket 4	0181 309 5960	www.meridian-software.co.uk
MESA UK	MESA	0181 303 7407	www.mesa.co.uk
Omega Research	Supercharts	0171 950 7711	www.omegaresearch.com
Qdata	Metastock	01594 810077	www.datasphere.ltd.uk/qdata
Synergy	Portfolio Advantage	01582 424282	www.synergy-software.co.uk
Ultra Financial Systems	Market Adviser	001 940 321 5423	www.ultrafs.com
Updata	Invest, Trader	0181 874 4747	www.updata.co.uk
Winstock	The Analyst	01962 715557	www.winstock.co.uk

UK software houses are increasingly becoming active on the web and information on the properties of their packages, price lists and what to do to obtain demo disks, are readily available.

Table 5.2 shows brief details of these suppliers, their packages, and details of their web presence.

The next chapter looks at what is fast developing into a highly significant area of the web for online investors—company web sites and the information they contain.

CHAPTER 6

Company Information Online

The world wide web has the potential to revolutionise communications between companies, their shareholders and investors at large. And to judge from the growth in the number of corporate sites in the last couple of years, the corporate sector as a whole is coming round to this view very quickly.

Why Companies Need Web Sites

Why is this? The answer is because the web offers the opportunity of distributing up-to-date financial and corporate information quickly and cheaply.

There are advantages to this on both sides: private investors need not feel inhibited, as they often do at present, about contacting companies to request basic information. From a corporate standpoint, investor relations personnel need not be burdened unduly with fielding mundane enquiries from small investors.

There are practical savings to be made, too. At large companies the cost of mailing out annual reports is substantial, in terms of printing, postage and staff time. One large British PLC reckoned that it had saved an annual £50,000 by making its accounts available on the web and so reducing the number of enquiries of this nature it had to field.

For investors, this aspect of the online revolution is linked closely to developments elsewhere on the net. If share prices are more readily available online for free or at low cost, and if investors can access cheap sources of daily and intra-day news over the web, and if they can deal in shares and buy other financial products online, then it makes sense for companies to make their detailed financial information freely available online, too.

It makes sense in other ways as well. As the number of online investors grows, they may come to regard the quality of a company's web site and the comprehensiveness or otherwise of the information presented on it as indicative of the quality of a company as an investment.

There are even indications that the government may get involved too, passing legislation to allow companies, if shareholders agree, to distribute documents to shareholders via web and email if desired. Electronic proxy voting is also reported to be on the way. Video and audio broadcasts of analyst presentations by companies are already available on the web, though they would scarcely set the average investor's pulse racing.

The response to this corporate information distribution challenge has been impressive in the US, but variable in the UK and elsewhere. Among European companies, as we shall see later, there are examples both of very good corporate web sites and truly awful ones.

The Growth of Corporate Sites

There has been a sharp increase in the number of large companies with web sites containing financial information. In the spring of 1995 I conducted an informal survey by fax of the top 100 companies in the UK, to attempt to find which companies (if any) had a net presence currently, imminently or in the planning stage. The survey produced about 40 responses. Of those that did respond, fewer than a dozen were at that time either contemplating a site or had one already operating. Many companies categorically ruled out any prospect of establishing a site. A logical deduction would have been that any such proposals would be thwarted by senior management's lack of awareness of the potential for effective communication offered by a web site.

At the time *The Online Investor* was published in 1997, just over 20 of the FTSE 100 listed companies had a web presence of some description. But a survey conducted at about that time—entitled 'The Corporate Cyber-Dash' and produced by the consultancy firm Manning Selvage & Lee—

suggested that many more large companies had web sites in the planning stage.

The survey polled over 500 multinational companies about whether or not they had a web site operating, under construction, or planned. While at that time in the USA 40% of the companies sampled had a web site operating, in Europe the figure was more like 30%. Even that was probably an exaggeration. The survey also claimed that 20% of the companies in both the US and Europe had sites under construction, while rather more European companies than US ones, about 15% of the total, had plans to do so. But the Luddites continued to hold sway. Around 30% of the European companies had no plans for a site, versus 20% of the US sample.

But things have changed dramatically. When I researched the topic again for this book, I was genuinely surprised to discover that the number of large UK and European companies with a web presence had risen sharply. It appears that some 90% or more of the top 100 companies in the UK now have a web presence of some sort, and the figures are not dissimilar when it comes to leading Continental European companies. Many medium-sized companies also have sites, especially those companies involved in technology or whose businesses entail direct dealings with the public.

Corporate communicators are clearly enthusiastic about using the web and other interactive electronic media as a means of communicating with investors, financial analysts, customers, suppliers and journalists. Where no web sites have been constructed or are planned, the reason is most likely to be that a stop has been placed on the idea much higher up in the organisation.

For and Against

What are the key issues to be borne in mind when creating a site, and what makes companies shy away from the notion of one? For a start, it is clearly hard to reconcile the different objectives of the various constituencies of web users in a single site without it becoming unwieldy.

Many companies can see advantages in using the web as a cheap means of delivering information to and interacting with customers and communicating with suppliers, particularly where such a project can prove likely to cut costs by reducing employee numbers.

The site often held up as an example here is Federal Express. Its web site enables customers to check the progress of their parcel via the web rather than, as was previously the case, by contacting a telephone enquiry number. Another company, Dell, has built a huge direct selling business in computer hardware and is increasingly using the web to allow customers to configure their orders and, once ordered, to check on the progress of the product up to the point of delivery.

But there are companies which, for a variety of legitimate business reasons, wish to keep a low profile and not display any more information to the public than they are legally obliged to do by listing requirements, companies legislation and the like. Among such companies, for example, might be defence contractors and cigarette companies. It is noteworthy that the UK-based BAT Industries has no web site; likewise, Philip Morris in the USA, an otherwise aggressive marketer and brand-builder, is the only Dow Jones index constituent not to have a web site. Having said that, it is possible to configure a web presence that simply reflects already-published statutory information: another tobacco group, Gallaher, has a web presence which does just that.

There are also some corporate web sites (especially in the UK) that simply contain consumer information and material of an educational nature or, if they do contain financial information, place it in an inaccessible position in the site, almost as an afterthought. Many consumer products companies rightly view the web as primarily an exciting marketing tool because of the demographic and socio-economic profile of Internet users.

Internet users are—so the theory goes—likely either to be relatively young and affluent, susceptible to new ideas and technologies, and have above average educational attainment. This makes them an ideal target group not just for up-market consumer products but also for books, CDs and other products. The success of Amazon.com in the book area has been well publicised, but at a more mundane level Tesco is building a good business for its online grocery ordering and delivery business.

Innovative consumer-oriented web sites like this are designed to hold the interest of the consumer and to generate loyalty by offering benefits in the shape of competitions, downloadable software such as screensavers and other gimmicks. They generally come complete with heavy graphics and other 'bells and whistles'.

These characteristics seem to conflict starkly with the interests of online investors, who require a speedy and efficient delivery mechanism for company information such as annual reports, results announcements, press releases, and other background information, perhaps a means of accessing a live share price on the company, and a mechanism by which an email response can easily be generated from the company to a specific question of a financial or corporate nature.

It should be possible, for instance, for a private shareholder to email a question about, say, a results announcement to a designated contact in the investor relations department of a large company and to receive a prompt official response. Yet only a minority of the sites established by UK and European companies offer such a facility.

But combining the interests of consumers and investors on the same site is by no means impossible, as many US companies have proved. The bigger issues to be addressed lie elsewhere.

Practical Issues

In practice, setting up a web site involves any company in a host of practical business-related and legal dilemmas, which are not easily solved and which, more importantly, can be and have been used by entrenched and traditional-minded management as an excuse for ruling out the whole idea. Fortunately, these potential problems all have comparatively easy solutions, or else arise from misconceptions about the way the web works.

These issues fall into a number of areas, which are outlined briefly below:

Domain name. The first main issue is registering a name. This is not especially difficult, but there have been cases of enterprising Internet users—so-called cyber-squatters—registering popular ones in the hope of persuading a corporation to part with some cash to buy the name from them. Is there much point having a web address, unless you can have one that is closely identifiable with the company itself? Arguably it doesn't matter, but the issue can lead to corporate heart-searching. Even if a company has no immediate plans for a site, registering a name is a comparatively simple matter and can be done for a negligible cost.

Security. A more serious issue is security. Corporate managements in general—justifiably in some cases—fear that establishing a web site which has any form of interactive content may lead to its defences being breached. In other words, that malicious hackers or those with a straightforward commercial motive may be able enter its computer systems and browse around in sensitive areas. Though companies are becoming increasingly networked internally, it is possible to overstate the importance of this particular issue. The security which should in any case exist for external connections to a corporate network can be adapted to prevent any spillover from the 'public' web site side of the network to the 'private' corporate side.

Cost. The establishment of a web site can entail substantial set-up costs, especially in the area of security. Employing consultants to design and create a secure web site insulated from the company's own internal computer system can eat up money. The issue of cost is related to the extent of in-house computer expertise. Large organisations, however, sometimes find that their web sites can be set up and maintained by a minimum of personnel if they are institutions with highly sophisticated technical expertise and long experience of managing secure systems. For a small organisation, setting up a simple site is easy enough with proprietary desktop publishing software. The key, in both cases is that it is vitally important to keep the site up to date, and the personnel cost of doing this needs to be factored into the equation.

Management Time. Related to the issue of cost is the fear that a web site will lead to a rise in the volume of enquiries into the company and be a drain on management time. This is nonsense. Not only does the experience of operators of large interactive sites suggest that this will not happen, but also, if a site is being used either to market and generate interest in the company's products, or to promote the image of the company to investors, then email responses are something to be welcomed rather than feared.

Legal. A more potent consideration relating to corporate web sites is the legal issue, especially if a site is dispensing information to investors. Companies need to be conscious of not disseminating any information different from that distributed officially via stock exchange and other normal investor channels, or any form of advice or information that is not in the public domain.

It is this factor which may limit the degree to which UK companies are prepared to make investor-related websites interactive, for instance by inviting questions by email. But it does not invalidate the idea of making more information available to ordinary investors at the same time as it is received by institutional investors and their representatives.

Indeed stock market regulators are believed to take a relatively relaxed view of corporate web sites, while even those marketing investment products such as PEPs, unit trusts and the like are on fairly safe ground provided that their sites have some method of filtering out unregulated applicants (i.e. non-residents) and abide by the existing guidelines covering print and broadcast media advertisements.

A company offering to answer investor questions individually by email may be on slightly shakier ground, but making information available to private investors that has already been disseminated to another class of shareholders by definition should have no adverse legal consequences. Indeed it should be applauded for potentially widening the opportunity for private shareholder involvement.

It is clear that legal and indeed any other obstacles to the creation of corporate web sites can be overcome if sufficient will is there to make it happen. With the huge quantity of corporate web sites set up in the USA as a guide, especially in that most litigious of countries, it is perhaps no surprise that corporate web sites in Europe and the UK have risen sharply in number in the past couple of years.

The goal of the remainder of this chapter is to examine where we are now in terms of the provision of web sites by major companies in both the UK and other countries, to outline some pointers for finding them, and to measure their usefulness as objectively as possible.

How to Find Them

Finding corporate web sites has become somewhat easier than it once was, although the UK still lacks a definitive source of *listed* company websites.

Sheila Webber's guide to Business Information Sources on the Internet at www.dis.strath.ac.uk/business/ contains a rundown of directories from which to access information on companies, but many of the links are to directories of basic information on companies (names, addresses and telephone numbers) rather than links to corporate web sites. Many of the sites listed are also ones where information must be paid for. One of the

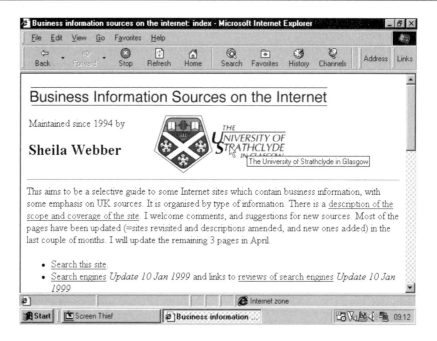

Figure 6.1   Business Information Sources on the Internet at the University of Strathclyde

philosophies behind this book is that the information investors seek should be available either wholly free, or for a very modest cost.

The most comprehensive guide to UK company home pages used to be UKCom's 'UK Businesses on the Web'. The site contained around 1500 links arranged alphabetically. However, the vast majority related to private companies and other organisations. These also include government departments, universities and other semi-official organisations. The site no longer appears to be operating.

However, other sources of information have emerged in its place. The Financial Times web site at www.ft.com has a series of 'net directories' including one giving links to UK FTSE 100 companies with web sites containing financial information, and a brief commentary on what is available. The FT's net directories also include similar lists of corporate web sites for Dow 30 companies, and French and German blue chips.

My web site at www.cix.co.uk/~ptemple/linksite, also accessible via the New Online Investor home page, has a series of links to UK company

Figure 6.2   The New Online Investor's Linksite

corporate web sites, as well as those of Dow 30 companies, the leading NASDAQ companies, European companies and a wide range of other sites.

In addition, Northcote Internet, a firm specialising in web site design, has established a site containing links to FTSE 100, FTSE 250 and several other categories of UK listed company at www.northcote.co.uk. The site is regularly maintained but does not as yet appear to include all of the large company sites and may also miss out on several smaller ones. FTSE International www.ftse.com has a list of sites of FTSE 100 index constituents, although at the time of writing this was incomplete.

Another good site is CAROL (Company Annual Reports On Line). This site, at www.carol.co.uk, contains links to a large number of companies with corporate web sites and also includes companies which have chosen to put their annual report and in some cases other material on the web via the CAROL system. Another one, EMAR's www.ukonlineinvesting.com, has links to a large number of brief company reports and related links.

Another useful source of information is the Market Eye web site mentioned in the previous chapter—www.market-eye.co.uk—which contains some company web addresses at the bottom of the price and price chart pages for individual companies. Although new sites are added from time to time, the site does not include mentions of every corporate web site available, understandably because its primary purpose is the dissemination of market price information.

In the US, the process of identifying web sites is considerably easier. One very good site is the Dow Jones Business Directory http://bd.dowjones.com which has a well-organised list of reviews of corporate web sites, not only for the components of the various Dow Jones indices, but also for other stocks in the market, all arranged by sector. This site is searchable and the site reviews contain considerable detail about what is present at each site.

There are two other good alternative approach routes to US corporate web sites. One is the Fortune 500 site at http://pathfinder.com/fortune/fortune500.index.html. This site has links to a thumbnail sketch of each of the Fortune 500 companies, with links to web addresses included in the contact details for US companies. For smaller companies and high technology stocks the NASDAQ web site at www.nasdaq.com has a complete set of web links to companies listed in the market, available either alphabetically or arranged by sector and index category.

Most US public companies, and certainly the larger ones, have company web sites. At the time of writing I counted 29 of the DJIA's (Dow Jones Industrial Average) 30 constituents as having web sites (the exception, as previously mentioned, is Philip Morris), and 98 of the NASDAQ 100. Doing the same exercise for the Standard & Poors or Fortune 500 is more time-consuming, but the obvious point is that a higher proportion of large US listed companies have corporate web sites than is the case in the UK, although the gap is narrowing.

Looking elsewhere, the Strathclyde directory also has a number of other links to corporate web site directories in Asia, Continental Europe and some other territories. Some of the best links to listed companies in other countries can be found at local stock exchange sites, which often have built-in links to company web sites at the pages giving price information on the larger listed companies. An examination of the web sites of the main European stock exchanges can be found in the previous chapter.

Assessing Corporate Sites

In the remainder of this chapter I compare a number of different web sites in the UK and elsewhere, assessing their usefulness or otherwise from the standpoint of the online investor.

The tables on the following pages derive from the CoWeS database, a large Access database of corporate web sites and their characteristics created specifically for this purpose. The database currently contains up to date information on more than 420 corporate sites covering mainly UK and European companies.

One of the aims of creating this database was to arrive at an objective ranking of the quality of the sites, in terms of the ease of navigation around and the depth of information it contained, of which more later. (Note: To find out how to purchase the full database on diskette, email cowes@ptassoc.u-net.com.)

One of the big problems with corporate web sites is that the companies that create them—supposedly as a vehicle for effective communication with the outside world—often have a different design agenda from the one that online investors might find useful. As one commentator put it a couple of years ago: 'Corporations love graphics, and the bigger the better.' Web sites can easily become corporate virility symbols. Rather than creating a simple and effective site which communicates its message efficiently, companies often get side-tracked into a competition to display more sophisticated graphics than their corporate rivals. The result is that sites become a triumph of style over substance.

In surveying a wide variety of sites of companies in different companies it is tempting to conclude that sites reflect national characteristics. It is often noticed for instance, that web sites of Japanese companies all conform closely to each other and have a markedly different style to those of Western companies. German sites are generally a model of brisk Teutonic efficiency; Swedish sites are somewhat similar. French sites often have heavy graphics and lots of style. Italian sites are chaotically organised but sometimes have arresting design qualities. And so on.

One reason for the problem of overly heavy use of graphical images may also be that company bosses and web designers, with access to ISDN lines, high-powered computer networks, and state-of-the-art communications media, often forget that the average 'hitter' of the web site is doing so via a 17-inch monitor, a standard telephone line and a

56 K modem. Sites are often not structured with the interests of the user in mind.

What most users want is a fast download, hard facts, easy navigation around the site, and a site that is updated frequently.

The Corporate Web Site Database

In compiling the database I considered the following broad characteristics:

Ease of navigation. This is a difficult characteristic to pin down and calls for a subjective judgement to be made. However, it is a combination of the intensity of the graphical images on the site, the speed of the server the site is connected to, and the way in which the site is laid out. Put simply, low graphics content is basically considered good, high graphics content bad. Making this judgement is not straightforward. Some sites have home pages which take a long time to download, but once in place mean that getting round the site can be easy. The worst sites have heavy images which have to be downloaded again each time a new page is viewed. A well laid out site map with simple links is a plus point. Because bandwidth and speed of download are problems that will eventually be solved by technology we have tended to bias our rating of sites in this context to their ease or otherwise of navigation.

Whether an up-to-date annual report is available. This is pretty much a minimum requirement for a site to be useful. It is important too that the report is well laid out on the site, with clear links to different aspects of its contents. Some reports require a PDF download and viewing via an Adobe Acrobat reader, which I consider an acceptable way to display such information. I do think, however, that it is important for investors to have access to the entire contents of a report and not just 'edited highlights'. Some of the more obscure parts of accounts are those which make the most interesting reading.

Whether press releases are available. The availability of company-issued news releases in full is also an important aspect for online investors. If they are available, you can then rely on the company site rather than keep voluminous files of paper news releases and press clippings. Company news releases should encompass both financially oriented releases and those related to trading, new product introductions, management changes, and so on. The more progressive sites have archived press releases categorised into different subject areas, which makes retrieving ones of interest an easier task.

Whether there is any additional useful general information on the company. Examples are product descriptions and prices, separate sections on the site giving information about the company's main streams of activity, operating companies, or divisions. Some form of description of the company's evolution is sometimes given, and can be useful.

Whether there are any other special features available. Web sites, particularly those of US companies, have developed hugely in this regard in the last couple of years, and among the items of interest that crop up frequently are: video and audio clips of analyst meetings and management presentations; downloadable PowerPoint presentations of the slide shows given at these meetings; downloadable fact books of financial and operating data; lists of the analysts and firms offering research coverage of the company and links to their web sites; and the facility for those using the web site to register for a service whereby future press releases from the company will be emailed as they become available.

Whether there is the facility for investors to email queries on the company and its financial performance to the investor relations department or senior management at the company, and—more important—have the reasonable expectation of an intelligent prompt response. Clearly this goes some way beyond the usual invitation present on many sites to offer comments on the construction and style of the site. Sites where a named investor relations contact's email address is stated are no more common in the case of large US companies than in European ones. On other occasions the site may include a general email area where one of the options is to email a question to an investor relations contact without having direct email access to the individual. It is, however, bizarre to observe how many otherwise highly sophisticated sites will include the name, address, telephone and fax numbers of an investor relations person, but not their email address.

Whether there is an online share price and price chart. Share prices and price charts (often with a short delay) are now readily available from a variety of sources and arguably this reduces the need for them to be present at a corporate site. It also means, however, that there is little excuse for a company to omit such data from their web sites. In the main we see no reason for a company not to have a direct display of their share price at the site, without the user having (knowingly at least) to link to another site. Where price displays and charts (see below) are provided by an indirect source, this should be accessible via a single 'click'. Sites which contain links to sites which have prices available only up to the previous day's close of business (for some reason a predilection of French corporate sites) are clearly unsatisfactory. Companies also vary in the degree of information they present if a share price chart is available at the site, the information ranging from a basic line chart, to some sites which have very sophisticated charts, complete with price movements relative to an index and trading volume data, moving averages and other indicators.

Whether there are useful links to other sites. Companies sometimes fall down in not providing visitors to their site with opportunity to explore in more depth by offering links to the web sites of subsidiaries, industry organisations and other related sites. Some companies are particularly good on this score (drug companies, for instance, often provide exhaustive links to sites concerned with the medical profession and clinical research), but others are more isolationist.

Corporate Web Sites Compared

The tables in this section provide a 'score' for each site in terms of the presence or otherwise of the characteristics listed above. In compiling the score for corporate web sites, I have worked on the following basis:

Step 1: Two, one or zero points are awarded depending on whether the site has easy navigation, medium navigation or cumbersome navigation.
Step 2: A point is awarded for the presence of each of the following: online annual report; online information on other company results; online press releases; online background information on the company; online share price (delayed if necessary, but not the previous day's close); online share

price chart; investor relations email facility; and links to other internal or external sites.

Step 3: The above eight categories (for each of which a company site will either score 1 or 0) are then added to the navigation score to arrive at the total score, giving a maximum of 10 for a site which has easy navigation and all the requisite elements, and zero for a site with heavy navigation and none of the required features.

Note: sites often change, for better or worse, without warning. The tables are based on the sites' features at the time they were visited prior to the submission of final proofs for this book in September 1999.

UK Major Company Web Sites

The Best

At the time of writing, well over 90% of the top 100 UK companies had web sites with some information of interest to investors. However, the quality of the sites is quite variable, with some big names having relatively poor sites.

Table 6.1 shows the characteristics of the best of the FTSE sites. These are the sites which, according to the criteria above score 9 or better. Eight of the sites fall into this category, all of which score well through having easily navigable sites, and many of which offer the facility for investors to email questions to named investor relations personnel.

Table 6.1 The best of the FTSE sites

Company	Web address	Gra-phics	Annual report	Results info.	Press releases	'Live' price	Chart	Investor relations email	Score
British Airways	www.british-airways.com	Low	Yes	Yes	Yes	Yes	Yes	Yes	10
Kingfisher	www.kingfisher.co.uk	Low	Yes	Yes	Yes	Yes	Yes	Yes	10
National Grid Group	www.ngc.co.uk	Low	Yes	Yes	Yes	Yes	Yes	Yes	10
Reckitt & Colman	www.reckitt.com	Low	Yes	Yes	Yes	Yes	Yes	Yes	9
Reed International	www.reed-elsevier.com	Low	Yes	Yes	Yes	Yes	Yes	Yes	10
SevernTrent	www.severn-trent.com	Low	Yes	Yes	Yes	Yes	Yes	Yes	9
SmithKline Beecham	www.sb.com	Low	Yes	Yes	Yes	Yes	Yes	No	9
WPP Group	www.wpp.com	Low	Yes	Yes	Yes	Yes	Yes	Yes	10

Severn Trent and in particular Kingfisher have been consistently among the best corporate sites around, and were two of the first to be launched, but of the newer sites National Grid scores highly.

Diageo, the company that resulted from the merger of Guinness and Grand Metropolitan is an interesting case. The site scores a respectable 8 and would have done better but for the absence of any share price information at the site. The interesting point, though, is that neither of the predecessor companies were particularly noted for their web presence. The emergence of the new company has allowed a good site to be constructed from scratch.

Reckitt & Colman is another example of a company which uses the web well, with a site that is easy to navigate, has share price information and falls short of a perfect 10 only by virtue of the absence of any links to industry or subsidiary web sites.

The media group WPP is another very good corporate site, packed full of information about its various subsidiaries through links to their sites or, if they do not themselves have a web presence, to a standard page of information about them.

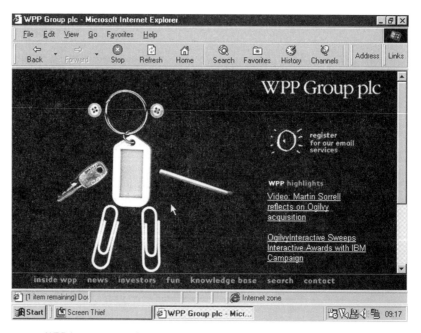

Figure 6.3   WPP is a very good corporate web site

The Worst

Unfortunately several companies fall into the opposite category, typically with sites that have heavy graphical content or poor navigation, and relatively sparse content of use to investors.

There are some common themes to these sites (see Table 6.2). One is that though sophisticated in their own right, they may be more oriented towards marketing the companies' goods or services to consumers. Financial services companies and retailers used most commonly to fall into this category, but improvements of late have meant that only two financial services groups, Lloyds TSB and Sun Life, and one retailer, Boots, now field below par sites scoring four or less.

It is, however, pleasing to report that some of the worst offenders—such as Safeway, BSkyB, Rolls Royce, Bass and 3i—have registered some improvement. Boots and Bass for example, have recently unveiled corporate 'head office' sites separate and distinct from their consumer related offerings, which though not scoring highly do represent some improvement.

It is self evident from the table where the improvements could be made—most notably in offering sites which contain lighter graphics and easier navigation, and which offer annual report information on line, a share price and price chart and an investor relations email contact.

Table 6.2 The worst of the FTSE sites

Company	Web address	Gra-phics	Annual report	Results info.	'Live' share price	Chart	Investor relations email	Score
Alliance & Leicester	www.alliance-leicester.co.uk	High	No	Yes	Yes	No	No	4
Bass	www.bass.com	Medium	No	Yes	No	No	No	4
Blue Circle	www.bluecircle.co.uk	Medium	No	Yes	No	No	No	4
Boots Co	www.boots-plc.com	High	No	No	No	No	No	4
GKN	www.gknplc.com	High	Yes	Yes	No	No	No	4
Hays	www.hays.co.uk	High	Yes	Yes	No	No	No	4
Land Securities	www.propertymail.com/lands	Low	No	Yes	No	No	No	4
Lloyds TSB Group	www.lloydsbank.co.uk	Medium	Yes	Yes	No	No	No	4
Scottish & Southern Energy	www.scottishsouthern.co.uk	Medium	Yes	No	No	No	No	4
Sun Life & Provincial Holding	www.sunlife.co.uk	Low	No	Yes	No	No	No	4
Williams	www.williams-plc.com	High	Yes	Yes	No	No	No	4
Anglo American	www.angloamerican.co.uk	High	No	No	Yes	No	No	3

However trenchant these criticisms may seem, all of the 90 or so 'footsie' companies who have web sites at the time of writing have at least made the effort to establish a web presence.

As an aside, FTSE Mid 250 companies—the companies next in the market pecking order to the Top 100—have also been taking to the web. Around 75% of them now have sites, with more being added week by week. In general these are more variable in quality than those of larger companies, but many are very good. Links to the Mid 250 sites can be found at the URL www.cix.co.uk/~ptemple/linksite or by following the link at www.new-online-investor.co.uk. More than half of the remaining top 500 companies have sites, to which links are also available at the New Online Investor 'linksite' pages.

US Company Web Sites

US corporate web sites are (or should be) of interest to UK and European online investors for two reasons.

First, as the increasing use of the web breaks down geographical barriers, it will no longer seem that unusual or that difficult for investors to buy and sell shares across national boundaries. Certainly for most US companies of any size, pretty much all the information that investors need for making an informed decision about whether to buy, sell or hold their shares is available on the web.

Second, some US companies, particularly those in Silicon Valley, have been innovators in terms of the content they seek to include on their web site that might be of use to investors. So much so, in fact, that it might be argued that their corporate sites almost contain too much information for investors to assimilate easily, or at least sometimes rather more than they need. Few experienced investors would complain about this. Almost no information is irrelevant or too trivial when it comes to making a judgement about a company.

It is also the case that (with some horrific exceptions) US companies on the web have paid attention to the concept of investors having ease of access to the information, in the sense of relatively uncluttered design, high-speed computers to serve up the pages, and ease of navigation around the site. Often investor information is collected together at a single point in the site (almost a 'site within a site' concept).

The US sites commented on here are those of the 29 Dow stocks with corporate sites and the top 20 NASDAQ stocks by market capitalisation at the time of writing. This is clearly a restricted sample of the sites available, but helps to give a flavour of the various sites and their characteristics. The same scoring methods were used as described previously.

The Best

There were 18 sites scoring 9 or 10, split roughly 50/50 between the Dow and NASDAQ top 20. These are shown in Table 6.3.

Low graphics is by no means a universal feature of these sites, but they score well in many other respects and some have features that leave others standing.

The ability for investors to log onto a list for automatic email receipt of future company press releases is a common feature of the best sites, and Cisco Systems and Dell also have audio of executive speeches and presentations to the financial community available for download.

Table 6.3 The best of the US company sites

Company	Web address	Gra-phics	Annual report	Results info.	Press releases	'Live' price	Chart	Investor relations email	Score
3 Com	www.3com.com	Medium	Yes	Yes	Yes	Yes	Yes	Yes	9
AMGEN	www.amgen.com	High	Yes	Yes	Yes	Yes	Yes	Yes	9
AT&T	www.att.com	Low	Yes	Yes	Yes	Yes	No	Yes	9
BMC Software	www.bmc.com	Low	Yes	Yes	Yes	Yes	Yes	Yes	10
Chevron	www.chevron.com	Medium	Yes	Yes	Yes	Yes	Yes	Yes	9
Cisco Systems	www.cisco.com	Medium	Yes	Yes	Yes	Yes	Yes	Yes	9
Comcast	www.comcast.com	Medium	Yes	Yes	Yes	Yes	Yes	Yes	9
Compuware	www.compuware.com	Medium	Yes	Yes	Yes	Yes	Yes	Yes	9
Dell	www.dell.com	Low	Yes	Yes	Yes	Yes	Yes	Yes	10
DuPont	www.dupont.com	Low	Yes	Yes	Yes	Yes	Yes	No	9
Ericsson	www.ericsson.com	Low	Yes	Yes	Yes	Yes	Yes	Yes	10
GE	www.ge.com	Medium	Yes	Yes	Yes	Yes	Yes	Yes	9
IBM	www.ibm.com	Medium	Yes	Yes	Yes	Yes	Yes	Yes	9
JP Morgan	www.jpmorgan.com	Low	Yes	Yes	Yes	Yes	Yes	Yes	10
Kodak	www.kodak.com	Medium	Yes	Yes	Yes	Yes	Yes	Yes	9
MCI Worldcom	www.mci.com	Medium	Yes	Yes	Yes	Yes	Yes	Yes	9
Oracle	www.oracle.com	Low	Yes	Yes	Yes	Yes	Yes	Yes	10
United Technologies	www.utc.com	Low	Yes	Yes	Yes	Yes	Yes	No	9

Microsoft, a company which is absent from the 'best' list primarily because of its unwillingness to have links to other sites and give an email address for its investor relations personnel (maybe the US Justice Department case could be blamed for this) has a startling innovation, to UK readers at least. This is an Excel spreadsheet available online at which investors can enter their own assumptions and produce their own profit forecast for the company, guided by the historic numbers and the Wall Street consensus. Intel also has extensive links to tables of historic financial ratios and charts. Oracle has a system for online proxy voting.

The best Dow stocks (GE, Kodak, DuPont, Exxon and AT&T) also innovate in their own ways. AT&T has an A to Z of its web site to aid navigation. Exxon has a commission-free shareholder investment programme. Links to consensus earnings forecasts and details of which analyst and firms cover the stock are, if not common, beginning to feature more than they used to.

Among those which score less well there are some with other interesting features. Sun Microsystems has links to analyst websites; Union Carbide has a page where investors can get details of surplus plant being

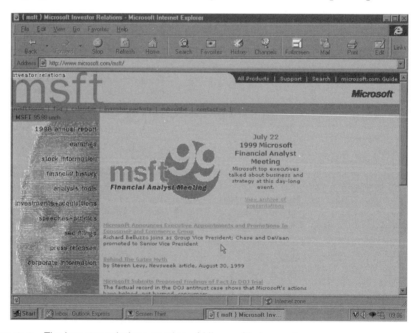

Figure 6.4   The investor relations section of Microsoft's huge site

auctioned off; General Motors provides an SEC handbook of advice for investors; and Johnson & Johnson gives comparison of shareholder returns over various time periods.

Lower Scoring Sites

There are few US sites that by international standards score poorly, but some are less helpful than others. Table 6.4 below shows five sites scoring six or less. The most common failings are less in the navigation area (although Disney's is cumbersome) but in failing to include live prices, charts or investor relations email addresses (Disney has two out of the three).

Of others one could mention that otherwise score reasonably well, Caterpillar has been prone to over-heavy reliance on graphics and obscure navigation, while Coca-cola in the past has stuffed its site with hard-to-read graphics that appear to have been designed by geeks for geeks.

However these criticisms are mild when set against the very high quality information that is generally made available by US companies. Even low scoring US sites are better than the majority of the ones produced by UK and Continental European companies.

Table 6.4 Low scoring US sites

Company	Web address	Gra-phics	Annual report	Results info.	Press releases	'Live' price	Chart	Investor relations email	Score
Allied Signal	www.alliedsignal.com	Low	Yes	Yes	Yes	No	No	No	6
American Express	www.americanexpress.com	Medium	Yes	Yes	Yes	No	No	No	6
Disney	www.disney.com	High	Yes	Yes	Yes	Yes	No	Yes	6
Maxim Integrated Products	www.maxim-ic.com	Low	Yes	Yes	Yes	No	No	No	6
Union Carbide	www.unioncarbide.com	Medium	Yes	Yes	Yes	No	No	No	5

Continental European Company Web Sites

Continental companies have on the whole embraced the web with as much enthusiasm as those in the UK. Companies in Scandinavia are noteworthy in this respect, but many mainstream companies in France, Germany, Italy, the Netherlands and Switzerland have good corporate sites.

In finding sites to input into the database I have tried as far as possible to identify those companies which are constituents of France's CAC40 and the German DAX index and which have corporate sites. For the remainder, I have looked for those companies in territories other than the UK, France or Germany which have sites and which are constituents of the Eurotop index of Europe's top 100 companies by market capitalisation. This produces a database with a range of companies spread across most European countries. Those sites which do not have an English version available are excluded.

The Best

In looking at the best of Continental sites we have taken those sites which score 10. Nine companies fall into this category (see Table 6.5).

In contrast to the UK, financial groups and chemical companies feature in the list of the best. UBS is there, as are Hoechst and Rhone Poulenc, one of four French companies in the top echelon. The latter two companies are shortly to merge. The earlier drawback to many Gallic and Latin sites, an emphasis on over-heavy graphics, appears to have been moderated, at least in the case of the French sites.

Rhone Poulenc's site quite simply has light graphics, easy navigation and all the requisite information easily available. Investor, the Swedish investment group, also has a site devoid of any pretensions with plenty of information readily available on its complex web of investments.

ING's site (just out of the top group) is easy to navigate and lacks only an email contact address for investors. Among its unusual features is a 'photo-tour' of its building, which can be varied by clicking on directional

Table 6.5   The best of the continental European company web sites

Company	Web address	Gra-phics	Annual report	Results info.	Press releases	'Live' price	Chart	Investor relations email	Score
BASF	www.basf.de	Low	Yes	Yes	Yes	Yes	Yes	Yes	10
Eridania Beghin Say	www.eridania-beghin-say.fr	Low	Yes	Yes	Yes	Yes	Yes	Yes	10
Hoechst Group	www.hoechst.com	Low	Yes	Yes	Yes	Yes	Yes	Yes	10
Investor AB	www.investor.se	Low	Yes	Yes	Yes	Yes	Yes	Yes	10
Rhone Poulenc	www.rhone-poulenc.com	Low	Yes	Yes	Yes	Yes	Yes	Yes	10
RWE	www.rwe.de	Low	Yes	Yes	Yes	Yes	Yes	Yes	10
UBS	www.ubs.com	Low	Yes	Yes	Yes	Yes	Yes	Yes	10
Usinor	www.usinor.com	Low	Yes	Yes	Yes	Yes	Yes	Yes	10
Saint-Gobain	www.saint-gobain.com	Low	Yes	Yes	Yes	Yes	Yes	Yes	10

Figure 6.5   The Investor site has plenty of information (English version available)

buttons. Some way from virtual reality, but an interesting feature nonetheless.

Many of the sites have few special features, but simply include all of the required information in an accessible, unfussy format.

The Worst

Sites scoring 4 or less are—it has to be said—dominated by the French and Germans, with a smattering of motor companies (see Table 6.6). Fiat, Volkswagen and Peugeot all feature. Three of the eight are French and four German.

The problem with the car company web sites is perhaps simply that they aim to sell cars, rather than promote their own attractions as companies investors might like to find out about. Among the others scoring badly (although just out of the table) is a broadcaster, Canal Plus, which falls into the trap of giving more attention to schedules and not enough to displaying its financial profile. And stores groups feature as

Table 6.6 The worst of the continental European company web sites

Company	Web address	Gra-phics	Annual report	Results info.	Press releases	'Live' price	Chart	Investor relations email	Score
Adidas-Salomon	www.adidas.de	High	Yes	Yes	Yes	No	No	Yes	4
Fiat	www.fiat.com	High	No	No	Yes	No	No	No	2
Karstadt	www.karstadt.de	Medium	No	No	Yes	No	No	No	3
La Redoute	www.redoute.com	Medium	No	No	No	No	No	No	1
Peugeot	www.peugeot.com	High	No	No	No	No	No	No	1
Volkswagen	www.volkswagen.com	High	No	No	Yes	No	No	No	1

ever, with Karstadt and La Redoute present, the latter with a site which has a similar lack of information to that of some UK stores group sites.

Some of the sites not included, again especially the French ones, have respectable content marred by extremely heavy or irritating graphical interfaces. This was particularly true of Legrand, a domestic electrical group while both Accor and Alcatel had heavy, poorly laid out sites. Renault's site was particularly hard to access. Several of the companies, by no means exclusively French ones, had no English version at the time of writing, including Bougyues and Credit Local de France, Edison, Generali and TIM. Volvo had an annual report available online, but only in Swedish.

Among those with truly awful design qualities (admittedly a subjective judgement of the site at the time of writing) was the cement group Lafarge, and the Belgian utility Electrabel.

Contents of the Ideal Site

After dishing out all these bouquets and brickbats, it is perhaps worth spelling out what we feel are the contents of the ideal site from the standpoint of the international online investor.

❏ In English, or an English version easily available.
❏ An easily memorable URL.
❏ Easy navigation and light graphics, the simpler the better.
❏ A site map, giving an overview of and links to all parts of the site.
❏ Up to three years of annual reports, in both HTML and downloadable PDF format.

❒ Archived press releases back for at least the same length of time, indexed by subject area (or as a minimum, into 'financial' and 'other').
❒ A bullet point summary of the company's activities.
❒ Links to subsidiaries' and affiliates' web sites—where present.
❒ A live share price quote, and historical share price charts.
❒ A direct email contact in the company's investor relations department.
❒ An automatic email server for financial press releases and other corporate information.
❒ Downloadable background information, including slide presentations and audio from meetings with analysts.
❒ Links to other sites in the same industry.
❒ Details of analyst coverage and consensus earnings estimates.

With data like this at a web site, the online investor has a one-stop shop of authoritative information on which to base an investing decision. Many US company web sites possess all of this and more. European corporate web designers, please note.

CHAPTER 7

The Online Investor in Action—
Building up the Picture

In the previous chapters of this book we have looked at various sources of online information. But the real key is how these sources can be used to build up an accurate picture of a company quickly and efficiently and at low cost.

Not all companies are equally favoured in this respect. The bigger the company, the more likely it is that more information will be available about it. We saw in the previous chapter, for example, how the overwhelming majority of large companies in the UK now have a corporate web site with financial information available on tap, whereas smaller companies are less likely to have one.

But one of the positive features of the net is that information on some foreign companies (especially, but by no means exclusively, US ones) is readily available, too. It is as easy for a UK online investor to build up a dossier of information on Microsoft or Mannesmann as it is to do it for Marks & Spencer.

Before selecting some companies to show how the online investor can operate in practice, we'll review the type of information we want to discover about these companies. This falls into the following broad categories:

❐ Financial information about or published by the company.
❐ Other background information about or published by the company.

149

❏ Recent press comment on the company.
❏ The views of other investors on the company.
❏ A share price chart.
❏ The current share price.

We'll look at each of these in turn and how to get the information from the web.

Case Study 1: A Large UK Company—Logica

Logica is a UK IT-based consultancy group with customers in the finance, telecommunications and utilities industries. By market capitalisation it ranks in the top 100 of UK listed companies at the time of writing.

Company Web Presence

Logica has made a particular point of having information readily available to investors over the web through its corporate web site at www. logica.com. The site differs from some other corporate web sites. At the home page investors are channelled from it into a separate and specially constructed 'investor relations' site (the URL is www.logica.com/ir/).

This sub-site contains additional information. As well as access to an online version of the company's annual report and recent press releases, there is also the option of contacting both the company's own investor relations staff by email and contact details are also given for the company's official broker and its financial PR company. This is unusual. Many companies do not allow quite such close potential contact to be established.

A select few companies, of which Logica is one, also make available for downloading a copy of the slide presentation made to brokers and professional investors following the results. These documents usually contain interesting additional information. As we noted in an earlier chapter on tools and utilities, information in this form generally requires the user either to have Microsoft PowerPoint installed on his or her computer, or at least a PowerPoint viewer, which enables documents like this to be read without the whole program being installed. The PowerPoint viewer is itself downloadable from the Microsoft web site (www.microsoft.com).

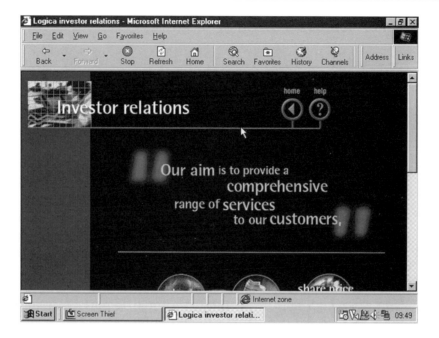

Figure 7.1 Logica's 'investor relations' site

In Logica's case, the slide presentation is available, but access is controlled (presumably to prevent competitors getting easy access to the material). Investors need to email the company's investor relations contact (which can be done direct from the web page) to get the password to enable the slide show to be viewed.

Press releases from the company, covering both financial topics and business-related issues are also available in a chronologically archived form. On occasion in the past there has been a minor drawback to the press release issued at the time of the company's results announcement. This was that the web version of the press release, while containing detailed analysis of the performance of the group's various businesses, did not contain the full range of hard profit and loss, balance sheet and cash flow numbers, but only a descriptive summary of the salient features.

In the most recent release, however, this deficiency was remedied. This is important so that, in the period between the results being issued and the annual report being released, investors relying solely on the web for the figures have access to the full range of financial information.

Other Sources of Data

As I've highlighted previously, information is usually also available from other sources, and it's always good to have a back-up. A good one is UK Equities Direct, an online version of Hemmington Scott's Company Guide. This can be found at the URL www.hemscott.com.

The drawback to using this as a back-up is that the figures are not usually updated to include the latest year until the Annual Report is released. Equities Direct does, however, provide a five-year history of the basic balance sheet and profit and loss items and has a system whereby stock exchange announcements other than results released in the previous couple of weeks can be accessed. There is also the option to access the Company REFS financial statistics service on a pay-per-view basis at £10 per page.

As noted previously, a quick and easy way of ordering an annual report (or a number of them) free of charge and without having to repeat your name and address over the phone incessantly, is to go to the site at www.icbinc.com and select the FT Annual Report Ordering Service. Reports for selected companies (many—although not all—companies participate) can then be selected. Your mailing details have to be entered. Although the site says to allow 7–10 days for delivery, my recent experience is that reports for UK companies will usually arrive within two to three business days.

Searching for Information

When it comes to accessing other information about the business, investors interested in Logica are well served. There is a comprehensive archive of past press releases available at the company web site. This isn't always the case, however, and a good 'fallback' is to do a search on a comprehensive search engine such as AltaVista (www.altavista.com) or Northern Light (www.northernlight.com), specifying quite tightly the particular aspect of the company's operations one is interested in. Even this can produce a large number of hits. Specifying 'Logica' or 'Logica consultancy' (the latter put between quotation marks to retrieve only pages containing that phrase) in AltaVista produced over 50,000 hits in the case of the company name and 14 in the case of the more complex two-word phrase. In Northern Light the result was around 64,000 and seven respectively.

Press Comment

There are several sites where press comment is available, often (although not exclusively) via a searchable archive. The *FT*, *The Times*, *Telegraph*, *London Standard, Mail on Sunday* and other papers can be searched for comment. Searching the *FT* archive (accessible via www.ft.com) currently allows investors to retrieve the last 30 days of company comments free of charge, and earlier ones are priced at $1.50 per item. At the time of writing, performing such a search for comments on Logica produced 42 references (large and small) over the previous six months.

The *Daily Telegraph* archive (www.telegraph.co.uk), which is free to use at present, is easily searchable and normally throws up a decent range of articles to peruse. In this instance, however, there were no comments on Logica results. The back issue of *The Times* for the day after the most recent results contains a brief comment on the results. Accessing back issues on the graphically heavy *Times* site (www.the-times.co.uk) is a cumbersome process. The *London Standard/Daily Mail* site (www.thisismoney.co.uk) is easily searchable and throws up a selection of articles on the company, several of which are price-related market report comments, but some of which contain interesting information on the company.

As we saw in Chapter 4, a particularly good, quickly available source of news from a variety of sources can be found at Newsnow (www.newsnow.co.uk). To recap, this site covers business and finance as well as current affairs and IT stories. Essentially it produces aggregated news from a variety of sources which by and large do not overlap with the sites of the heavyweight broadsheets. The coverage also includes web-based news services including those of the BBC and Sky. The site has a searchable 30-day archive, and entering 'Logica' as the search term recently produced six bona fide news stories mainly relating to recent results, only one of which (from This Is Money) overlapped with those sources mentioned previously.

Other Investors' Views

Seeking out the views of other investors, particularly on a technology stock like Logica can pay dividends. A good starting point is Deja, which archives comments posted to Usenet newsgroups. As we explained earlier, these are unrefereed forums containing comments on a wide variety of topics. Searches can be restricted to newsgroups likely to contain comments of interest, such as *uk.finance*.

In Logica's case, performing a Deja search (www.deja.com) on *uk.finance* throws up a large number of hits, most of which are represented by posts from those with a *logica.com* email address (i.e. Logica employees). Clearly one needs to look elsewhere. A more fruitful avenue of enquiry are the web-based bulletin boards profiled in Chapter 4.

We can take two as examples, namely the UK Motley Fool site (www.fool.co.uk) and the Market Eye 'Eye to Eye' board (at www.market-eye.co.uk). Both of these are searchable and, in the case of the Motley Fool, a straight search of mentions of the company name in the body of a posting (i.e. not necessarily the title of the message) produces no less than 38 messages discussing Logica, often in the context of other IT stocks. This is clearly a good way of getting a useful insight into the way other investors are viewing a stock. In the case of the Market Eye site a similar search can be performed with somewhat similar results.

Another interesting source of information specifically on IT-related stocks is a daily commentary produced by Richard Holway, a leading commentator on the sector. This is available at www.holway.com and includes sometimes brief but usually germane comments on the gamut of IT stocks, including Logica. At the time of writing, Holway's comments on the most recent set of results were extensive and included the results of a detailed phone conversation with the chief executive.

Share Prices and Charts

In the case of a share price chart the choice is more limited, but there are nonetheless some useful alternative sources of information. The UK Equities Direct web site has a very basic share price chart included in the service. For greater detail you need to look elsewhere. At the Market Eye site (www.market-eye.co.uk), all of the shares for which prices are quoted have a chart with a share price graph and trading volume information.

It is also worth remembering that some companies include up-to-date share prices and share price charts at their corporate web sites. Logica

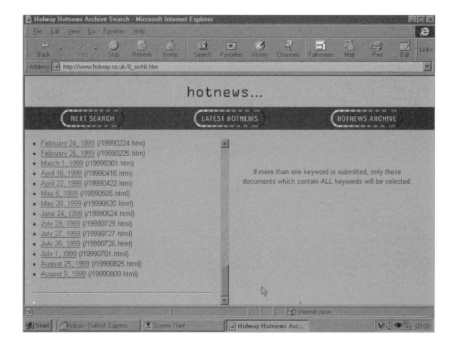

Figure 7.2 Richard Holway's comments on Logica

offers some help in this respect. The company's web site contains the following: the share price at the previous day's close; the company's market capitalisation; its earnings per share and price-earnings ratio: its position in the pecking order of companies (96th at the time of writing); a graphical representation of the trend in earnings per share; and an abbreviated five-year record.

Accessing share prices is a comparatively easy matter these days. Yahoo!'s UK finance site (http://finance.yahoo.co.uk) has an easy to use interface which requires users to type in the company's ticker symbol (in this case LOG). The system returns the current bid and offer price (20 minutes delayed) as well as the day's change and volume of shares traded.

Market Eye has a similar interface although a little more information is given, including price–earnings ratios, yields, highs and lows and other information. The price page can be accessed either via typing the company's symbol or through a conventional index. Clearly prices like these are not sufficiently current to deal on, but most online dealing services offer a facility whereby up-to-date indicated prices are given when submitting, but before confirming, an order.

There are other sites with prices available. Interactive Investor (www.iii.co.uk) offers the ability to display a limited number of stocks in 'portfolio' form. The portfolio page is bookmarked in the web browser and can then be called up at will and several prices checked simultaneously. This also gives access to a discussion list containing a few comments on the company from investors.

Summary

This shows that for a reasonably large company it is usually possible to build up a pretty good picture from sources of information which are, in virtually all cases, free of charge.

Case Study 2: A Small UK Company—Euro Sales Finance plc

Euro Sales Finance is a small company capitalised at around £42 million and listed on the main market in London, having moved up from the UK's AIM (Alternative Investment Market) smaller companies market in the autumn of 1998. It had the distinction of being the only successful start-up company to be listed on AIM, and is involved in factoring and invoice discounting for a wide range of UK clients dealing with businesses in Continental Europe, and also for clients originating in Continental Europe, especially Germany.

Company Web Presence

ESF has a corporate web site, but one that is primarily designed to communicate with its clients rather than investors. Having said that, there is some financial information available at the site (www.eurosalesfinance.com) including selected portions of the annual report available in PDF format.

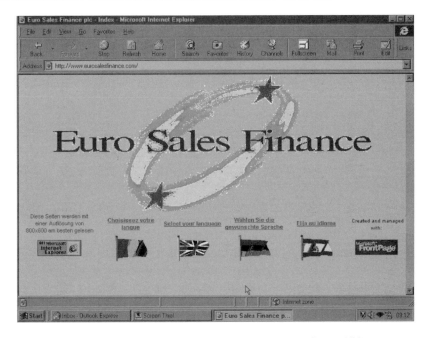

Figure 7.3   Euro Sales Finance was the first start-up company to list on AIM

The site also has scope for investors to offer some feedback and have their questions answered, and the hard copy version of the annual report can be ordered online. This is quite useful because at the time of writing the company's accounts were not available to be ordered electronically via the annual report ordering service described elsewhere in this book.

Other Sources of Data

In the case of smaller companies where a corporate web presence may not give as much detailed information as is required, investors need to employ a little more lateral thinking to get hold of the information they require. This might involve, for example, looking at the web sites of larger competitors in order to get a fix on industry trends, or using trade associations for background information, including the 'big picture' trend for the industry concerned.

In the case of Euro Sales Finance this approach produces some interesting results. The UK Factors and Discounters Association web site (www.factors.org.uk) yields industry statistics, explanations of how the industry's various products work, and links to the web sites of some of the other main players in the industry.

Searching for Information

Using the normal search engines to locate information on a small company produces fewer hits than is the case for a larger company. In ESF's case putting the company between inverted commas and searching AltaVista produces 42 hits and adding 'plc' to the search string reduces the number to 30.

These hits do, however, include the company's web pages and some other sources relating to the industry in which it operates. Using Northern Light in the same way produces respectively 30 and 15 hits, many of them the same as those produced by AltaVista.

An alternative approach in the case of some companies is to use a search tool specific to a particular industry. This is not possible in all cases, but in the case of the financial services industry, there happens to be Financewise (www.financewise.com). Here, however, the problem is what to put in the search string. Using the company name may not yield much extra, but using a narrow industry term could restrict the field too tightly.

Experimentation is therefore necessary, to find out which phrase produces the best response. Putting the term 'invoice discounting', one of the generic products that ESF offers, as the search term produces several hundred hits from Financewise, although many of them do not appear to be that relevant. Smaller companies involve more detective work from investors to dig out the information.

Press Comment

Comments in the press are rather less common for many small companies than they are for big ones, unless some particular event has brought the company into the news.

At the time of writing a search of the FT archive produced four hits, of which one represented a short comment on the company's most recent results and the other three simply mentions of price changes in the shares. *The Times* site, the Electronic Telegraph, the Financial Mail Online, and other press sites similarly drew a blank, although this would probably be unusual in the case of most smaller companies, where at least one of the main papers would carry some comment. Newsnow, which can be searched over the previous aggregation of news stories, drew a complete blank. More accurately this site produces a large number of hits about the Euro (in fact more than 1000) when searching for the company name, but none when searching for 'invoice discounting'.

Other Investors' Views

Like press commentary it is more difficult to find other investors with views if the company is a small one. Searching the Motley Fool UK message board for mentions of the company yielded a complete blank at the time of writing. A search of Deja produced 11 hits, all of which were comments that simply included the words 'Euro', 'sales' and 'finance' within the message.

In the case of the Market Eye 'Eye to Eye' message board, one hit results: inclusion of the company in a list of recommendations made by one small company newsletter posted on the board by a subscriber.

The important point here, though, is to remember that message boards are a two-way street and it is perfectly possible to post a message asking for any information or gossip about the company up on one or more of these boards and see what response you get.

Share Prices and Charts

Because ESF is a main market listed company, share price quotes and price charts are available from all of the sources mentioned in the section earlier in the chapter related to Logica.

Summary

The difference between the ease of getting information about Logica and about a much smaller company is perfectly illustrated here. However, by using a little ingenuity, the diligent online investor can winkle out more information than is at first apparent and always has the option of soliciting the views of others.

This could be a good instance of when using the pay-per-view Company REFS service at the Hemmington Scott site could pay dividends. This and the conventional UK Equities Direct entry for the company might provide further clues about where to go for more information (such as the company's broker or financial PR adviser).

The advantage of an under-researched company where information is harder to come by—it hardly needs saying—is that it is more likely that the shares are incorrectly priced by the market and offer scope for a better than average return.

Case Study 3: A Continental European Company—Deutsche Telekom

Deutsche Telekom (DT)—the former German state telecoms operator—is one of the largest companies in Europe and was privatised recently in an issue which made history by being the first large-scale public offering of shares to private investors in the Federal Republic. Using the same framework adopted for the two previous examples, we can discover how easy or otherwise it might be to find out about a company that is largely unknown to UK private investors.

Company Web Presence

DT has a good presence on the web via its site at www.dtag.de. The site has an English version and features a short explanatory profile of the company as well as a 'facts and figures' section which essentially is a compendium of the material issued in connection with the company's results, which are reported on a quarterly basis. However, as well as press releases and other financial information, the site also has details of management speeches at analyst meetings and similar material.

News releases at the site are organised into news of general interest and that of interest to investors. The result is that building up an initial picture of the company can be accomplished quite easily simply by using the company site as a one-stop shop.

Other Sources of Information

Although DT has a version of its annual report online, it is not (at the time of writing) participating in the online ordering system for annual reports described earlier. However, since the company has a widespread presence and international offices (contact details are available at its web site), this is not too much of a drawback. The usual sources of company data (such as Hemmington Scott and Company REFS) do not yet cover European companies and so are of no help in this respect. CAROL now takes in European companies. Its site (www.carol.co.uk) includes an entry for Deutsche Telekom, but in this instance it simply replicates what is available at the DT web site.

Searching for Information

Using the standard search tools we have used for the previous two examples in this chapter also throws up a useful number of hits. AltaVista produces some 24,000 hits using the company name as a search term, while putting AG after it (the German equivalent of 'plc') reduces the hit numbers to around 6,000.

With numbers of hits of this magnitude the problem of managing and classifying the information assumes greater importance. This is where the Northern Light search engine comes into its own. In this instance, the Northern Light power search option produced approaching 29,000 hits when searched using the term 'Deutsche Telekom' and 7,500 hits when AG was included between the quotation marks.

These were categorised automatically by the system into those relating to the company's web pages and several other categories, including one on voice telecommunications, another on internet telephony, and so on. This makes identifying the information required somewhat easier.

Press Comment

Searching for press comment on larger European companies is not as difficult as it might seem. You are not, for instance, confined to reading articles in the original language although in the case of DT, German speakers will find more detailed information available. However, the *Financial Times* in particular takes pride in its European content.

Searching the *FT* archive both using the *FT* alone as the source of material and ticking the options in the *FT* search form to include press releases, newswires, and other European business sources yields a large number of hits (more than 200 in each case). In the case of the more broadly based option, some of the sources retrieved required payment to be made.

This can either be accepted or the publication noted and a separate search made of its web site for the appropriate material. For example, the *FT* search reveals comments in both the *London Standard* and *Handelsblatt*. Both of these have a free search facility. In *Handelsblatt*'s case the free search available in English is confined to summary stories included in the previous two weeks, but even this option throws up several interesting stories.

Searching Newsnow (www.newsnow.co.uk) also throws up 45 matches relating to Deutsche Telekom over the last 30 days. Elsewhere, searching *The Economist* archive produces 14 articles including mention of Deutsche Telekom over the past year, of which three are particularly relevant and one is an in-depth feature on the company. Even without searching more exhaustively than this it can be seen that, for a large European company, there is no shortage of sources for interesting and useful press comment.

Other Investors' Views

The usual message boards are somewhat sparser in their comment, although no doubt specialist German language boards may contain a fair amount of debate on Deutsche Telekom. The Motley Fool site contains only a very small number of comments (just two hits at the time of writing). Comments in the message boards in the Yahoo! system are mainly confined to comments on companies supplying DT rather than specifically about it, although in themselves these may shed some light on the way the company operates.

A search of Deja using the company name produced 26 hits, none of which appears to have any relevant information, although perhaps by widening the search to take a search term such as 'German telecoms industry', or something similar might yield a few extra nuggets of information.

Share Prices and Charts

The usual Yahoo! quote server produces a quote and basic price chart of Deutsche Telekom.

In addition the Deutsche Borse web site at www.exchange.de has 15-minute delayed price quotes and charts for constituents of the DAX share index, including Deutsche Telekom. These are not that easy to find from the front page of the site, but a simple search of the site will produce the necessary result. The site defaults to German but has an English version. The share price information is basic but useful.

Summary

The preceding sections demonstrate quite readily that it is as easy, if not easier to find out information about a large European company as it is to do the same for a medium-sized or smaller UK one. Investing overseas, especially in Continental Europe, may or may not be a good idea, but online investors no longer need fear an information gap when it comes to deciding whether or not to deal offshore. The advent of the Euro is likely to increase pan-European investing, and the web enables investors in all the relevant countries to have equal access to the information they need to make a decision.

Case Study 4: A US Company—General Electric Company

US General Electric, universally known as GE, is one of the most successful companies in America. It is the only company that was a constituent of the Dow Jones index when it was founded more than a hundred years ago that is still a constituent. GE is essentially a conglomerate, operating in a wide range of industries including aero engines, domestic appliances, financial services, industrial control systems, information, lighting, medical systems, as well as the NBC TV network.

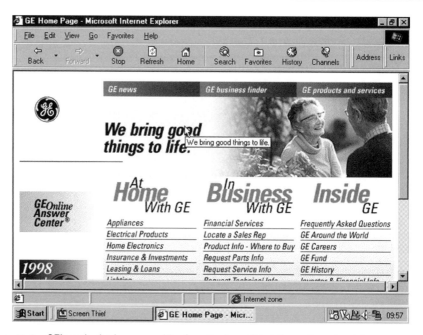

Figure 7.4　　GE's web site has a wealth of easily-digestible information about the company

Company Web Presence

GE's web site at www.ge.com has a wealth of easily digestible information about the company including a basic fact sheet, and sections which give easily accessible financial and corporate information, recent news releases, and detailed information (presented in a standard format) on the company's many subsidiaries. Within the section on investor information is a section on the stock price which, as well as giving an up-to-date quote and chart of the share price, also has detailed financial ratios and the profit and loss account and balance sheet history. For a complete picture of the company, there is little need to look elsewhere.

Other Sources of Information

US investors are well served when it comes to in-depth financial information about companies by the presence of EDGAR, the online document filing service operated by the SEC. Not only is EDGAR accessible to the general public for free, but its very presence has spawned additional free services which are commercial (i.e. include advertising) but still free and slightly more user friendly than the standard EDGAR interface. One of the best of these is EDGAR Online (www.edgar-online.com), which will sort the documents filed on a particular company by type of document and by time filed.

Many of these documents are boring administrative ones, but detailed quarterly and annual financial reports (so-called 10Q's and 10K's) filed by companies are readily available and sometimes contain more detail than the documents published on the company web site. The presence of EDGAR and the SEC generally has tended to mean that most US listed companies operate a full disclosure policy, so online investors have little trouble getting hold of a wealth of financial information on even the smallest listed company.

Searching for Information

With a company as large and pervasive as GE, searching for information can be a frustrating business simply because of the sheer quantity of data available. AltaVista and Northern Light each produce around 500,000 hits, many of which are likely to be duplication. There is no way round this unless you narrow the search for information to a particular aspect of the company's business, but this approach would arguably be too detailed for most investors. The problem of information overload is, therefore, perhaps best attacked through searching press archives.

Press Comment

To produce the best results, a slightly different subset of publications is needed for a US company. However, the FT archive remains as good a starting point as ever. Inputting 'GE' as the search terms solely for comments in the *FT* produces 174 hits, while excluding the newspapers but including newswires, press releases and US business sources produces over 200 hits.

Forbes (www.forbes.com) is one of the best free sources of business information for US companies. Searching the Forbes archive produces 180 articles, including some very topical ones about the company and, for example, its management succession issue (a very germane issue at the time of writing).

A search of *The Economist* archive produced 21 hits, including one or two especially relevant pieces while Newsnow's 30-day archive generated 753 stories mentioning the company, although not all of these were relevant.

Other Investors' Views

There is, in general, a much greater opportunity to sample other investors' views when it comes to US stocks. The problem is that the quality of the comment is sometimes distressingly low. The Motley Fool (www.fool.com) has a separate message board for GE that appeared, at the time of writing, to be producing around 60 messages a month. At Yahoo! the message board on GE produces around a dozen messages a day, although some of the comment ranges between the unduly brief, trite and blatantly self-serving.

Share Prices and Charts

With US companies there is rarely any shortage of opportunities for obtaining price quotes and charts. The quote servers section of Yahoo! lists 39 separate real-time quote sites of this type for US companies. All that is required to access such services is the ticker symbol (in this instance GE). Six of the sites offer free real-time quotes (provided users register).

Summary

Many of the comments made about assembling information about Continental European companies can be applied to US companies 'in spades'. In fact the difference between the two is that in the case of the USA there is much less distinction between small and large companies in terms of the amount of information that is readily available. In the US smaller companies may demand more searching to track down non-official information, but a much greater proportion of US companies (even small ones) have web sites, and quotes and charts, and financial information courtesy of EDGAR, is available for all companies, however small.

CHAPTER 8

Dealing Online

In the first version of this book, we covered the topic of online share dealing in some detail. Rather as has happened with corporate web sites, online dealing has developed very rapidly indeed in the past couple of years.

This is especially so in the USA, where it has become arguably the main way in which private individuals, or at least active private investors, deal in stocks. Some estimates suggest that more than 20 million individual investors will manage their portfolios online by 2003.

In the UK the development of online share trading has been much slower, although it has speeded up recently with the advent of the CREST settlement system, the SETS electronic order book, and computerised order execution by the so-called 'retail service provider' (RSP) systems operated by some major stock exchange firms. This means that private investors can, for the first time, effectively deal direct with the market, have a firm price quoted electronically, accept it and deal instantaneously, in the knowledge that the price is guaranteed and the deal will be settled automatically.

We will return to this topic later, and in particular to the differences between internet based share trading in the USA and in the UK. First, though, we'll look at a little background.

The Development of Electronic Markets

Traditionally, all stock market dealing was conducted on the basis of personal contact. A client would instruct the broker to buy or sell some shares, by letter or by telephone. The broker's dealer would then go onto the stock exchange floor and deal face-to-face with a jobber (the wholesaler of shares) at the best price available. Very often a wealthy client would meet his or her broker face-to-face, perhaps over a City lunch table, to review shareholdings and plan a dealing strategy for the following few months.

This system changed in 1986 in the Stock Exchange's so-called Big Bang. Dealing migrated from the Stock Exchange floor to large dealing rooms and trades were conducted over the telephone with the help of electronic displays giving price information.

Floor trading still ostensibly continues in some markets, such as the New York Stock Exchange (NYSE). But in many financial centres, electronic trading has all but replaced face-to-face contact as the preferred method and even in the markets that do have a floor trading presence, in many respects it is a shadow of its former self, with much of the business taking place electronically. The trend appears to be for markets ultimately to go all-electronic. Competition from electronics-based European futures exchanges forced LIFFE, for example, to migrate all but its most heavily traded contracts to a new electronic system in early 1999. The remainder are set to follow.

There are many reasons for this change in the way business is being done. One is, of course, cost: electronic networks are cheaper to run.

The old method of trading—whereby a dealer would have to scurry around a crowded market floor to check a price with a number of market-makers to ensure that the best price was obtained—was positively antiquated for the late twentieth century. In futures exchanges, the crowd of dealers in brightly coloured jackets shouting and gesticulating is being overtaken by a system which guarantees speed and anonymity at low cost.

Anonymity is important. An order being entered over a screen has less impact on the market than a dealer from a large broker checking a particular share price prior to dealing. Electronics can also permit the process of price setting to be conducted automatically, with a computer setting the price that best accommodates the highest numbers of bids and offers entered for a particular share.

This is known as 'order driven' trading, distinct from the old 'quote driven' system of competing market-makers for each individual share. Its introduction in London was the source of some controversy, with objections from market-makers, whose livelihood it threatened. However, despite occasional complaints about its efficiency, the system has now been accepted by most users of the market. So much so that the talk now is of so-called Electronic Communications Networks (ECNs) which bypass the official market and allow big investors to trade directly with each other.

Aside from this latest aspect of electronic markets, large market-makers and the brokers who trade with them some years ago developed a system whereby orders received from small investors could be aggregated and transacted automatically at the best price available. This is clearly advantageous to all concerned. Investors are guaranteed 'best execution'—still a fundamental principle of most major exchanges—while the Stock Exchange firms concerned are spared the labour-intensive process of dealing with a large number of small orders.

Once this system of automated order execution developed, and it is also a feature of other advanced markets such as the USA, it allowed a new category of broker to develop. A broker who could site his premises in a low-cost area and offer a no-frills dealing service to clients.

But combined with SETS, the CREST electronic settlement system, and the universal access possibilities offered by the web, this so-called 'retail-service provider' (RSP) automated dealing system also means that there is theoretically no bar to clients being given direct access to the automated aspects of the system. In other words, instead of a client calling a dealer, who then checks a price on an RSP system and asks the client's permission to go ahead, the web means that the client can access the RSP directly via the broker's system. Instead of the dealer being quoted a price and given a brief time period to accept it or not, this option can, through the web, be offered direct to the client.

From Execution-only To E-broking

Some private client brokers take a client's existing investment portfolio and look after it without the client having to make any investment decisions at all. This type of broking account, known as a discretionary account, in effect makes the broker the individual's personal fund manager and is only really economic in the case of wealthy individuals with large portfolios. In this instance deals are done by the broker and the client is informed about them some time later. Clearly the onus is on the broker to perform well and 'beat the market'.

While the broker would once normally be rewarded in the form of commission, in the case of many discretionary accounts the broker is now paid on the basis of a percentage annual fee, which rises as the value of the portfolio grows.

For many individuals a discretionary broking account is either too expensive, or the antithesis of what investment is all about.

Those with a limited amount of money to invest who do not want the bother of picking investments can always buy a unit trust. Some are indexed to the market, removing the risk that particular share selections will underperform the index. Funds are also available that are insulated against any drop in the market and will capture a certain percentage of any upward move in the index. These can be a good option for investors whose priority is preservation of capital.

Those investors who want to participate in making their own investment decisions, picking shares they like the look of and deciding when to buy or sell, have two options when it comes to choosing a broker. These boil down to whether or not the individual concerned wants investment advice.

Many brokers offer a 'portfolio advice' service. The client retains the final say over what to buy and sell and when, but may ask the broker for advice about a particular course of action, or ask his or her opinion about a particular share or other investment. At the up-market end of the scale the service can include advice about the client's tax position and other relevant matters, but more often than not the service is based on an exchange of ideas between the client and the individual broker servicing the client's account.

The broker makes money out of dealing commission from the client's orders and from fees charged for additional services such as portfolio valuations and the like. The service the client gets will depend to a degree on the frequency with which deals are done.

However, the new wave of the late 1980s and early 1990s was execution-only broking. This mimicked an earlier trend in the mid-1970s in the USA, following the deregulation of commission there. 'Execution-only' broking means that the client is not offered any advice (in fact, execution-only brokers are prohibited by City regulations from offering advice of any description), and the broker will simply transact an order without question at the best possible price.

The quid pro quo for the lack of advice is that commission charges will typically be much lower than the dealing-with-advice or the discretionary service. Charges are kept low because of the high-tech systems at the heart of the execution-only brokers' operations. These route calls to a team of dealers, who can then deal electronically using the order-execution systems operated by RSPs.

Administration is also kept streamlined. Many execution-only brokers insist that clients keep their shares in a nominee account and link their purchases and sales to a high interest cash management account. This account can simply be debited when a purchase is made and credited with sale proceeds—without the need for cheques to flow back and forth. The CREST electronic settlement regime is also tailor-made for a system of this type. An alternative to the nominee account is CREST-sponsored membership for the individual investor, which costs £10 a year and preserves the identity of the individual on the share register.

The establishment of execution-only broking services came in the 1980s with the abandonment of fixed commissions. But the plethora of privatisation issues in that decade was also a big driving force behind the growth of no-frills services like this.

Privatisations left many individuals with small parcels of shares. Often they had not dealt with a stockbroker before. Brokers competed to sell these shares in the hope that the individuals concerned would stick with the investing habit and become regular clients.

In many instances this proved a vain hope. Nonetheless, many regular investors who might previously have dealt through a higher-cost dealing-with-advice broker discovered that execution-only services offered a way of cutting their dealing costs. This was provided they were independent-minded enough to make their own decisions and research their own shares.

Seeing the advent and success of execution-only firms, led by ShareLink (now called Charles Schwab Europe) and quickly followed by other leading players, many other brokers—offering a range of other services to their clients—have since also begun offering an execution-only services as an option, and orders traded through execution-only services have dramatically outstripped those dealt via conventional services.

But the real point about the development of execution-only broking is that it is tailor-made for online dealing. One of the main reasons for having an account with a full-service firm is conversing with the broker to exchange ideas and advice. For the execution-only client, however, this is not the case. Here, communication between client and broker is restricted to giving an order and having it confirmed that the transaction has been done at a particular price. Human intervention in this process is not essential.

Although in my experience most staff at execution-only brokers are sympathetic and patient with clients who may not be fully conversant with stock exchange jargon and the intricacies of dealing, some people—perhaps those who deal infrequently—find calling up a broker a forbidding prospect. Others are irritated by the fact that calling up the broker may result in the call being held in a queue until a dealer is available.

This scenario adds to the pressure on the client. Having got through to an obviously very busy dealer, originally intending simply to ask a price, the client may feel some obligation to deal anyway, even though this need not have been the purpose of the call. This is not conducive to good investment decision making. A client should feel able to deal only when required, and the process of dealing (sometimes mistakenly characterised as the glamorous part of investing) should be reduced to the status of a functional transaction, no more and no less significant than ringing up a cinema box office to book a couple of tickets for Saturday night.

The most important part of the investment decision is deciding which share to buy and when. The act of placing the order should be simple and quick, and is not the end in itself. This being the case, any execution-only broking client ought to consider the possibility of transmitting orders to and receiving dealing confirmations from the broker by electronic means, as an alternative to the disembodied voice of the dealer on the phone.

A later part of this chapter will look at the alternatives currently on offer for electronic dealing through the dozen or so UK brokers that now offer it. But let's look first at some of the points that need to be established at the outset.

These can be summarised as follows:

❏ You need to be comfortable making your own investment decisions without the benefit of any advice or research from the broker.
❏ You need to be familiar with normal dealing vocabulary. For instance, the web site interface at an Internet-based broker may offer the opportunity to input orders either 'at best' (the best price then ruling), 'limit' (where you specify a limit above which a purchase or below which a sale will not take place), and whether the limit is 'good for the day', 'good until cancelled', or 'fill or kill'.
❏ You need to shop around. Investigate what facilities—such as news, information, research, and 'live' share prices—are provided as part of

the online trading service, and whether commission charges are competitive. Brokers who offer online accounts ought by rights to charge considerably less than they would for a telephone-based service, since there is less (costly) human intervention involved. This principle has yet to be firmly established in the UK, although forecasts are for commission rates to be cut further as competition for online trading accounts intensifies. Some US electronic broking services are extremely cheap.

❑ Establish at the outset whether order confirmation is received while online, or whether you might have to wait for a subsequent email message to provide information that it has been completed. Brokers differ in this respect, some transacting orders via dealers' screens, and some providing direct RSP access. The latter system looks set to take over.

❑ Make sure the service you choose offers the ability to check the current best bid and offer prices prior to an order being entered and allows you to enter a dealing limit. The ability to check your portfolio's value, and the amount of unused cash in the account, is also handy.

❑ Security is also a vital concern of many contemplating online trading for the first time—or indeed at any time. How good is the password protection and encryption? Can orders be sent in secure mode from a browser? Security issues can be overstated but in view of the sums involved you may wish to have the reassurance that access to your investments is secure.

❑ For settlement purposes an electronic broker will require you to have a linked money market account from which funds can be debited and to which they can be credited as necessary. Virtually all online brokers require either the stock to be lodged in a broker nominee or for CREST sponsored membership to be taken out by the client.

❑ If going electronic entails a change of broker, make sure first that the dealing and administration service being offered is at least as efficient as the one operated in the conventional way by your existing broker. If, for example, you are happy with your existing execution-only service, it may be better to wait until your broker offers online trading as an option, rather than switch to another's electronic service whose dealing and administration is an unknown quantity.

Later in this chapter we'll look at how the services currently on offer in the UK stack up, but in the meantime, since these innovations in the sphere of online trading originated in the USA, let's check on how services have developed there, what type of product is typically offered by US online brokers, how much it costs, and what the recent experience there has been.

Web-brokers—the US Experience

In other chapters of this book we have commented on the tendency of the USA to lead the way in terms of the take-up of Internet-based investment techniques. And this has been as true in online dealing as anywhere. The figures quoted vary somewhat, but best current guesses suggest that around 40% of all 'retail' investor trades are conducted electronically.

Some other random facts show the increasing pervasiveness of online dealing among private individuals within the USA.

❐ Yahoo!'s Business and Economy/Investing index gives a list of US Internet-based broking firms, with some 84 entries.
❐ The average US online investor does 25 trades per annum, compared to the UK figure of three.
❐ The cheapest US online broker charges around $5 a trade in commission. Compare this to around £20 a deal in the UK.
❐ Some estimates suggest that more than half of all financial transactions (including banking) will take place online by the end of the year 2000. Around 40% of 'retail' investor transactions in the USA now take place online, and the figure is growing rapidly.
❐ The top five US online brokers are estimated to have more than 5 million accounts. Charles Schwab alone is believed to have 2 million and E*Trade recently claimed to have logged its millionth customer. Around 60% of Schwab's orders from retail investors are now transacted online and a further 20% or so by automated touch tone phone and voice recognition phone systems.
❐ Forrester Research, an independent consultancy specialising in market research related to the Internet, has estimated that by 2002 there will be some 14.4 million online accounts in the USA with some $688 billion in assets.

One lesson of the US experience is that competition is likely to drive down dealing costs as the online trading habit expands. Since the essence of the services is that the customer can in effect tap directly into the automated execution services used by the brokers themselves, the broker becomes no more than a conduit for orders, and a site for processing bargains and ensuring that trades are settled correctly.

The corollary—one that will hold good in the UK, too—is that the marginal cost to the broker of doing the trade is extremely low. No highly paid dealers need be involved, and the charge to the investor can in theory just represent the cost of processing and settling a trade, moving cash and stock back and forth, plus a profit margin on top.

Many execution-only services have tried to add value to the package they offer by bundling information services, either free or at a discounted price. They fall short of offering advice, but represent useful information for which the investor might otherwise have to pay a full price.

Table 8.1 shows some characteristics of US-based internet brokers, together with an indication of where they fall in the commission charging structure and the other services they offer. Merrill Lynch, doyen of US retail brokers, is also shortly expected to offer web based dealing to its private clients—to the consternation of some of its more traditionally-minded 'account executives'.

As with other tables in this book we have attempted to give these brokers a score on the basis of several factors. UK (and a selection of US) brokers with web sites have been assessed on: ease of site navigation;

Table 8.1 Characteristics of US-based Internet brokers

Broker name	Web address	Web dealing	Commis-sion rates	Market comments	Company comments	Price service	Score
Charles Schwab	www.schwab.com	Yes	Yes	Yes	Yes	Yes	9
Accutrade	www.accutrade.com	Yes	Yes	Yes	Yes	Yes	9
Amex Financial Direct	www.americanexpress.com/direc	No	Yes	Yes	Yes	Yes	7
Ameritrade	www.aufhauser.com	Yes	Yes	Yes	Yes	Yes	8
Scottrade	www.scotttrade.com	Yes	Yes	Yes	Yes	Yes	8
Dreyfus Brokerage	www.tradepbs.com	Yes	Yes	Yes	Yes	Yes	9
Computel	www.computel.com	Yes	Yes	Yes	Yes	Yes	8
Datek	www.datek.com	Yes	Yes	Yes	Yes	Yes	10
Discover	www.dbdirect.com	Yes	Yes	Yes	Yes	Yes	8
DLJ Direct	www.dljdirect	Yes	Yes	Yes	Yes	Yes	9
eTrade	www.etrade.com	Yes	Yes	Yes	No	Yes	8
Jack White	www.jackwhiteco.com	Yes	Yes	Yes	Yes	Yes	7
JB Oxford	www.jboxford	Yes	Yes	Yes	Yes	Yes	10
National Discount Brokers	www.ndb.com	Yes	Yes	Yes	Yes	Yes	10
Quick & Reilly	www.quick-reilly.com	Yes	Yes	Yes	Yes	Yes	8

whether or not web dealing is available; whether or not commission rates are quoted; whether or not prices, company research and market commentaries are available online; whether or not the site includes downloadable software tools or some useful interactive calculators; whether or not there is email contact and whether or not there are external links at the site. Allowing two points for easy navigation (one for moderate and zero for difficult) and a point each for the presence of the other characteristics, gives a score out of 10.

Most US brokers score well, with Datek (www.datek.com), JB Oxford (www.jboxford.com) and National Discount Brokers (NDB) (www.ndb.com) being the best. NDB has particular software tools that clients can download to make market monitoring and order entry especially easy.

Cost comparisons are difficult to make because of differential scales of charges for different sizes of order, hence the categorisation of the brokers into high, mid and low cost. The categorisation is that used by Xolia (Expert Online Investment Advocates) at their web site at www.xolia.com. Mid cost brokers are those which generally charge less than $100

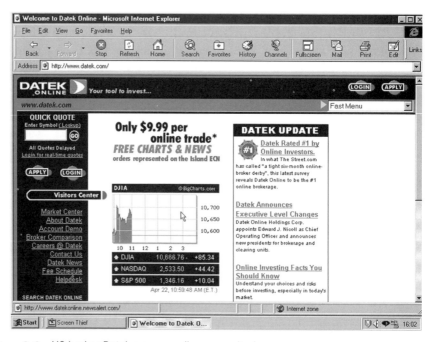

Figure 8.1 US broker Datek scores well on our criteria

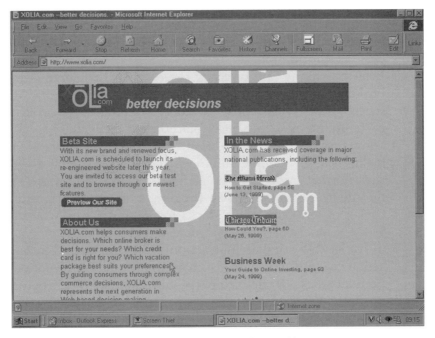

Figure 8.2 Xolia categorises brokers into high, medium and low cost

commission for a 5000 share order (this would perhaps be the equivalent of £25,000 order in UK terms, given the higher weighted prices generally on US stocks.

The deep discount brokers typically operate a fairly spartan service, but charge single figure dollar commissions. Their web sites often have tables which give flattering comparisons with the higher charges elsewhere.

The Xolia site is a useful one to look at anyway. It gives an interesting history of the development of online share trading in the USA as well as detailed objective reviews of the service provision and charges of US web-based brokers.

The web offerings of UK brokers will be covered in the next section, but for now it is worth recording some of the characteristics demonstrated by their US peers' sites. These can be summarised as follows:

❐ Virtually all of the sites reviewed score highly in terms of the provision of market information and company research, but this is typically provided by inbuilt links to third party services such as Zacks Company Reports, PC Quote, BigCharts and others.

❏ In many sites delayed quotes are free, but users either have to register or be existing clients of the broking firm to get access to all but the most basic of information.

❏ Real-time quotes are typically reserved for registered clients and some brokers, especially the deep discount variety, operate a system whereby a new client is allowed 100 free real-time quotes and 100 for each buying or selling order placed over the web.

❏ Some brokers offer other incentives. American Express's web broking business offers membership reward points for each trade placed. Datek says normal trades will be commission free if they take more than a minute to execute. Discover Brokerage offers the opportunity to buy a basket of ten Dow Jones stocks for a commission charge of less than $40. The stocks can then be freely added to or sold.

❏ E*Trade, the original Internet-only broker, has a special service for active traders which feeds changes in analyst recommendations on popular stocks (from third party sources) to members before the market opening. E*Trade has also been active in promoting bulletin board discussion groups for its 'members' for discussing stock tips and is believed to have 150,000 users for this service.

It is this latter point which verges on the controversial. Internet bulletin boards have been blamed for the dramatic swings noticed in Internet-related stocks in particular and technology stocks in general.

While freedom of speech is as much a right for investors as anyone else, it is perhaps noteworthy that monitoring of these discussion groups is under way. NASDAQ, where many of the stocks are listed, has been developing software to monitor these groups on a regular and automatic basis, to combat possible abuses including fraudulent price manipulation. Regulatory moves of this type are also taking place in other countries.

It is unlikely that the online revolution will stay so effectively confined to the USA for long. The take-off has been much slower in the UK, but it is beginning to happen.

The Electronic Share Information Story

It is often the case that what takes place in the USA will happen in the UK five years later. Execution-only broking was a US idea that caught on in a big way in the UK after being extensively developed on the other side of the Atlantic. Online trading is its natural extension, but it has been much slower to develop in the UK. There are signs that the logjam of investor conservatism may be breaking down.

It actually has an additional selling point to offer in the UK. Here, stockbrokers, and dealing with them, was once regarded as the preserve of the affluent middle and upper classes.

Since almost everything in Britain is deemed to have something to do with social class, it would be unrealistic to expect this attitude to disappear overnight. But privatisations and the development of execution-only services in the past 15 years has done a lot to democratise and demystify the process of share dealing.

It was perhaps natural to expect Sharelink (now Charles Schwab Europe) to have been in the forefront of moves to introduce online trading to UK investors. Its management roots were in the telecoms industry rather than the more traditional City firms. And that was perhaps the point. The problem of introducing wider share ownership within the UK has always lain, however, in the vested interests of more conventional Stock Exchange firms and in the conservatism of the London Stock Exchange itself.

The reason is simple. In the years since Big Bang, the Stock Exchange has been struggling to find itself a new role, and to preserve as much as possible of its old one. It has since lost much of its influence. Its role as market regulator was subsumed into the SFA and SIB (now the FSA), its role as a standard-setting and examining body moved into the Securities Institute, its role as a disseminator of price display hardware and software hived off into firms such as Reuters and Datastream/ICV, and its role in settlement, after the TAURUS debacle, moved into CREST, initially directed by the Bank of England and owned by City institutions.

The Stock Exchange's attitude to the online revolution encountered something of a watershed in its early dealings with Electronic Share Information, which brought the whole question of the exchange's attitude to the web, and web dissemination of share prices into sharp relief.

At the time Electronic Share Information (ESI—www.esi.co.uk) was a comparatively young company set up by Herman Hauser, the entrepreneur behind the founding of Acorn Computer. Its mission was to allow its users access to share price information and other company information via the world wide web and to provide the links to brokers to allow its subscribers to transact orders electronically. It offered the capability for the first online dealing service in UK stocks for private investors.

The Stock Exchange's well-chronicled objections to the ESI service did not lie in its making available electronic trading to the private client, but in the way in which ESI was disseminating price information. The Exchange withdrew permission for the company to distribute live price information over the Internet two days before the launch of the service.

In the event, the threat was withdrawn soon after, at the cost of some embarrassment to the Exchange who, though it clearly feared that the system might be used as a way for some ingenious individuals getting expensive share price information on the cheap, failed to understand precisely how the service might be used by individual investors.

From June of 1997, the Exchange introduced a new system whereby it would charge exchange fees only for live share prices and allow delayed prices to be distributed to investors free of charge.

Ironically Sharelink was subsequently acquired by Charles Schwab and ESI has recently entered into a partnership with E*Trade to enable the latter to launch a web-based dealing service, which it has now done. Market Eye has launched a 'trading gateway' at its popular price dissemination site which is used by several small firms to promote their web dealing services and several other brokers have launched services independently.

ESI's role was crucial in creating the conditions for online trading to flourish and, by linking with E*Trade, the original Internet-only broker, it signalled it intended to play an ongoing part in the market's development. E*Trade's UK service has recently been launched.

UK Brokers Online

The world wide web is now coming to be used more and more by brokers wishing to interact with their computer-networked clients. Although we deal here mainly with UK brokers and their services, this is equally true in Continental Europe where online dealing is very well established in Germany and Sweden, and developing strongly in France.

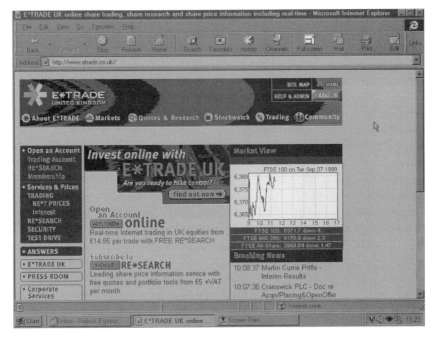

Figure 8.3 E*Trade's web-based dealing service

As more brokers come online, however, and as the online investing habit becomes more broadly based so it is likely that commission rates will drop, albeit not perhaps to the levels seen in the USA, which has the benefit of a deeply ingrained personal investing habit and greater receptiveness to online information in its various forms.

As the experience of Charles Schwab in the USA showed, embracing online trading takes a great deal of management courage, because it needs to be keenly priced yet it can cannibalise more profitable business previously transacted in non-online forms.

Schwab was converted to e-trading very quickly, and got its systems up and running in a matter of months. It has since been rewarded with substantial increases in trading volume but went through a quite lengthy period when volume gains were insufficient to compensate fully for tighter margins.

Schwab's experience is instructive because of its ownership of Sharelink (now known as Charles Schwab Europe). It is a fair bet that Schwab's US experience will mould the way it tackles the UK and other European share

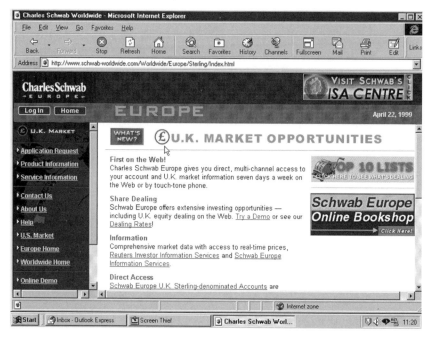

Figure 8.4   Schwab's e-trading web page

dealing markets. The partnership between E*Trade and ESI will also bring US experience to bear. DLJ Direct's recent debut extends this US influence. The way in which the market develops will, however, ultimately be determined in part by the way in which investors and other UK-based brokers react.

As with the US broker web sites examined earlier in this chapter, we have also taken a critical look at the web offerings of the UK entrants onto the online scene. There are currently around 25 UK equity brokers with a web presence, and we have attempted to assess all of them in as objective a way as possible. The fact remains that only around a dozen offer web-based dealing (see Table 8.2). The remaining sites represent essentially promotional material for a telephone-based service, albeit on occasion quite useful and informative.

In general terms, and with some exceptions, the sites appear inferior to those of US online brokers in a number of respects.

In contrast to the USA, where the provision of some form of stand-ardised market information, quotes and basic research on companies is considered essential, in the UK the provision of information like this is haphazard. Some brokers are even coy about revealing commission rates.

Table 8.2 Characteristics of UK-based Internet brokers

Broker name	Web address	Web dealing	Commission rates	Market comments	Company comments	Price service	Score
Barclays	www.barclays-stockbrokers.co.uk	Yes	Yes	No	No	No	4
Cave & Co.	www.caves.co.uk	Yes	Yes	No	No	No	5
Charles Schwab Europe	www.schwab-worldwide.com	Yes	Yes	Yes	Yes	Yes	8
DLJ Direct	www.dljdirect.co.uk	Yes	Yes	Yes	Yes	Yes	8
E*Trade	www.etrade.co.uk	Yes	Yes	No	No	Yes	5
Goy Harris	www.ghcl.co.uk	Yes	Yes	Yes	Yes	Yes	8
Halifax	www.sharexpress.co.uk	Yes	Yes	No	No	Yes	8
James Brearley	www.jbrearley.co.uk	Yes	Yes	Yes	No	No	6
Stocktrade	www.stocktrade.co.uk	Yes	Yes	Yes	Yes	No	5
Torrie	www.torrie.co.uk	Yes	Yes	Yes	Yes	No	7
Xest	www.xest.com	Yes	Yes	Yes	Yes	Yes	9

Most of those with web-based dealing services provide some form of price information, but others do not. Company research where it is provided (in a minority of sites), is generally a web version, or PDF format version, of print-based research that is mailed out to clients in the normal way.

Some sites, such as Beeson Gregory's and Collins Stewart's, are very clearly not aimed at private investors but, respectively, at potential new corporate clients and at institutional investors. Others combine some good ideas with irritatingly heavy graphics. At the Killik site, for example, the design is very heavy and rather confusing, but the site has a visitor sentiment meter, where those visiting the site can register their current views on the market.

Brewin Dolphin's site has a good selection of company comments, while Durlacher, a broker increasingly specialising in research and corporate finance for Internet-related stocks and other technology issues, has summaries and ordering information for its very comprehensive research on a number of investment-related aspects of the Internet market but, as yet, no web-based dealing.

The best sites are those operated by Schwab Europe (www.schwab-worldwide.com/europe) and Xest (www.xest.com). The latter is the web dealing offshoot of Charles Stanley (which also itself has a basic web presence). Schwab's site reflects the sophisticated experience of its US parent and the firm probably (at the time of writing) offers the best all-round service, albeit at commission rates that are slightly on the expensive side compared to some firms, operating as they do on a sliding scale rather than the flat rates of £20 and £25 per trade respectively offered by Xest and Stocktrade.

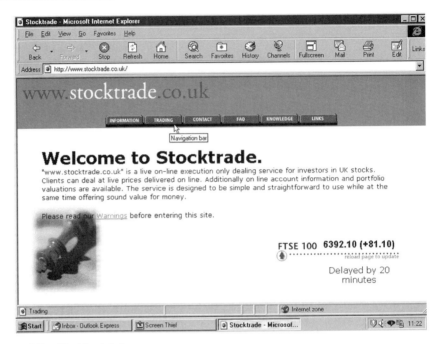

Figure 8.5   Stocktrade's home page

One of the newer entrants, Barclays offers a fairly spartan broking service online, but interestingly has linked its offering to a parallel initiative in Internet banking and an offer of free Internet access. Several other brokers are contemplating offering a web-based dealing service. Freeserve is also launching a web share dealing product in conjunction with a US financial institution.

A Personal Experience

How do online trading services work in practice? In my own case, when Fidelity Brokerage, of which I had been a client for a number of years, shut up shop I opted for the Xest service mentioned previously, if only because Charles Stanley, the firm of which the service is a part, was a broker I had used some years earlier.

Account opening in the case of the Xest service is relatively simple, and takes place in hard copy format, although the forms can be requested online. Xest's settlement operates via the firm opening a CREST sponsored membership account for each client, and this takes a week or two to set up. In contrast to a nominee set-up, for a modest cost (now only £10 a year) this method preserves the client's identity on the share register of companies invested in. A money market account has to be set up and funded, much like a normal execution-only client of a telephone-based broker.

Data for the Xest service is supplied by S&P Comstock. Commission rates are a flat £20 per deal. The order entry screen is easy to use and order transmission is encrypted and protected by a complex password, substantially more secure than the conventional system of phoning up the broker and only having to give a five-digit account number as identification.

For much of my experience with the system, the Xest account has not operated on the basis of a direct RSP link. That is to say, the order crops up on the dealer's screen and is executed via an RSP if appropriate (or through negotiation if price improvement is possible) by the dealer and confirmation sent back. Following the service's redesign, a limit service has been instituted to protect the client from sharp market movements. The broker has found that in 50% of cases, the option not to use an RSP results in a better price for the client. Valuations and a record of past deals are also now available online.

In the several deals I have done since opening the account, the system has worked pretty well, delivering confirmations at or inside the 'touch price' at the time I placed the order in every case.

The only point that does require some explanation is that communication with the broker is normally exclusively by email. It is clear that brokers save costs and offer deeply discounted commission rates by doing this, but for the client it does mean that waiting for a reply to a complicated settlement query can take a little time and be frustrating. Only by using the system for a while will the user gain confidence that it really does work.

The other drawback is that whereas with a telephone-based broker the service can be accessed on the move, a PC with access to the web is required to input orders—there is sometimes no alternative method. I have personally not found this a problem. Some brokers do, however, offer a telephone service in the event that web dealing services are interrupted.

Whether or not it makes sense switching to a web broker now or sometime in the future really depends how 'net aware' you are, how price (i.e. commission) sensitive you are, and to a degree how confident you are of your ability to make investing decisions independently.

For my money, though, just sign up for a basic dealing service without the extras like prices, valuations, news and so on. Those are just as likely to be available elsewhere for free on the web or in the case of a valuation, capable of being constructed in packages like Quicken or Excel. In the case of Xest, real-time prices and news are available free of charge for clients, but this is not usually the case with other online brokers.

In fact there is clear scope now for externally provided sources of information to take the place of the rather inadequate offerings of some brokers in the area of prices, news, company information and the like. Not only are there resources on the web that brokers can link their sites to or embed in their web presence, but organisations such as Reuters have developed packaged information products tailor-made for financial web sites that are being actively marketed to banks and brokers in the UK and Europe.

These take the form of both a cut-down price and news service intended to be provided free of charge to the client, and in the form of a more detailed premium service for which the broker can charge the client either all or part of the cost if so desired. The Schwab Europe web presence was one of the first broker web sites in the UK to offer this service.

Until these services are more freely available at broker sites, it makes sense for the active online investor to look elsewhere for free information if necessary, armed with the experience gathered from reading this book.

CHAPTER 9

Personal Finance Online

As we have already seen, the web has lots of comprehensive and cost-effective information about investment in shares, whether it's share prices, charting software, financial news, or information displayed by companies themselves. But it also has its uses for those in search of information on other personal finance matters.

Personal finance is often a loosely defined term. Here we'll take it to mean anything related to your savings and investments, but excluding investment in individual listed company shares. This means that personal finance can encompass banking, the merits of different types of savings accounts, savings and investment vehicles such as life assurance and personal pensions, PEPs, TESSAS and ISAs, taxation, collective investments such as unit trusts and investment trusts, and many other topics.

It is easy to neglect this crucially important aspect of your finances. If you have a demanding job, there never seems to be enough hours in the day to sort out the best deal on a savings product, to work out how best to minimise your personal tax bill, pick a unit trust with a good performance record, or plan how best to provide for an adequate (not to say generous) personal pension—one of the biggest financial decisions you can make.

The events of recent years, especially the furore over the mis-selling of personal pensions, have rightly or wrongly led some investors to be suspicious about what a supposed financial expert might want to sell them. As a consumer of a personal financial product, you want independent advice, but you may very well be searching for a truly objective source.

And you need an easy way of comparing the individual characteristics and relative merits of different savings and investment products.

The web offers a number of ways of resolving these problems and addressing these issues. A few of them are:

- ❐ There are several sites on the net where the basic nuts and bolts of personal finance are outlined in plain language and where issues can be raised and discussed.
- ❐ Over the past three or four years several large UK personal finance web sites have been launched which offer the opportunity to explore pretty well all of the issues described above, and to search databases of performance statistics to select investment trusts, unit trusts, and other funds and products that fit your specific criteria.
- ❐ An increasing number of pensions and unit trust product providers are setting up web sites to promote their products. Most providers worth their salt now have a web presence, although the quality of the information on offer can vary considerably.
- ❐ One of the most basic personal finance services is a bank account, and the notion of online web-based banking is slowly gathering pace. Having said that, whether or not they offer online banking, most banks and building societies now have sites, although again the information on offer does vary.

For the purposes of this chapter we have excluded any mention here of sites that offer more general insurance products (such as car insurance, house insurance and travel insurance) although it is now perfectly possible to buy cover of this sort online. A good one-stop shop for this type of product is Screentrade. This can be found at the URL www.screentrade.co.uk; it offers online quotations from most major providers and is fully searchable.

In common with many online purchasing options, completing the details can take some time, and the Screentrade interface at the time of writing was not particularly quick to download each of the multiple pages required to be filled out in order to buy, say, a car insurance policy.

The point is, however, that consumers are increasingly willing to buy financial services online, and will become more attuned to this way of doing business as time goes by. A recent survey by Reuters revealed, for example, that around 30% of consumers were prepared to operate an online current account, while 20–25% would buy car insurance and household contents insurance online. Acceptance of purchase services such as life policies, mortgages and the like is currently around 10% and rising. Virgin, for one, is ready to promote pensions over the net, presumably with tight regulatory safeguards built in. However, a recent survey by Pearl Assurance found that only 1% of individuals would contemplate buying a pensions product over the web. The message is clear. Though it is early days, online trading cannot be ignored by providers of personal financial services.

'Educational' Sites

In parts of this book, and particularly when we published *The Online Investor* originally, it was and has been very apparent that a big chunk of the Internet and world wide web's content originates in, or is relevant to the USA. US web sites often illustrate the way things may develop in the UK and Europe. While more non-US content is emerging all the time, US users still account for perhaps around two-thirds of global Internet use.

Using US sites to illustrate the type of services that, for instance, stockbrokers offer online is one thing, because the service they provide is essentially a generic one. Features are similar across borders, and so those looking to make comparisons between the way these services work and new or potential services of a similar type in the UK or Europe can do so in the knowledge that they are comparing like with like.

For personal finance advice the generic approach will not work. The different ways in which the tax system operates in the UK and Europe versus the USA, and different types of financial products available, and even different traditions relating to personal finance, and differences in attitude to different types of investment, all mean that we must consider European sites (and in particular UK sites) alone in this section.

General UK-oriented personal finance sites are, if not overly numerous, then at least pretty comprehensive in the way they tackle the material. Product provider sites have grown substantially in number in the past two to three years and are examined in detail later in this chapter.

We'll look first at those which offer a general grounding in personal finance topics, or which offer compendiums of links to a range of personal finance sites and topics.

If you are not a devotee of online investing, you might ask whether or not all this is worth the effort. After all, it is always possible to buy one of the many publications that deal with personal finance topics or to subscribe to magazines and newspapers that cover them. Personal finance is routinely looked at in the quality week-end press, for instance, and there are many personal finance books that look at the different options open to individuals in this area. The problem with this approach is partly cost, partly the way the content is presented, and partly the assumption made by many writers of a greater degree of knowledge than the reader may possess.

What the world wide web offers is the opportunity to satisfy oneself on basic questions and concepts in a sufficiently detailed but relatively anonymous manner—with the minimum of effort and cost. On the web you need not feel embarrassed by hunting out the answers to even the naivest of questions.

Two sites currently stand out when it comes to getting general background information on personal finance products.

The first is Moneyweb (www.moneyweb.co.uk). Moneyweb is the creation of Ian Dickson, a one-time independent financial adviser (IFA) and now a personal finance writer and Internet consultant. The Moneyweb site is primarily educational in content, and includes FAQs (frequently asked questions) on a variety of personal finance topics, including investments, mortgages, insurance and so on. The FAQ answers are given in direct and clear language and cover most of the topics on which individuals are likely to want to seek clarification.

The site is particularly good on the pensions front, with a number of interactive calulators to help users decide, for example, what level of pension contributions are appropriate and what level of pension a particular sized fund would buy. Another calculator looks at the monthly contributions needing to be made by a person of a particular age in order to retire on a given income in a specified number of years' time.

The site also includes a large number of essays and articles on a wide variety of investment and finance topics including financial scams, electronic money, traded options and so on.

Another very good site of this type is the AAA Investment Guide at the URL www.wisebuy.co.uk. Again the creation of a financial journalist and author, the site has clearly worded explanations that run the gamut of investment and personal finance topics, linked together in a logical form.

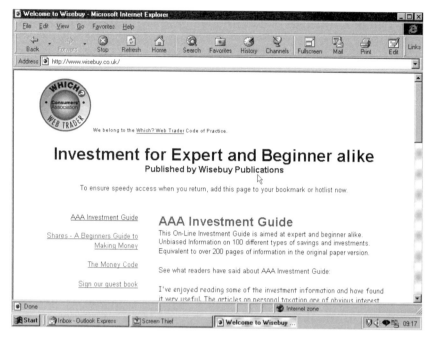

Figure 9.1   The Wisebuy web site is a good first step for personal financial information

All types of possible investment vehicle are examined (the site claims to have details of 94 different savings and investment products) and the essays on each aspect are interspersed with external links where more information can be obtained.

This is a very good first step for any investor confronting the sometimes confusing world of personal financial products. The author of the site, however, does charge a fee for accessing the most popular pages, among which (inevitably) are those on shares, gilts and other popular topics. An icon indicates which pages are for subscribers only. A lifetime subscription to the site costs £25 and, for a modest extra payment, the subscriber can purchase a CD-ROM containing all the information in an easily accessible form.

If you are not bashful over posing those unanswered questions and initiating a more interactive discussion on the merits of different types of investment and savings products, then the Usenet *uk.finance* newsgroup offers a convenient forum. It has a reasonably consistent number of participants, a tendency broadly to stay on-topic, and an orientation towards personal finance rather than exclusively stock market investment issues.

There are also personal finance-oriented discussion groups operated by bulletin board systems such as CompuServe, AOL and CIX. Some of the sites discussed later in this chapter also offer the opportunity for bulletin board style discussion on general investment and personal finance topics. It may be worth re-reading the comments in Chapter 4 about how discussion lists and bulletin boards work, and what 'netiquette' should be observed.

Finding personal finance related sites is not that hard, particularly as there are so few large-scale ones related to the UK scene. A good starting point is the financial links index site of FIND (Financial Information Net Directory) at the URL www.find.co.uk. This has expanded considerably in the last year or two and now includes links to a very broad spread of sites, including banks, life assurance companies, unit trust groups, and various other sites grouped together under several broad categories including 'banking' and 'savings'.

Some of the broader-based sites described below also have classified directories of sites which enable the user to search and get down to a relatively small list of relevant web addresses without going through the laborious process of sifting through the results of a non-specialist search engine. On the other hand, information in directories such as Yahoo! Finance (even the UK version) is disappointingly slight, listing only a few of the more commonly used sites.

Financewise, the specialist financial search engine (www.financewise. com) has a selection of links in its directory section loosely based on an 'investments' theme, which includes insurance company and unit trust web sites and similar links. However, these are very broad brush categories indeed and the links thrown up in each one are confusingly jumbled between country, type of product provider, and so on. Users would normally need to define a search much more precisely to retrieve anything of greater value.

All-purpose Personal Finance Sites

Although the operators of some other sites might disagree, there are basically only two UK large-scale all-purpose sites—personal finance 'portal' sites, as it were. By this I mean sites that contain information on all aspects of saving and investment, including prices and performance data, news, useful financial calculators and other interactive tools, educational material and links to the sites of providers of products and services. The two sites in question are MoneyWorld and Interactive Internet Investor (iii).

As time has gone by, these two sites, which arguably had different starting points, have converged significantly in terms of their product offering, although their philosophies are still quite different.

MoneyWorld (www.moneyworld.co.uk) has recently undergone an extensive site redesign, but in content terms remains wedded to free information funded by advertising and sponsorship.

The site has been a pioneer in offering free delayed prices (now 15 minutes from real-time rather than 20), and comprehensively searchable performance data on a wide variety of savings and investment products. MoneyWorld also offers its own edited personal finance news highlights, rather than simply being a passive 'wholesaler' of news.

The site also has a series of brief FAQs on different aspects of personal finance, a glossary of personal finance and investment terms, personal finance news, and an extensive library of links to personal financial product providers, advisers and other sites of interest. This list, known as Start! in the site's new guise, is also searchable, even down to the point of being able to do a postcode search to find your nearest stockbroker.

So, if you want to check out the web sites of a range of personal finance product marketers, and perhaps have a brief objective grounding on a chosen topic in the personal finance arena, MoneyWorld is hard to beat.

The MoneyWorld Club (entry is free, subject to providing a certain amount of personal information about yourself in order to register) has a variety of attractions, including discounts on investment books and software, and the ability to create and monitor portfolios of shares.

According to MoneyWorld director Danny Bowers, the site is currently getting around 20 million hits a month and has about 150,000 users, of whom about one-third have signed up for the MoneyWorld Club. Extra functionality has been added to the system, including the ability to add funds data and cash to the portfolio monitoring system and charts and company profiles (from the Hemmington Scott database) are being added.

Interactive Investor (www.iii.co.uk) began life seemingly as an umbrella site which, as well as a limited amount of internally provided content from the site's sponsors (the *Financial Times*'s stable of personal finance and offshore investment magazines), also had inbuilt links to product providers.

This rather gave the impression that the site was simply a mouthpiece for the industry, rather than offering an independent voice. If this ever was the case, it is no longer true. Just as MoneyWorld began with a news, share prices and personal finance directory approach and then filled out its offering to encompass other parts of the personal finance and investment scene, so Interactive Investor began from an IFA, product provider axis and spread more into the mainstream of the investment scene.

The headings in iii's contents page include: quotes, news, performance, product providers, and advice, as well as email discussion lists on a variety of topics, and a portfolio section. There is a good site map.

The news section of the site used to be particularly good in that the database included several performance finance and IFA-oriented publications produced by the Financial Times Group, providing a unique resource for searching for news items specifically from the personal finance press.

Figure 9.2 iii's home page

Now, however, the news database is limited to *Money Marketing*, a weekly magazine-cum-newspaper for IFAs, and Two-Ten, a database of company press releases, plus a link to the *MoneyWise* personal finance magazine web site.

The quotes section includes the ability to derive quotes using either company name or ticker symbol, for a wide range of markets, but there is no facility for displaying large numbers of quotes together (for instance, no FTSE 100 index page as on MoneyWorld). However, quote pages like this are readily available elsewhere.

Performance data includes a particularly good section on investment trusts, with data provided by BT Alex Brown, now part of Deutsche Bank. The site also enables users to search for performance data on a wide range of funds, including unit trusts, with data courtesy of Micropal and Lipper.

Interactive Investor's site was comprehensively redesigned in September 1999 with the company focusing on the theme of giving new and would-be new investors the confidence and information to take control of their finances. The site is now divided into a number of 'centres', which include, for example, ISAs, New Issues, Traded Endowments, Life Assurance, Shares, Students, Banking, Mortgages, and so on. Interactive also operates separate sites for IFAs and offshore investors.

There is no question that the formula has been successful. At the time of writing, just after the re-launch of the site, iii's chief executive Tomas Carruthers claimed that the site was averaging well over a million hits per day from some 300,000 users, most of which were taking advantage of the free online 'portfolio' valuation and monitoring service available there. Interactive Investor is also involved, in conjunction with Dresdner Kleinwort Benson, in offering hosting services for several online broking services.

As a slight digression, there are two additional specialist sites well worth looking at for information.

The first is Moneynet (www.moneynet.co.uk). This site focuses essentially on savings, loans and credit cards and has data from, it claims, 100 lenders and 90 different investment product providers. Data on investment funds is provided via a link to MoneyWorld, but the information on savings accounts, mortgages and the like allows the data to be screened on various criteria and the user come up with the 'best buys' that fit his or her personal circumstances.

Once a seemingly appropriate product is identified, fuller information is displayed and the user can follow up by moving direct to the product provider's web site or contacting them by telephone.

Lastly, among the general sites, is TrustNet (www.trustnet.co.uk). When it launched, this site was something of a one-off, and quite simply one of the best sites on the net for personal investors—or at least those interested in UK investment trusts and closed end offshore funds. This is still true, but TrustNet has now expanded to include comprehensive information on unit trusts as well.

Basic information is available on each trust and is accessible from an easy-to-use index. It includes: the name of the management group; its address and phone number; the trust's investment objectives; its gross assets; the date of its most up-to-date NAV (net asset value) calculation; the sector in which it appears (with a link to a comparative table of similar trusts); and so on.

Performance tables are available which look at all trusts (including a separate table for investment trust warrants) or separate them out by

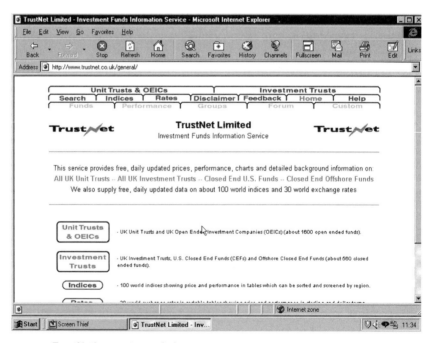

Figure 9.3   TrustNet's easy-to-use index

geographical region or investment sector. The tables can analyse their constituents on the basis of the alphabetical order of fund or management group name, discount or premium to NAV, or their performance over one, three and five years.

But an attractive features of the tables is an ability to alter the ranking criterion without leaving the table. Simply clicking on the 'sort' button above each column in the table will re-order the ranking on the basis of the descending order of the parameter in the column selected. Hence you can, for instance, look at the trusts in the sector alphabetically at first, then click to view them ranked by discount to NAV, click again to view the same trusts ranked by five-year performance, and so on.

The trusts in the stable of each management group can be viewed, although not ranked. But tables are available which rank 100 world stock market indices and 30 exchange rates on the basis of their performance in local currency and sterling terms over one, three and five years.

TrustNet does not offer advice, and indeed it is precluded from doing so by City regulations. But the site is a fantastic resource for those looking for an investment trust and seeking an easy way to find out the basics. Armed with this site and a telephone to ring the manager for copies of the selected trust's annual accounts, little more is needed for successful picking of the appropriate vehicle.

Product Provider Sites

When describing product providers' web sites, the epithet 'fantastic' (used above to describe TrustNet and which could equally be applied to iii, MoneyWorld, and Moneynet) is not the one that springs readily to mind.

Let's define what we mean by product providers. In the context of this chapter, we are talking about any financial institution which provides a savings or investment-based financial service, whether a bank, a unit trust or OEIC (open ended investment company) fund management company, or a life and pensions provider such as an insurance company. We have not included in this chapter any reference to providers of general insurance, property services, stockbroking, investment trusts or any other products of this type—some of which are covered elsewhere in this book.

As a broad generalisation, many of the sites (with some honourable exceptions) are awful, examples of the worst kind of distracting 'brochureware'. There are bright spots, companies which do get it right. The best sites only show up the inadequacies of the others. The irony is that although many banking and insurance groups were early onto the web, their sites have not moved on significantly from those early efforts.

Regulation is not to blame for this state of affairs, although it is sometimes used as an excuse for inaction. All of the characteristics cited later in the chapter as making a good site are present in the list because at least one site has included it. If a feature is present in one site, there is clearly nothing to stop anyone in the same peer group from incorporating it in theirs.

However, rather than talking in abstract terms, let's get down to specifics.

Life and Pensions Companies

The ideal site contents for each different category of product provider differs according to the type of product involved. The features relevant for life and pensions providers are different from those required from banking and savings providers, and different again from the sites of unit trust managers.

All sites need to have easy navigation, searchablity and perhaps news releases available about new products and services (although in many cases these characteristics are absent).

Looking first at life and pensions providers, my view is that the most important attributes of a site, as well as easy navigation, are: the provision of pension product information; performance data; an online illustration form; some interactive calculators; news releases on company or product information; the ability to search or use a site map to track down information; and the ability to email the company for information. Last but not least, some companies offer a special section of the site for IFAs, which can be useful if you fall into that category.

Let's just look at some of these requirements in more detail.

IFAs typically produce printed 'illustrations' or projections of what a particular monthly or lump-sum investment in a specific pensions product would be worth once the investor reaches pensionable age. There is, however, nothing to prevent the investor from generating this for him or herself, provided he or she understands that the illustrations are precisely that, and do not constitute any form of guarantee. Few pensions providers actually incorporate this in their site, perhaps fearing regulatory repercussions.

Simple interactive calculators, which illustrate the effect of compounding on monthly investments made over a period of years, and the amount that could then be taken as a tax free lump sum, and as a pension at a specific point in time have little regulatory impact because they do not incorporate any form of product selection. For an illustration of the type of calculators that can be produced, the previously mentioned MoneyWeb site (www.moneyweb.co.uk) has a good selection.

Performance data is another feature conspicuous by its absence, although again a couple of companies, perhaps those which feel they have a good story to tell, do include it at their sites. Although the standard disclaimer is that past performance is not necessarily any guide to the future, it is probably safer to invest in the fund that has performed well than one that has performed badly. So performance figures are perhaps the single most useful guide for investors. They are available from other, independent sites. MoneyWorld (www.moneyworld.co.uk) has a section in its site which enables users to search for the best performing life funds and similar animals.

On the plus side, most product provider sites allow for visitors to register their details by email and receive information by post, and many sites, not unnaturally perhaps, have special sections for IFAs. Indeed some only do their marketing through IFAs and will not allow access to the non-professionals.

How does the group as a whole score? (See Tables 9.1 and 9.2 for the best and the worst.) For the purposes of this exercise we looked at 20 life and pension providers' sites. Surprisingly perhaps, only 11 out of the 20 actually provide any form of product information at their site. Only three sites (CIS, Equitable Life and Scottish Amicable) provide good performance data, only two (Equitable Life and Marks & Spencer) offer the option of an online illustratrative projection. These two sites, plus Scottish Widows have interactive calulators. The majority of sites have news releases, but only nine out of the 20 make navigation easier by offering a site map or site search facility. Half of the sites allow potential

Table 9.1   Personal finance—a selection of the best sites

Company name	Web address	Category	Overall rating
Citibank	www.citibank.com/uk	Bank	7
Equitable Life	www.equitable.co.uk	Life/Pensions	8
Fidelity	www.fidelity.co.uk/direct	Unit trust manager	9
Fleming Asset Management	www.flemings.lu	Unit trust manager	7
Lloyds TSB	www.lloydsbank.co.uk	Bank	7
M&G	www.mandg.co.uk	Unit trust manager	7
Marks & Spencer	www.marks-and-spencer.co.uk/financial-services	Life/Pensions	7
Martin Currie	www.martincurrie.com	Unit trust manager	7
Nationwide	www.nationwide.co.uk	Bank	10
Norwich & Peterborough	www.norwichandpeterborough.co.uk	Bank	7
Perpetual	www.perpetual.co.uk	Unit trust manager	7
Royal Bank of Scotland	www.rbos.co.uk	Bank	8
Sarasin	www.sarasin.co.uk	Unit trust manager	10
Save & Prosper	www.prosper.co.uk	Unit trust manager	8

Table 9.2   Personal finance—a selection of the lowest-scoring sites

Company name	Web address	Category	Overall rating
Alliance & Leicester	www.alliance-leicester.co.uk	Bank	2
AIB Asset Management	www.aibgovett.com	Unit trust manager	3
b2	www.b2.com	Unit trust manager	4
Exeter Fund Management	www.chameleon-isa.co.uk	Unit trust manager	2
Norwich Union	www.norwich-union.co.uk	Unit trust manager	4
Premier Asset Management	www.premierfunds.co.uk	Unit trust manager	1
Singer & Friedlander	www.singer.co.uk	Unit trust manager	3
Standard Life Investments	www.standardlifeinvestments.co.uk	Unit trust manager	3
Axa	www.axaassurance.co.uk	Life/Pensions	0
Cooperative Insurance	www.cis.co.uk	Life/Pensions	2
Pearl	www.pearl.co.uk	Life/Pensions	0
Prudential	www.pru.co.uk	Life/Pensions	3
Royal Liverpool	www.royal-liver.com	Life/Pensions	3
Scottish Provident	www.scotprov.co.uk	Life/Pensions	3
Winterthur	www.winterthur-life.co.uk	Life/Pensions	2
Allied Dunbar	www.allieddunbar.co.uk	Life/Pensions	0

investors to email for information and seven out of the 20 have an IFA-only area of the site.

Many of the sites have exceptionally heavy graphical content, the worst of which are Allied Dunbar, Pearl, Prudential and CIS. Some sites—Scottish Widows and Winterthur are examples—have obviously been designed on an oversized screen, making access difficult for those accessing the site from a more normal 17-inch monitor.

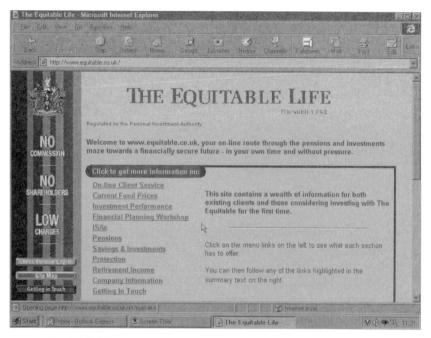

Figure 9.4 Equitable Life is the best of the life and pensions provider sites

On the principle that 'naming and shaming' is something with which pension providers are familiar, it is worth noting that several of the sites score zero. In other words, they have heavy graphical content or are hard to navigate, and have none of the attributes that we look for in a site. Those that fall into this category (see Table 9.2) are the sites of Allied Dunbar (www.alliedunbar.co.uk)—probably the slowest site of all those examined—Pearl (www.pearl.co.uk) and Prudential (www.pru.co.uk). These sites are simply online brochures with little or no practical content of use to investors. Inclusion of the Pru in this list may be a little unfair, since some of its other sites score better. Scottish Amicable scores a reasonable 6 out of 10, and the Egg banking site (www.egg.com) is also an interesting one.

On the positive side, two life and pensions companies make it on to our table of best personal finance sites (Table 9.1). Equitable Life (www.equitable.co.uk) is clearly the best of the life and pensions provider sites, its score marred only by slightly slow graphics and the absence of a section for IFAs.

Marks & Spencer (www.marks-and-spencer.co.uk/financial-services) also scores highly, dropping points only on slightly slow graphics, and the absence of performance data and an IFA section. In fact, in M&S's case these omissions are understandable. The store's group is clearly oriented towards using its brand name to market its products direct to the consumer, and probably does not need to pay commissions to IFAs to help sell its products. Equally, its track record as a financial services provider is too short for performance figures to have much meaning.

Unit Trust Managers

A similar set of essential attributes can be stipulated for the sites of unit trust managers. Aside from the fact that, like the life and pensions provider sites, they should be searchable, have easy navigation and a low graphical content, there are some other attributes which are unique to unit trust sites.

These include whether or not fund price data is posted at the site, whether or not there are details of the performance of individual funds also present, interactive calculators, the usual news releases, and the ability to apply for a fund online, even if the accompanying paperwork is later sent (as is normal) for signature via 'snail mail'.

Another important attribute for online investors is for a site to contain the ability for the fund holder to check the fund valuation from time to time and to be able to switch from one fund to another via the site.

Facilities such as this for existing unit holders cause few if any regulatory problems, and is perfectly feasible technically, although only a small number of unit trust managers offer this facility.

Unit trust managers' sites generally put up a better showing than those from life and pensions providers (see Table 9.1). All but six of the 36 sites surveyed are searchable, and only one, AIB Asset Management (www.aibgovett.com) has what could be described as heavy graphics. Fund performance data is available at 31 out of 36 sites although the presence of daily fund price data is less common, with 11 out of 36 not offering this. However, some of those not offering daily prices, do update their price information on a weekly basis. Interactive calculators are found on only two sites—Save & Prosper's (www.prosper.co.uk) and b2's (www.b2.com). Some 20 out 36 sites have news releases available on site, but only six offer the ability for potential investors to fill in an online application form. These are Aberdeen Prolific (www.iii.co.uk/aberdeen-prolific), Fidelity (www.fidelity.co.uk/direct/), Flemings (www.flemings.lu), Gartmore (www.iii.co.uk/gartmore), Global Asset Management (www.ukinfo.gam.com) and Save & Prosper (www.prosper.co.uk).

At the time of writing a similar number allowed online fund switching or some form of electronic dealing. These include Fidelity, Fleming and Global Asset Management (mentioned above) plus AIB Asset Management (www.aibgovett.com) and the Glasgow fund management group Murray Johnstone (www.murrayj.com).

Many fund groups, around 16 out of the 36 surveyed included some form of economic or market comment at their web site, either in the form of an online comment or a PDF version of a printed publication.

When it comes to bouquets and brickbats, those scoring best (7 out of 10 or over) include Fidelity and Fleming, both of which score 9, Fidelity lacking only an interactive calculator. Others rating an honourable mention would be Martin Currie (www.martincurrie.com), a traditional Scottish fund manager, and M&G (www.mandg.co.uk).

On the minus side (see Table 9.2), Exeter Fund Managers (www.chameleon-isa.co.uk) had one of the worst scores, with a site that had only a couple of the necessary attributes and combined this with excessively heavy graphics. Others in this less than distinguished company with only a couple of the necessary attributes or with sites which were spoilt by poor navigation, included AIB Asset Management, b2, Norwich Union (www.norwich-union.co.uk), and Premier Asset Management (www.premierfunds.co.uk), which was the lowest scoring.

Those whose primary focus is elsewhere (for example Norwich Union), might perhaps be excused, but it is hard to see why a new entity like b2 (www.b2.com) should have such a poor site, with no fund price information, no searchability at the site, no online application forms and no online fund switching.

Nonetheless, even some of the middle of the road sites have their plus points. Aberdeen Prolific, for example, offers online newsgroup contact with other investors, as does GAM, Hill Samuel Asset Management (www.hillsamuel.co.uk) offers an A–Z investment glossary, and Legal & General (www.landg.com) offers access to account details and valuations online. Some sites, such as Baring Asset Management and Credit Suisse Asset Management, are aimed solely at IFAs.

Figure 9.5   Sarasin's site scores highly in our assessment of unit trust managers

Savings Product Providers

This category essentially includes banks and building societies, although in theory the net could be widened to include any institution which accepts deposits.

Among the criteria looked for at the various sites surveyed is whether or not rate information is available online, whether there are details available on the various types of account on offer, whether there is information on branch locations, whether there is any other product information (such as particulars relating to lending activity such as personal loans or mortgages), whether or not background information can be requested online, whether there are the usual news releases available and whether or not the site is searchable or has an easy-to-use site map.

The bank sites vary on the amount of information of this type there is available. Some 11 of the 27 sites surveyed claimed to have web-based banking in operation or working in a pilot version. The services offered on the web may vary, however, with some offering balance checking and bill paying and not much more, and others offering a more extensive service.

Somewhat surprisingly, only 16 of the 27 banking sites contained information about the rates currently on offer on various savings accounts, and six sites failed to offer even any basic account information.

These sites include several building societies, among them Alliance & Leicester, Bradford & Bingley, Bristol & West and even Midland Bank. Some 11 of the 27 do not include any branch information at their sites, although in the instances of those such as Standard Life Bank, Egg, First Direct and BankNet, this is because these institutions operate solely on a telephone or web-based service basis.

Around 16 of the 27 sites have news releases available on site relating to the institution or its services, but only a handful allow application forms for an account to be filled in online. These four are Bank of Scotland (www.bankofscotland.co.uk), BankNet (mkn.co.uk/bank), Nationwide (www.nationwide.co.uk) and Egg (www.egg.com). Only 12 of the 27 sites offer a search capability or a site map to make navigation easier.

Which sites are the overall best and worst? (See Tables 9.1 and 9.2.) Nationwide (www.nationwide.co.uk) is the best overall and scored a perfect 10. Royal Bank of Scotland (www.rbos.co.uk) falls slightly into the slow graphics trap, but lacks only the ability to apply to open an account on line. Norwich & Peterborough (www.norwichandpeterborough.co.uk/), Woolwich (www.woolwich.co.uk), Lloyds TSB (www.lloydsbank.co.uk) and Citibank (www.citibank.com/uk) all score a creditable 7 out of 10, helped in the case of the first and the last on the list by the presence on their site of a web-based banking offering.

Among the sites with plenty of room for improvement are Alliance & Leicester, which rivals some of the unit trust management company sites in terms of paucity of content and has a site with very cumbersome graphics and irritating sound-effects to boot. Others with content of only limited use are Bristol & West (www.bristol-west.co.uk) and Bradford & Bingley (www.bradford-bingley.co.uk) though they are not the worst offenders in this respect.

Electronic Banking

This brings one naturally onto the whole notion of electronic banking, which is worth a paragraph or two in its own right, particularly as a number of new services are in the process of being launched.

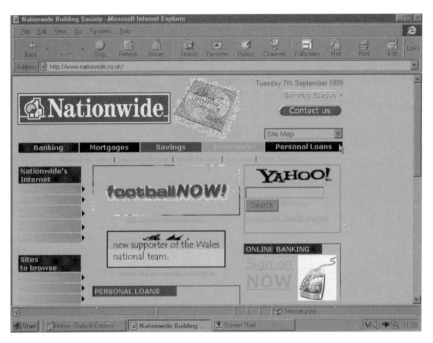

Figure 9.6   Nationwide's home page

The idea of electronic banking is not new, but the growth in the use of personal computers, increasing use of personal financial management software, and particularly the rise of the Internet and world wide web can take it out of its previous backwater and give it the critical mass to succeed. Moreover, the increasing offering of electronic sharedealing services also leads on naturally to electronic banking as a more efficient means of organising one's finances.

In the USA, where trends in many areas are often repeated in Europe a few years later, the idea of electronic transactions linked in to personal finance software on a home PC is now taking off.

According to an article in *The Economist* in October 1995, for example, a quarter of personal banking transactions in America were at that time done over a phone line, mirroring similar trends in the securities industry. Persuading those who telephone instructions to their bank to simply log in on their PC is likely to be the natural starting point for banks looking to develop online. A very recent estimate suggests that more than 40% of all banking and financial transactions will take place online by the year 2000.

Given the staggering success of Internet based broking businesses in the USA, such a statistic is perfectly believable. A contrary view suggests that growth may falter as users become disenchanted with the complexity of some of the security procedures.

It should be stressed that online banking is somewhat different from the concept of digital cash. This idea, like the Mondex concept (partly owned by NatWest and Midland) now being tested in some areas of the UK, and the competing Visa 'electronic purse' (Barclays, Lloyds and others) is a different concept and somewhat beyond the scope of this book.

Online banking is an interesting development for a number of reasons, not least because, like buying financial services over the Internet, the cheapness of the delivery mechanism means that the customer is likely to pay less for a level of service superior to the conventional branch-based bank.

The cost savings are dramatic. According to one source the cost of a transaction involving a teller in bank branch is approximately $1.50. The same transaction done via an ATM (automated teller machine) is around 60 cents, while the same transaction done over the web is reckoned to cost less than five cents.

Small wonder, then, that Citibank, the large American bank which is part of Citigroup, has already scrapped charges for personal customers who bank online, and other banks are following suit. One American bank has taken this even further, actually charging customers for each visit to a physical bank branch.

More interesting still is the potential that online banking offers for the convergence of the interests of specialist software producers like Microsoft and Intuit (both with a powerful position in personal financial software), banks, and providers of financial services and savings and investment products.

In other words, online banking can be a route into one-stop shopping for financial services—but banks can also tap into the ready-made customer network represented by the existing installed user base of personal finance software producers.

The best example of this comes from Intuit, the makers of Quicken personal financial management software. In late 1995 it signed agreements with 21 US banks to offer PC banking using private networks and a special version of its Quicken software. This has a Netscape browser and Internet access bundled into the package. Intuit has also announced a deal to provide access to online banking for the multi-million user base of AOL, the leading ISP. In the UK, however, it has so far signed up only one mass market bank's online service.

The US deal made sense for Intuit because not only does it sell more software as a result, it takes a tiny commission on each transaction going over the network. It works in another sense, too, because Quicken has an installed base of 12 million in the US, and 90% of the owners of the latest version also have computers with modems and probably Internet access too. Quicken's burrowing into the consciousness of savers and investors is highlighted in the UK by the joint web site venture that the group has with the *FT* (www.ftquicken.com). This provides financial news and share prices.

Not to be outdone, Microsoft has launched a similar initiative for its Money99 product, a site called MoneyeXtra (www.moneyextra.com). It has, moreover, had rather more success in signing up UK mass market banks to link into via its software.

Quite apart from the cost argument, banks are also attracted to the idea of online banking because of the socio-economic profile of the typical home computer user, which is oriented towards the higher income groups and the younger end of the adult population. Here, demand for banking and financial services is potentially more pronounced.

In the UK there have been several initiatives too. Barclays launched a pilot scheme with 2000 customers, was overwhelmed by the response and has recently rolled out the service nationally, offering a free ISP service at the same time. Bank of Scotland has long had an online banking offshoot known as HOBS (home office banking service). And Nationwide also has a PC banking facility for its FlexAccount customers. TSB operates an online banking service via CompuServe, and the Midland offshoot First Direct has now begun an electronic banking service.

Details of the services on offer are contained in the respective bank web sites which can, for example be accessed through the New Online Investor 'linksite' pages, or through a directory such as FIND. But the common thread running through all services of this type is that they offer the ability to: transfer funds from one account to another; set up standing orders; pay bills now or on a specified future day; and check on account balances. In some cases the banks offer reduced charges to those using the services.

However, worthy though these offerings may be, they have been partially eclipsed by the success of Egg (www.egg.com), the Prudential's internet banking operation, which has undoubtedly been a catalyst for greater competition in the banking market.

Services such as Egg are simply savings accounts linked to another conventional bank current account with deposits made into the online account acting as a base for other lending. Egg is for instance beginning to offer mortgages and plans other services such as unit trusts and credit cards.

Online banking in its different variants offers to the consumer the added convenience of not having to visit a bank branch and the ease with which such a service could theoretically be linked with personal financial management software, although there remain compatibility issues to be addressed here. Banks are also expected to collaborate with utility companies and others to deliver bills for payment electronically to those who wish to receive them in this way rather than via the postal system.

The big issue in electronic banking is security, although as previously explained, it is no larger an issue than it should be with telephone banking or with the normal use of credit cards. Credit card users are quite happy to present a card in the insecure environment of a public place such as a restaurant or a shop, or to read their credit card number over the phone to a theatre box office. Why then should they object to digital banking over a telephone line?

Yet Internet-based banking may not really make headway until the security issues related to it can be patently proved to have been solved. However, several techniques can be used to ensure security.

One simple way is by minimising the time spent online, by using an off-line 'out-tray' to record transactions and instructions to the bank. The out-tray is then emptied into the bank network in a single 'blink' of data of a few seconds in duration, minimising telephone charges and making it difficult for a hacker to sniff out.

Web banking systems typically operate through several layers of password protection. Large or unusual transactions will be flagged and extra password identification demanded before they can be implemented. Similarly an alarm will be raised if an attempt is made to access the account from a computer different from the normal one used.

The issue of watertight security also troubles banking regulators, since a totally secure electronic banking link has regulatory implications related to the power it gives to those intent on tax evasion, money-laundering and the like. For these reasons, governments tend to object to unbreakable electronic encryption in private hands but may have no choice but to agree to it.

The central point is that present banking rules and regulations (at least as they relate to 'retail' customers) are designed around face-to-face contact at bank branch level and paper records. They urgently need to be amended to take account of the digital age.

And an online banking revolution would bring casualties in its wake. The end-result of a move to online banking is likely to be large-scale redundancies of bank branch employees and greater competition for custom among the banks.

Banks should, though, end up less forbidding as a result, and customers will be able to access information on financial products without fear of embarrassment through showing their ignorance, and without invoking the unwelcome attention of a cold-calling rep.

As one commentator put it: 'When the world's banks are online, and you can switch accounts with a phone call or through a session on your PC, competition will be here with a vengeance . . . In five years, our personal finances will be organised around *our* choices and convenience, not those of financial institutions.' This comment was quoted in *The Online Investor*. It is possible to see now, two years later, that banking services are gradually evolving towards the position envisaged by this commentator, especially in the light of recent proposals which will make transferring standard order and direct debit instructions much easier.

CHAPTER 10

Futures and Options Online

While many investors confine their investing activities—online or otherwise—solely to the share markets, this does not represent the beginning and end of the choices available for those prepared to be a little more adventurous.

As with most other forms of investment, information is available online to help investors who might wish to invest a proportion of their savings in bonds (see next chapter) and other securities offering a fixed income, and those who wish to invest in derivatives.

Derivatives (futures and options) are so-called because their price derives from an underlying security or (in stock market speak) instrument. Thus there are derivatives based around baskets of government bond issues, short-term interest rates, stock market indices and—the place where most investors encounter them—those based on shares. Futures are largely the preserve of the professional, but options are frequently used by the more sophisticated private investor.

Options on shares give the investor the right (but not the obligation) to buy – in the case of a 'call' option—or to sell (a 'put' option) a specified quantity of shares at a pre-set price on or before a certain date in the future. The price of the option is usually a small fraction of the price of the underlying security and because of this, any movement in the price of the 'underlying' will produce a geared-up movement in the price of the option.

Because of this, options are often used as a way of speculating on a movement in the price (up or down) in a given share. Those expecting a price rise buy a call option: those expecting a fall can buy a put. However, it is not quite as simple as that. The price of the underlying share must move in the required direction before the option expires and also offset, not only the cost of buying the option, but also dealing costs.

Also important is the fact that as it approaches the time for it to expire, the option becomes inherently less valuable, because there is a lower probability of a profitable movement in the price of the underlying shares before it's too late. Lastly, changes in the market's view of the likely future volatility of the underlying shares can affect the price of the option, moving it either in favour of, or against, the interests of the holder.

It sounds complicated, and indeed there is rather more to it than meets the eye, but it should also be remembered that options have one great advantage. If the price moves against the holder, the option can be allowed to expire without any action being taken (the option gives the holder the right to buy or sell shares at a pre-set price, but it doesn't force him or her to take this action). Thus the maximum amount that can be lost is the initial cost of the option.

Options can also be used in other ways, as insurance. Buying a put option on a share you already hold can insure against most of the loss that might otherwise occur if there is a sharp fall in its price, but without having to sell the holding and perhaps incur capital gains tax. If the fall in the underlying share price does occur, the value of the put option increases accordingly and helps protect the holder against the loss.

Before contemplating dealing in options, it is essential that investors read up extensively on the subject, and attend one of the many training courses run on the subject of option trading for private investors. There are several books available on the topic suitable for private investors including my own *Traded Options—A Private Investor's Guide* (2nd edition, BT Batsford, 1998), and Michael Thomsett's book *Getting Started in Options* (John Wiley, 1993).

The advantage of options, however, is that the concepts underlying them are universally applicable. Reading one or more books about options equips one to understand the theory behind trading options in any markets. The concepts used to value options and the techniques used in trading them are applicable in any market.

The web is particularly useful for would-be option traders in a number of ways, which fall into several categories: company information; market prices and charts, a subset of which is the options exchanges that have a web presence; web-based dealing in options; options software online; and educational material on options available online.

Company Information

Option traders frequently need access to fundamental information about companies in whose options they may wish to deal. This can include: general economic news that might affect the company concerned; information and news about specific companies, including profit announcements; and other company information.

The web—as we have seen in earlier chapters—can provide this through the medium of online news and the information available at company web sites. Because options on individual shares tend to be available only in the shares of the largest companies in a particular market, these companies are more likely than not to have a corporate web site at which background information is available. Web sites of most UK companies with options can be found at the link page of the New Online Investor web site.

In other markets, a similar regime applies. In the USA there is probably scarcely a company whose options are traded which does not by now have a corporate web presence. And, as we have seen earlier, services such as EDGAR and the basic statistical information offered free on services such as Yahoo! Finance mean that US option traders are unlikely to be short of the fundamental information they may need to make a decision. Similarly in Germany, France and Sweden, most companies with options available on their shares appear to have a corporate web presence.

Online Option Prices

For a number of years one of the best free sources of periodically updated price information on options in the UK was via the BBC2 CEEFAX service. In late 1996 the BBC unilaterally decided to remove this service, despite the protestations from LIFFE and many individual equity option investors. Fortunately, other alternative sources have become available, not least from LIFFE itself, which has posted option price data on its web site for some time now, but also from other broadcasting organisations—

notably BSkyB—which runs options prices on its Sky News SkyText service.

The price service on the LIFFE web site is, however, much more comprehensive than the service on Sky, with a much fuller range of option 'strike' prices and expiry months, and an integrated service providing share price charts of the underlying securities, and recent news on the companies concerned. As an integrated source of information on the options scene in the UK, this site (www.liffe.com) can hardly be bettered, particularly now that data of relevance to private investors is gathered together in a single part of the site.

It is important for option investors to keep in touch with and analyse the movements in the price of the underlying shares. Charts can be a big help in working out accurately the likely short-term behaviour of the underlying share price and hence the best time to buy and sell individual options.

As mentioned in Chapter 5, there are now a number of good sources for this type of information. These have developed extensively since the freeing up of data on individual shares by the stock exchange. This has also

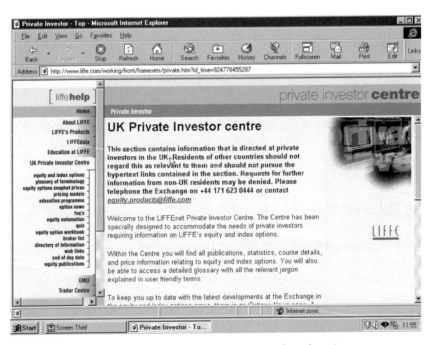

Figure 10.1   LIFFE gathers together data of relevance to private investors

been matched in the option area, and services such as E*Trade UK and Market Eye carry option prices on their web sites. These prices are typically in the form of a delayed continuous feed, or a system whereby prices are updated very frequently, normally every 15 or 20 minutes.

Despite this availability of information, the average private investor cannot possibly compete with the professionals in terms of speed of reaction to an underlying price change, nor in terms of the sophistication of the software which can be employed to value options and monitor option trading. This is not to say, however, that the astute and nimble investor cannot make money in this market.

Options Exchanges

As suggested previously, options exchanges represent a comprehensive source of the information that investors need to be able to trade options successfully.

LIFFE's own involvement in the web is a case in point and before going on to look at the information available from other derivatives exchanges, we look in more detail at the characteristics of the LIFFE site (www.liffe.com).

Like many other futures and options exchanges, LIFFE has had a presence on the web for some time, the site having undergone periodic redesigns.

LIFFE's first involvement with the web was in 1991. At that time, Internet access was made available to selected employees in its technology area and those who needed to use email. From these small beginnings LIFFE's exposure has grown considerably, so much so that during its recent streamlining exercise, its web presence remained intact whereas more conventional forms of information publishing and distribution were radically pruned.

LIFFE's staff's early access to the growth of the Internet had one result, however. It enabled the exchange to keep up to date with developments and launch its web presence quickly when it became obvious that the medium was likely to become more and more widely used by private investors and traders alike.

Like many exchanges, LIFFE decided early on to structure the site mainly as a vehicle for educating and informing investors—in other words, as a repository of resources about options—rather than using it actively to market options to private investors via the web. In so doing, some of the knottier compliance issues are, if not completely avoided, then at least reduced in force. Even so, accessing the site is only possible in the first instance via pages that contain heavyweight legal disclaimers.

The site contains information about courses for professional and private investors alike, exchange press releases, detailed historic data in a downloadable form for feeding into proprietary and commercial software packages, information on the technology behind the exchange, and, as previously indicated, intra-day prices, charts and other information for would-be traders.

The most recent major redesign of the site a couple of years ago moved it away from offering information segmented by product group (stocks, bonds, short-term interest rates, and commodities) towards a sharper dividing of the site between those areas intended for professional use, and those for private investors. At the same time the exchange also offered a Java version of the site as well as one written in conventional programming language. Users can opt for one or the other depending on the capabilities of their web browser.

The redesigned site had a 'private investor centre' which, in theory at least, contains all the data that such an individual investor would need, from information on courses, details of suitable software packages, equity and index option prices, downloadable data, company news and charts, and so on. This avoids the user having to spend time shifting between different parts of the wider site, with the inevitable delays caused by web traffic.

While the site has always been a popular one, early access statistics reflected the way in which the web was developing, with a predominance of US users especially so-called commodity trading advisers (CTAs) predominating. CTAs are a concept unique to the USA. They are independent traders who manage trading funds for both private investors and larger fund managers. Investors may allocate funds to more than one manager and select them on the basis of their published performance statistics. CTAs have a voracious demand for trading data and trade internationally, hence their early dominance among LIFFE's web user statistics.

Now the figures suggest that more UK users, especially private investors, may be using the site. So although the use made of the site by US traders and professional advisers has probably remained steady in absolute terms, it is decreasing as a proportion of the total.

Many organisations worry that setting up web sites may absorb an undue amount of management time. Because LIFFE started early and was a technologically aware organisation, it has been able to create and operate the site with the minimum of personnel.

There are legal complications of operating a site like this, or indeed any site containing information for investors. This is that, at least in the view of nervous compliance people, access to the site can involve a very large number of different legal jurisdictions, each of which may have differing laws relating to the distribution of information to would-be investors.

As previously mentioned, the LIFFE site skirts this issue by means of a carefully worded disclaimer as you enter the site. It is impossible to access the site without passing through that page. It is in this way that the exchange believes it covers itself legally in respect of any potential liability arising from the use or misuse of information contained in the site.

The surprise, perhaps, is that many other exchanges around the world offer web-based information, and allow information of this type to be accessed without passing a disclaimer page.

Categorising futures and options exchanges around the world in terms of the information they have on offer for online investors is not that easy.

One problem is that some exchanges encompass both the market for underlying shares (by convention known as the 'cash' market) and also trade in the futures and options that derive from them. Others, notably in major financial centres such as London, Chicago, Tokyo and elsewhere, have separate and distinct exchanges for the underlying instruments. In this case the derivatives exchanges, even if combined under the same ownership, have a separate presence on the web.

The categories employed in assessing options exchange sites are much the same as those described in the section on exchanges as sources of price information in Chapter 5. So you can, for instance, assess derivatives exchanges on whether they have easily navigable sites, with information about exchange members, publications, press releases, product and price information, including contract specifications, trade data (both intra-day and end-of-day for downloading into software packages) and so on.

In total we can identify some 40 sites for derivatives exchanges around the world. These are shown in the tables below.

In Europe, there are 14 exchanges (of which five are wholly derivatives-oriented and the remainder part of larger markets). These are shown in Table 10.1. The Oslo market scores best, with Prague and Amsterdam

Table 10.1 Derivatives exchanges in Europe

Exchange	Web address	Member-ship list	Publi-cations	Press releases	Type*	Country	Score
AEX	www.aex.nl	No	No	Yes	A	Netherlands	5
Belfox	www.belfox.be	Yes	Yes	Yes	D	Belgium	8
Copenhagen SE	www.xsce.dk	Yes	Yes	Yes	A	Denmark	8
Deutsche Borse	www.exchange.de	No	No	No	A	Germany	7
Helsinki SE	www.hex.fi	No	Yes	Yes	A	Finland	7
Italian SE (Milan)	www.borsitalia	No	No	Yes	A	Italy	6
LIFFE	www.liffe.com	Yes	Yes	Yes	D	UK	8
Meff	www.meff.es	Yes	Yes	Yes	D	Spain	7
Meff RV	www.meffrv.es	Yes	Yes	Yes	D	Spain	7
Monep	www.monep.fr	Yes	Yes	Yes	D	France	7
OM	www.omgroup.com	No	Yes	Yes	A	Sweden	8
Oslo SE	www.ose.no	Yes	Yes	Yes	A	Norway	9
Prague SE	www.pse.cz	Yes	No	Yes	A	Czech Republic	5
Swiss Exchange	www.swx.ch	No	Yes	No	A	Switzerland	6

* D = wholly derivatives-oriented; A = part of larger markets

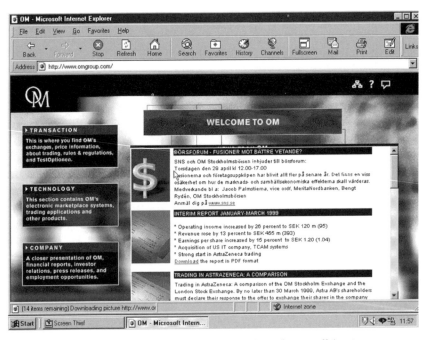

Figure 10.2 OM Group combines several markets and a software offshoot

(AEX) doing least well. Although a creditable mention should perhaps go to Sweden's OM Group which combines several markets, as well as a software offshoot, into one publicly listed entity.

Where the European exchanges falter is in being coy about their membership lists, and in being reluctant in some instances to put publications and news releases online. Some of the sites make up for this by having sophisticated Java-based price displays for both the underlying market and the derivatives based on it. If one can generalise in terms of site navigation and graphical 'heaviness', it is that Latin countries tend to overdo the images on screen, while the Nordics are altogether cooler and less demonstrative with their use of colour and design.

Derivatives exchanges in the Americas generally score well. Many of the best sites among these exchanges are the North American ones, as Table 10.2 demonstrates.

These sites contain a combination of easy navigation and full information on prices, trade data, plus background information about the market itself. The Chicago Mercantile Exchange (CME), the Pacific Exchange and the Toronto exchange score the best. One or two have some unusual features. At the Chicago Board of Trade (CBOT) there is an audio/radio commentary on trading, the Chicago Board Option Exchange (CBOE) has a Java-based option pricing model available online.

In other parts of the world the story is slightly different, with exchanges generally not scoring particularly well—the Tokyo Stock exchange, which

Table 10.2 Derivatives exchanges in the Americas

Exchange	Web address	Member-ship list	Publi-cations	Press releases	Type*	Country	Score
Chicago Board of Trade	www.cbot.com	No	Yes	Yes	D	USA	8
Chicago Board Options Exchange	www.cboe.com	Yes	Yes	Yes	D	USA	8
Chicago Mercantile Exchange	www.cme.com	Yes	Yes	Yes	D	USA	9
Colombian SE	www.bolsabogota.com.co	Yes	No	No	A	Colombia	3
Kansas City Board of Trade	www.kcbt.com	No	No	Yes	D	USA	6
Midam	www.midam.com	No	Yes	Yes	D	USA	8
Montreal Exchange	www.me.org	Yes	No	Yes	A	Canada	7
Nyce/Finex	www.nyce.com	Yes	Yes	Yes	D	USA	9
Pacific Exchange	www.pacifex.com	No	Yes	Yes	A	USA	9
Philadelphia Exchange	www.phlx.com	No	Yes	Yes	A	USA	7
Rio de Janeiro	www.bvrj.com.br	Yes	Yes	No	A	Brazil	7
Santiago SE	www.bolsantiago.cl	Yes	No	No	A	Chile	3
Toronto SE	www.tse.com	Yes	Yes	Yes	A	Canada	9

* D = wholly derivatives-oriented; A = part of larger markets

also trades some derivatives, scores particularly poorly. There are bright spots. The Hong Kong Futures Exchange (HKFE) has downloadable software available for users, while the Kuala Lumpur Options and Financial Futures Exchange (KLOFFE) has a true real-time price feed.

Imperfect though some of these sites may be, an online investor wishing to deal in options can now get the information necessary to do so. For any major derivatives market in Europe or North America, he or she will find information about the exchange, about prices of the various products listed on it, and about whom to deal through, all readily available on the web.

Option Brokers Online

Assessing and categorising broker web sites is rather like aiming at a moving target. Changes come thick and fast. But the select few brokers serving the option market have taken the lead in providing information of use to investors at their sites.

These sites are limited in number, not because UK brokers are necessarily averse to having web sites, but because many of those with sites offer a service only in equities and gilts, and not in traded options.

Among those with sites are Berkeley Futures (despite its name the firm also transacts option business for private investors), Durlacher, Options Direct, Charles Schwab Europe, and Union CAL. However, each site is different, some simply offering access to basic information and option market commentary, and some going all the way up to offering an electronic dealing service in traded options.

Electronic trading in options is big business in the USA. Trading in options is second nature to many investors and the leading options exchanges such as the CBOE offer options in many hundreds of stocks, compared to the 70 or so offered by LIFFE and rather lower numbers available at other European options markets.

E*Trade, the originator of web-based discount broking, reckons that its firm accounts for around 2% of all US stock option trades, a bigger market share than it has in ordinary stock trades. The mathematical nature of option trading and evaluation makes it something that is suitable for computer analysis. So what could be more natural than, after analysing an option trade on computer, to place the trade electronically as well?

For some years, the advent of electronic options trading in markets like the UK seemed a long way away, with the options exchange wedded to floor trading. However, LIFFE's new CONNECT system, launched in November 1998 as part of the exchange's move to automate trading on its less liquid products in order to save costs, has been a success and is leading to slow but steady changes in the way options are dealt with by private investors.

The second hinge of the electronic revolution is that the launch of the SETS system for UK equity trading has opened up the market to that of US-style fully automated electronic trading without the need for any physical intermediary. This was described in detail in Chapter 8. The result is that with the market in the underlying shares streamlined, and options trading now electronic, spreads on options should narrow as the market-maker's risk is reduced, making dealing in them more attractive to investors. Combine the two revolutions and the next logical step is full automated electronic trading of equity options direct from the client to the market system via the web.

Some are comfortable with this idea, others less so, preferring to opt for an advisory service to pick their way through the option dealing minefield. Whichever camp you fall into, it's probably a good idea, if you happen to be selecting a broker through which to trade options, to ask whether or not they have a web site. Ask too whether or not they plan to offer online trading of options via the web or another electronic means in the future.

Of the sites alluded to earlier, however, those of Options Direct, Schwab and Union CAL are worthy of special mention. Berkeley Futures' site is a relatively basic offering. Durlacher, though it is chaired by Geoffrey Chamberlain, a former chairman of the old London Traded Options Market (prior to its merger with LIFFE), is majoring more on technology issues than option trading these days. This is reflected in the content of its site.

In the case of Options Direct (www.options-direct.co.uk), the site contains much of the usual general information about the firm, but a particularly useful section accessible to the general public containing some simple spreadsheet programs related to options strategies. Client areas also contain special information including recommendations on strategies and market commentary. Options Direct has recently begun offering web-based trading of equity and index options.

Union CAL (www.unioncal.com) has adopted a slightly different approach, with a secure online dealing service in foreign exchange supplemented by other information, including links to sites containing downloadable software and other web links, and technical commentary (among other things) on the FTSE 100 index. Option trading accounts can be viewed online, even if dealing is by telephone at present. The company serves the more affluent trader, with a minimum account balance of £30,000.

Charles Schwab (www.schwab-worldwide.com/europe) has been one of the pioneers of automated trading of equities and options in the USA, and is bringing that technology to bear in Europe. The Schwab site is mentioned earlier in our section on broker sites. At the time of writing, although Schwab offers an option dealing service, at present this is not routed via its conventional web trading route, although a service of this type is expected to be introduced shortly.

E*Trade, through its European joint venture with ESI (www.esi.co.uk), has recently launched an online dealing service and, given its history in

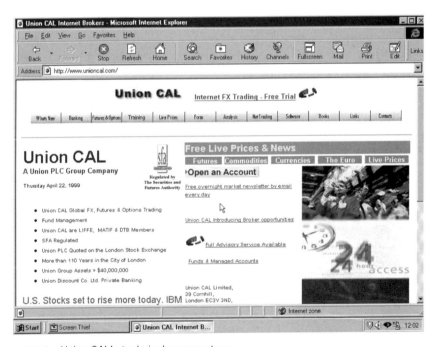

Figure 10.3 Union CAL's technical commentary

the USA, it is highly likely that this service will be extended to cover trading in options in due course.

Options Software Online

As we saw in Chapter 5, the web has a wide variety of software tools available for downloading. While many of these are personal financial managers, share evaluation tools and chart packages, there is also a subset of products related to futures and options products.

Newsgroups, specialist discussion lists and web-based bulletin boards, as well as press comment are probably the best way of finding out about packages like this. Alternatively, references can be found simply by typing the relevant search terms into a search engine such as Northern Light or a directory such as Yahoo!

As mentioned previously the vocabulary of the option market transcends national borders and because of this, software packages originally written, say, for US consumption can perfectly easily be adapted for use with options on UK and European stocks.

While some of the large-scale downloadable software sites (see mentions in Chapter 5 of Download.com and Winsite, for instance) have small sections related to options, for the most part specialist sites tend to be where these programs crop up. Where software does crop up outside of these areas, it may often be in the form of time-limited trial versions of commercial programs.

However, there is often academic input into this area too. Option theory is a topic that interests a lot of academics. There are well-flagged instances of university lecturers, especially in America, being prepared to post simple products—designed literally out of academic interest—on the web and make them available for use by the private investor.

Table 10.3 shows some examples of downloadable programs that are available either free of charge or on a shareware basis together with their web address and a brief description.

The variety of programs available indicates the interest that options generate, especially in America. These typically take one of three forms.

One form is the standard option pricing model. This will calculate the 'fair value' of an option or the underlying volatility implied by its market price, when certain variables are entered. The usefulness of software like

Table 10.3 Downloadable options software

Name of program	Type	Stand-alone (SA)/add-in (AI)	Company	Web address	Demo/free	Price of full version
Covered Option Writer	Strategy	SA	The Underground Software Group	www.tugsg.com	Demo	$40
Option Oracle	Pricing/strategy	SA	Deltasoft Financial Technologies	www.option-oracel.com	Demo	$695
Option Pro	Pricing/strategy	SA	Essex Trading Co	www.essextrading.com	Demo	$795
Options Simulator	Pricing/strategy	SA	Bay Options	www.bayoptions.com	Demo	$795
Option Wizard	Pricing/strategy	AI	John Sarkett	option-wizard.com	Demo	$99
OptionCalc	Pricing/strategy	SA	Austin Software	www.austin-soft.com	Demo	$295
OptionLab	Pricing/strategy	SA	Mantic Software	www.manticsoft.com	Demo	$90
OptionVue	Pricing/strategy	SA	OptionVue	www.optionvue.com	Demo	$1695
Optimum	Pricing/strategy	SA	Nigel Webb Software	www.warp9.org/nwsoft/index.html	Free	n/a
Option Driver	Pricing/strategy	AI	FIS Ltd	www.download.com/optdrv32.zip	Free	$49.50
Smartlog	Trading log	AI	IME Corporation	ourworld.compuserve.com/ homepages/svirsky/smartlog.htm	Free	$39.95

this is that it can determine the likely price of an option in the event of a sharp rise or fall in the price and/or volatility of the underlying instrument, and hence the probable profit or loss on the trade if this occurs. These 'what if' exercises are good things to perform prior to initiating an option trade, to get an idea of the probable risk and reward.

A second type of software product is one that monitors specific strategies, notably the returns available on trades that involve dealing in options in conjunction with a purchase of or holding in the underlying security (so-called 'covered option writing').

A third type of product is simply an accounting system, which will log trades and work out realised and unrealised profit and losses, returns, cash balances and other parameters as deals are input.

Option software like this usually crops up either in the form of simple stand-alone windows-based systems, or as spreadsheet add-ins, designed to work with packages such as Microsoft Excel.

But there are a number of things to remember before approaching this subject too enthusiastically. One is that when downloading a piece of shareware (just as when buying software), bear in mind that it may be one that is intended to be used with a particular type of data, possibly unique to the package's country of origin. It is therefore essential to check thoroughly that the package being downloaded will work correctly when UK data is input.

For most packages this is not normally a problem. The typical option pricing model, for example, will simply require an option price, underlying price, strike price, expiry date and one or two other pieces of data to be entered. The software works on the basis of statistical formulae and the relative values of the prices concerned. Currency values do not usually enter the equation.

Hence the packages will work perfectly adequately in any scenario, provided the requisite information is available to be entered.

In the event that a string of price data is required, perhaps for calculating volatility, remember that it is comparatively easy to download one for a particular underlying share from a free price source and simply cut and paste the data into the program. Web sites like Market Eye's, for example, offer this facility.

One of the simplest free software products is a spreadsheet add-in called !Options, which used to be available from Ray Steele's web site at Michigan State University. This simply adds extra functions to the basic Excel program and so can be used to value options contained in, say, the spreadsheet an investor might use to monitor his or her investments. Once the add-in is installed, the list of functions available expands to include standard valuation formulae for valuing put and call options and calculating a variety of other option-related parameters. This product sadly appears to be no longer available.

The Options Direct web site contains a spreadsheet that can calculate the returns available from a covered option writing strategy. As alluded to earlier, this is where a call option is 'written' against an underlying holding of the security in question. This can generate additional investment income and, even if the option is exercised, will result in the original stock held being called away from the investor at a significantly higher price. The Options Direct site also contains several other programs, all displayed in a ready-made tabulated form which makes it easy to calculate returns from a variety of standard strategies of this sort.

The site also contains a simple program for calculating the volatility of a stock simply by pasting in the values from a price series downloaded into Excel from another source (perhaps one like the Market Eye site referred to earlier).

Another relatively new site is The Underground Software Group (www.tugsg.com). This contains a package known as the Covered Option Writer (COW). Once downloaded, this package enables the profitability of various alternative covered writing strategies to be compared and ranked. Several different option series can be entered, and the covered write returns calculated and the most potentially profitable one picked out.

For those of more sophisticated bent, and deeper pockets, MBRM— standing for Mamdouh Barakat Risk Management, a firm whose products are used by hundreds, if not thousands of professional traders—has a range of Excel add-ins which evaluate option strategies down to the nth degree. Many of these are not particularly useful for the private investor assessing the market for conventional traded options, but MBRM offers liberal free 30-day trial versions of its software. A fully working version of the software can be downloaded from the firm's web site at www.mbrm.com. The would-be user downloads the software and emails MBRM for a code number to activate the program.

Lastly, Nigel Webb Software at the web site called Warp 9 (www.warp9.org) offers a free (at the time of writing) version of a program called Optimum. This will perform the normal option valuation calculations in a conventional Windows format. An earlier version of the

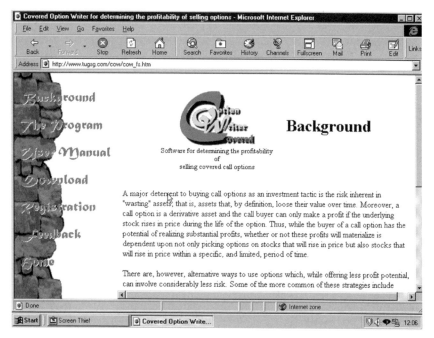

Figure 10.4 The Covered Option Writer from The Underground Software Group

program also provided 3D representation of the option 'delta', 'gamma' and other measures of its sensitivities in a 'wireframe' format often only found on much more expensive packages. However, this feature has since been discontinued because of copyright problems.

Investors should, however, check out all these products thoroughly for themselves before using them. Any preferences expressed here are purely personal and should not be taken as, or implied to be a recommendation.

It is also worth mentioning that a number of sites, including some options exchange web sites, offer interactive on-screen calculators which in effect operate in the same way as downloadable option pricing software. The best examples of these can be found at the CBOE web site (www.cboe.com), which has an easy to use Java-based tool, and at a general derivatives-oriented site, Numa (www.numa.com) where several different calculators are offered, covering conventional derivatives, but also related products such as warrants and convertibles.

The Numa site has sections offering links to likely sources of option software (freeware, shareware and commercial packages). Other sites that are good sources for various types of option software include Wall Street Directory (www.wsdinc.com). This has a comprehensive range of products for investors, including software of all types.

The original design of the site made casual browsing easy, but the volume of products now offered means that precise searching is required to identify the product required. The advantage of the Wall Street Directory site is, however, that extensive contact details for the products are given as well as pricing information and mini-reviews of the products' functionality.

Options Education

The web has many sites related to options and to the wider derivatives scene which explain the topic in terms that range from the simplest to the most complex.

There are many parties interested in the provision to investors of further options education, not least market regulators and trade associations, derivatives exchanges, brokers, firms offering professional risk management and option valuation software, as well as specialist publications and newsletters devoted to the topic, and those offering training courses.

It is as well to remember, however, that each of these has an axe to grind in terms of the information they offer at their sites and the angle they take. Only by reading widely can a would-be online option investor get a true insight into what makes the market tick and how best to trade (if at all).

Several exchanges in the USA and Europe offer web sites with useful material for online investors. Their web addresses are contained in Tables 10.1 and 10.2. Good exchange sites include the Chicago Board Options Exchange, Philadelphia Exchange, Deutsche Borse, and OM Group—all of which have extensive educational material on options.

Among specialist publications, *Futures and OTC World*, a well-known publication read by professional and amateur traders alike, has a web site (www.fow.com). Its counterpart, perhaps, can be found in the web site of Applied Derivatives Trading (www.adtrading.com), which is a wholly online newsletter devoted to derivatives (including options).

Sites devoted to specific option strategies crop up occasionally and one, with a US bias, is All In The Money (www.allinthemoney.com), devoted to information about covered call writing. The US bias is a disadvantage, however, as is the $49 per month subscription, which puts it out of reach of all but the most ardent enthusiast.

Another interesting site is OptionSource (www.optionsource.com), again US in origin but with educational information applicable to readers in any option market. Another good site for futures and options links, originating from a US university, can be found at the URL http://w3.ag.uiuc.edu/ACE/ofor/resource.htm (Futures and Options resources on the Web).

Mentioning these sites does not imply an endorsement: they are simply a random selection designed to give an idea of the variety of resources available.

Yahoo!'s investment section has a comprehensive range of links to futures and options-related web sites, and is a useful starting point. Of particular note is a link in the 'glossaries' section to Derivatives Research Unincorporated. This site contains a series of more than 60 essays on various aspects of the derivatives scene, including many relevant to options traders. All of the essays are written in non-technical language. Equally important, the site also contains a 'list of lists', giving links to large-scale compendiums of information on options, including some of those mentioned above.

If trading in options is a relatively unfamiliar activity for many investors, then bonds and other fixed income securities are equally closed books to many as well. The next chapter looks at how online investing techniques can dig out information on bonds and the information that drives them, notably economic statistics and commentary on the economy background.

CHAPTER 11

Bonds, Statistics and Economic Commentary Online

So far this book has concentrated primarily on information relating mainly to investment in shares. But with the seemingly permanent move to a lower inflation environment that has been the case for much of the post-war period, bonds have again begun to excite the interest of investors.

So that the online investor has all the necessary information at his or her disposal to pursue a rounded approach to investment, this chapter looks at the availability of information on bonds and the related issue of economic commentary and economic statistics on the web in various countries around the world.

This may seem somewhat drier fare than the earlier parts of this book, but it is worthwhile for budding online investors to remember a couple of points. One is that many large companies have operations in various markets around the world and that, to be thorough, researching the prospects for a particular company or share arguably ought to include an appreciation of the economic outlook in the countries in which they operate. A good way of doing this is by looking at and getting to grips with the basic statistics for the economy concerned. As we shall find out later, this is easier than it might seem.

Perhaps the more important point is that, rightly or wrongly, at the moment the share market as a whole is being driven by perceptions of the outlook for the major world economies (especially that of the USA), and especially the outlook for US interest rates. The slavish attention being paid to the utterings of the Federal Reserve chairman, the effect that nuances in his speeches have on Wall Street and hence on other world stock markets, means that it is vital for investors to have a good understanding of what makes these big economies tick, when major policy statements are expected, and the significance or otherwise of releases of official statistics.

Bond Prices and Analysis

When it comes to prices and other basic investment information, there is generally somewhat less information available for ordinary investors who wish to invest in bonds in their various forms. But this is, however, perhaps less of a handicap than it might seem. Bonds, or at least government bonds, are traded in highly competitive markets with generally much narrower spreads than is the case in equity markets. There is less likelihood in the bond markets of an investor dealing at the 'wrong' price because of illiquidity.

More importance can therefore be placed in analysing the factors that drive bond market performance: yield curves, credit ratings, the economic background; the outlook for inflation; the rate of return on competing investments, and so on.

Prices

Finding share prices on the web is comparatively easy. For bonds the task is somewhat harder. Many bonds are traded only in over-the-counter inter-bank markets and hence the availability of price feeds to the person in the street is very limited. Government bonds, the sort most commonly invested in by private investors, are a slightly different matter.

In the UK, for instance, gilt-edge security (i.e. government bond) prices are available on some, but not all, quote systems.

I tried and failed, for instance, to find UK government bond prices on Yahoo!'s finance page. But other quote systems—such as the Standard & Poor Comstock system used by some online dealing services such as Charles Stanley's Xest service, and the Interactive Investor site at www.iii.co.uk—do allow access to bond prices through their system.

Bonds being somewhat more homogeneous than equities—for instance, many gilts are simply termed Treasury Stock, Exchequer Stock, Conversion Stock and similar names and identified only by the coupon and maturity date—the stock codes for these securities are somewhat more cryptic than most equities. But inserting the word Treasury, Exchequer (and so on) into a look-up facility will usually locate the appropriate one.

Another good site for general information on the bond market and some government bond prices is the Bloomberg site at www.bloomberg.co.uk, which has several pages devoted to bonds, including a news page and a page giving prices and statistics for a series of benchmark UK (and other) government bonds. The bonds included are by no means an exhaustive list, but probably the more actively traded ones.

A more professionally oriented site is Money & Bonds (www.moneyand bonds.com) run by an offshoot of a City money market dealing firm. This site has extensive statistics on government bonds in various countries. It also has data on other related bond and money market instruments including forward rate agreements, swaps and other items. However, it costs around £50 a month for the basic feed, and is probably too detailed for most private investors in bonds unless they also happen to work as corporate treasurers.

Bond Background

Bond vocabulary is sometimes puzzling, but there are one or two points on the web which offer some guidance. One is the general personal finance-related sites on the web mentioned in the previous chapter, some of which contain reasonable explanations about what bonds are, the variations available, and how they work. These are for beginners only.

A particularly good site, however, is one set up by Kauders Investment Management, a specialist broker dealing in UK government bonds. The site, at www.gilt.co.uk, has a useful collection of essays and explanations about the rationale for bond investing and the mechanics of undertaking it.

Those seeking more meat need to look elsewhere. There are a number of ways of doing this. A key element in assessing bonds, for example, is the assessment of the credit standing of the issuers. In theory, one of the main drivers of bond yields is the credit standing of the borrower. In the case of

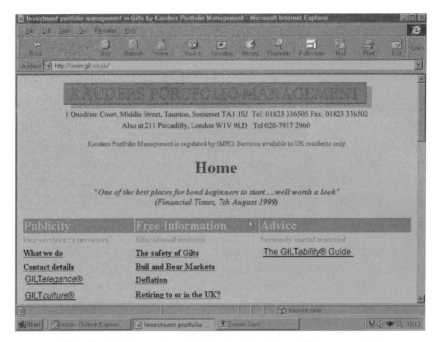

Figure 11.1 Gilt edge background on the Kauders Investment Management site

a company or indeed a government, the worse the balance sheet and prospects for the company (or economy) the higher the risk of default and the higher the yield. This is to compensate for the extra risk that interest payments may not be received on time (or at all) or that capital may be lost.

In the case of most OECD (Organisation for Economic Cooperation and Development) government bonds this risk is perhaps a less important parameter—although a very important one for bonds issued by emerging market governments. So, within the Euro zone, especially now that the underlying currency risk is now a thing of the past (with rates locked into the Euro), government bond prices do move around on the back of changes in perceptions about the soundness or otherwise of individual governments' economic policies.

In all bond markets, borrowers are rated by specialist credit rating agencies who assign borrowers a code letter in a strict pecking order based on various objective characteristics. Different rating agencies vary slightly in the codes they use and the rating criteria they apply. The Syndicate web site at the URL www.moneypages.com/syndicate/bonds has an explanation of the ratings system adopted by Moodys, one of the big rating firms.

Moodys' web site (www.moodys.com/economic) itself has brief comments on various topics which range internationally as well as covering the domestic US bond markets in their various forms. The comments, in the form of executive summaries of longer reports, are available on a subscription-only basis.

Other rating agencies are generally more generous in their provision of information for investors at large. Standard & Poors, for example, another large firm, keeps its most recent reports reserved for subscribers, but has an extensive archive of research reports (at www.ratings.standardpoor.com) which are downloadable in PDF format.

Two other firms, Fitch ICBA and Duff & Phelps, also provide extensive news and press releases on ratings topics over the web. Detailed rating reports can also be viewed once the user has completed a (wholly free) registration process. The Fitch ICBA site is at the URL www.fitchicba.com, and the Chicago-based Duff & Phelps has a web presence at www.dcrco.com.

Although the main thrust of both sites is US bond investors and issuers, and national government bonds, these two sites in particular do occasionally carry in their archives detailed reports on UK and European corporate bond issuers and industries. As an adjunct to the normal research information on companies, these 'warts and all' reports about the individual companies' debt servicing capability make interesting reading, the more so because they are prepared from a more dispassionate standpoint than most broker reports.

Broker and Bank Research

Large investment banks seek to portray a caring public image, particularly those which have an extensive retail investor client base, and a number of them allow reasonably unfettered access to their research on the web.

Among those that fall into this category are JP Morgan, Morgan Stanley Dean Witter and Merrill Lynch.

JP Morgan's site at www.jpmorgan.com (also one of the best corporate sites on the web) has detailed data on global government bond markets including their size by nominal value and market value, amounts in issue at various maturities, returns over time and volatility.

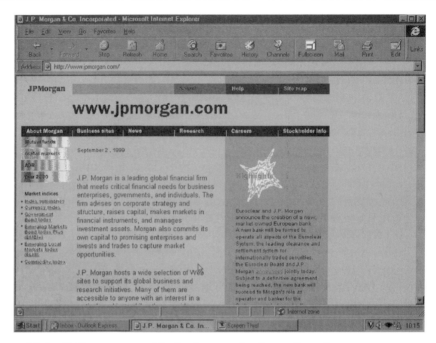

Figure 11.2   JP Morgan—one of the best corporate sites on the web

In this case the returns measured are a combination of the income yields on the bonds plus their price changes in local currencies and in dollars over the period. Volatility is typically used as a proxy for risk. In other words, earning a higher return may generally (though not always) be accompanied by bigger than average price swings in the bonds.

This is part of a wider research effort undertaken by the bank which also takes in analysis of emerging market government bonds and bonds issued by international bodies in the local currencies of emerging markets.

Taken as a whole this is an extremely useful resource for investors anxious to get some form of perspective on the bond markets in which they might invest. Anyone looking, for instance, to invest in the domestic government bond markets of any European country would do well to consult this site.

Merrill recently extended the offer of free access to all investors to the whole range of its research publications, including commentary on bond markets and market strategy. Users can access the research at www.askmerrill.com but have to complete a registration form and wait for a password to be emailed before access is enabled.

Morgan Stanley's site at www.deanwitter.com has a more limited range of market commentaries, but included, at least at the time of writing, commentary on general bond market topics. Among other US investment banks, Salomon Smith Barney also has a site, at www.sbil.co.uk, which gives access to some articles about topics of interest to bond investors.

In general the sites of large banks in the country of origin of an individual investor can be a good starting point for investors looking for information on their local bond market. A good starting point here is the Qualisteam site (www.qualisteam.com), which claims to have links to 95% of all banks' web sites world wide and categorises them conveniently by country and continent.

Economic Statistics

There is widespread provision of economic data on the web although, as is the case with corporate web sites, there is also considerable variation in the way in which it is presented. The sources of statistics relevant for investors are typically—in OECD countries—the central bank of the country concerned and its national statistics collection and dissemination agency or agencies. A number of international organisations also provide statistical information.

Outside of the OECD group, information is typically provided by national statistics organisations. Even the smallest of countries have these. Rather like a national airline, having a national statistics organisation with a website is seemingly a necessary concomitant of statehood even if (and again like a national airline) the service offered in some cases is poor and does little to enhance the country's standing.

We'll look in turn at the various links to and sources of statistical information of this type on the web.

Directories

A good starting point for tracking down the sources of statistics is the directory entry in Yahoo!'s Business and Economy/Statistics section. The 'economic indicators' group lists a number of directories and lists of links of which the best is probably a resources page assembled by a technical university in Singapore at the web address www.ntu.edu.sg/library/statdata.htm. This is a simple but comprehensive collection of links, particularly good on Asia and the USA, but also containing links to very many other statistics-related sites in the world.

Another good directory-style site is Alta Plana. This site, originally constructed for the OECD provides resources for economists in the form of links to a series of other guides and directories with brief comments on each. The URL for the site is http://altaplana.com/gate.html.

The US Census bureau (www.census.gov/main/www/stat_int.html) also has a page of links at its web site giving access to the statistical agencies of most world economies.

Economist Mark Bernkopf also has a good site (www.patriot.net/users/bernkopf) with a variety of links related to central banking. This site contains, among other things, a regularly updated set of links to the web sites of world central banks, as well as links to sites offering analysis and commentary.

As an aside, central bank sites themselves can often be good sources of background information on national government bond markets and economic background generally. Many produce monthly bulletins oriented towards these areas, often with articles that are downloadable free of charge.

As we shall see later, however, many of the easiest-to-use set of links to national statistics organisations are contained in one or two key sites of this type. For instance, the Federal Statistical Office in Germany and the Central Bureau of Statistics in the Netherlands both have excellent links to other similar organisations at their sites.

General Sites

There are a number of general sites related to economics and economic statistics generally. In fact there are probably too many to choose from. But two of the best are The Dismal Scientist and the Yardeni Economic Network.

The Dismal Scientist (www.dismal.com) takes its name from the nickname for economics as 'the dismal science' first coined by the philosopher and historian Thomas Carlyle. The site is quite simply one of the clearest on the web when it comes to identifying the timing of announcements and consensus expectations for major economic statistics. Much of the content is US-oriented, but other major world markets—notably Japan and Germany—are covered and the site is put together in non-technical language, with a good page of classified links related to economics and statistics.

Ed Yardeni is chief economist at Deutche Bank Securities in New York and Yardeni Economic Network (www.yardeni.com) has a comprehensive selection of research and statistics available for access by the general public. Among the offerings are an archive of research notes (although the most recent are in a 'client-only' area) and several pages of economic charts mainly, although by no means exclusively, related to the US economy.

The Yardeni site also has an extensive selection of links to statistics organisations on the web (although the list on offer is far from being comprehensive) and to economics research, think tanks, central banks and other organisations plus newspapers, online research services and other

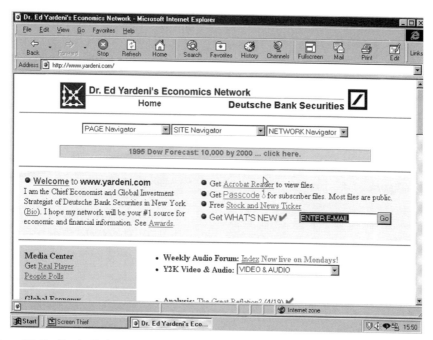

Figure 11.3   Yardeni's home page

sources of information. This is probably the best one-stop shop on the net for economics information.

A good home-grown (for UK readers) site along similar lines is a site from Lombard Street Research (www.lombard-st.co.uk), a consulting firm led by Professor Tim Congdon. This site has a number of publications available online (normally in PDF format) including a lengthy monthly commentary on economic matters, as well as periodic daily notes commenting on recently released economic and financial statistics.

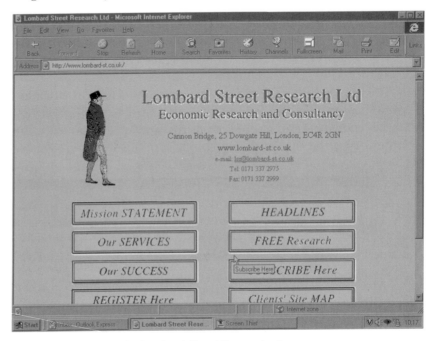

Figure 11.4   The menu at the Lombard Street Research site

Also worthy of note is Intermoney (www.intermoney.com), a site operated by the economics consultancy IDEAGlobal. This contains crisply written comments on economics and bond and foreign exchange markets.

International Organisations

One might suppose instinctively that international organisations, such as the United Nations (UN), the International Monetary Fund (IMF) or other similar bodies would be helpful sources of information for investors wanting perhaps to get a picture of several different economies at the same time.

This is true up to a point, but on the whole the web site content of many international organisations is disappointing.

Some statistics are available at the EU's Europa server (www. europa.eu.int) via a link to Eurostat, which is responsible for collecting statistics across Europe. The site offers a number of statistics and a forward calendar of releases, but the server itself is very slow and the site's navigation is poor with an incomprehensible menu bar. The EU is said to be conscious of these shortcomings and eager to improve its web offering—but progress in this direction is slow.

The European Central Bank (www.ecb.int) manages slightly better with a similar offering related to the financial system. The site has an advance calendar of release dates, past press releases and archives of the European Monetary Institute, its predecessor 'shadow' organisation. The download area for statistics appears promising, but the statistics when downloaded (at least at the time of writing) have puzzling headings which make them of little use to the casual reader.

The UN Statistics Department has a site which is mainly oriented towards paying subscribers.

Elsewhere in this category are a number of organisations such as the World Trade Organisation, the IMF, and supranational agencies such as the World Bank and its sister organisations, and the Inter-American Development Bank (IDB), the Asian Development Bank, the European Bank for Reconstruction and Development (EBRD) and so on.

As a broad generalisation, sites like this do have statistics available, but the tendency is for the approach to be fairly broad brush and for the statistics on offer not to be particularly up to date. An exception is the IDB, which has a useful site devoted to Central and South American economies at the URL www.iadb.org. The site also contains news releases and research papers.

The World Trade Organisation (www.wto.org) also has a site, but the content is disappointing for those in search of insights of use in the investment sphere. The content of the site is confined to press releases and some downloadable reports.

The World Bank (www.worldbank.org) has a range of national statistics on offer analysed by country and by region. The information is detailed but far from up to date, reinforcing the conclusion that better information is generally available by going to the site of individual national statistics organisations.

There are two interesting exceptions to this. One is the OECD (www.oecd.org) which has a good statistics section at its web site including economic statistics for the OECD countries and a table of composite leading indicators, as well as some analysis and comment on the figures. The latest statistics are available in a so-called 'hot file' which users have to subscribe to. Subscription may be worthwhile only for convenience's sake, since much of the data contained there will be available separately from the national statistics organisations of the countries concerned.

Finally in this section mention should be made of the IMF's attempts to enforce uniform disclosure of economic and financial statistics. The Dissemination Standards Bulletin Board site at www.dsbb.imf.org has standardised statements of most countries' compliance with the IMF's standards in this area, with links to a standard set of national statistics where these are available. However, not all countries comply with these standards, even though they may have perfectly adequate statistical disclosure made by their national organisations.

National Statistics—US vs UK

From the standpoint of easy availability of free and timely releases of important data to financial markets and investors, the USA stands head and shoulders above the rest. Having said that, there is a proliferation of statistical organisations within the USA, making the accessing of the appropriate ones something of a chore.

There are some short-cuts. The Financial Statistics Briefing Room (FSBR) site (www.whitehouse.gov/fsbr) has links to the full range of relevant statistics of interest to financial markets, information on the timing of future announcements and a huge variety of supporting information, all available in a graphics-free environment. The Federal Reserve's own news releases site at www.bog.frb.fed.us has a variety of additional information, including (most significantly perhaps for investors) details of the Federal Reserve chairman's public speeches and evidence to congressional committees.

In addition to these specifically financially oriented statistics sources, the USA has several other statistics-related sources, notably Fedstats (www.fedstats.gov) and Stat-USA (www.stat-usa.gov). These have general data on the US economy away from the financial scene, some of which is available free of charge and some, mainly the Stat-USA information, has to be paid for.

For most investors, however, the FSBR is the single best site for official statistics and can be supplemented by a visit to the Yardeni site referred to previously for additional material.

The UK is generally somewhat less well served in this respect. Although some of the general sites mentioned above include information on the UK economy, official provision of statistics in the UK happens on a rather piecemeal basis.

The two key sources of information are the Office for National Statistics (ONS) (www.ons.gov.uk) and the Treasury (www.hm-treasury.gov.uk) web sites. The Bank of England site (www.bankofengland.co.uk) offers some interesting information and a recent redesign has made its content more relevant to investors. Available at the site, for instance, are details of the minutes of the bank's monetary policy committee, responsible for setting interest rates in the UK, as well as details of other speeches by bank officials and various working papers and other documents and statistics.

The ONS site offers a variety of material and details of the organisation's press releases and paid-for services, but also has access to a section called Statbase. This is a separate part of the site from which statistics can be downloaded free of charge (although they are heavily copyrighted to prevent their unauthorised use). Use of Statbase requires the user to download either one of two special software readers (either Navistar or Beyond 20/20) to display the figures from the ONS database. The Beyond 20/20 reader is approximately 1.8 Mb in size (around half the size of the other) and allows the user to view the data in spreadsheet format.

It is not immediately obvious that once one of these tools has been downloaded the user then has to go to a part of the site known as Statstore to access and download the figures. Once there, however, a huge variety of statistical options is available, but the drawback of the system is that although the statistics can be downloaded and saved on the user's hard disk, they cannot be viewed while at the web site. Hence you could download the wrong table and have to return to the site to look for an alternative—a potentially frustrating process.

The Treasury site has a sizeable quota of resources of relevance for investors, including details of ministerial speeches and a particularly interesting section which gives a detailed comparison of the forecasts made by the three dozen or so independent forecasters who publish analysis on the UK economy. This table in particular is an extremely useful guide to the broad expectation of leading so-called 'expert' forecasts.

Another useful facility is the ability to receive press releases direct from the Treasury as they are issued by subscribing to an email list. Sadly this is 'read-only'; investors are unable to reply with comments on Treasury policy! Details of how to subscribe can be found at the Treasury site in the heading 'other useful information'. Whether or not you feel it worth subscribing to this list may depend on how interested you are in the course of economic policy. Many of the releases are mundane ones relating to the nuts and bolts of government policy, and not solely confined to material of direct interest to financial markets.

Other National Statistics Organisations

As previously mentioned, any nation worth its salt has an organisation dedicated to producing national statistics for government and general consumption, both inside the country and for the outsiders who monitor it.

Rather like the web sites of major corporations, these sites can tell you quite a bit about a country and its government, and their approach to provision of information. Also as is the case with corporate sites, the sites are sufficiently similar in terms of their content to permit analysis and 'scoring' on the basis of the presence or absence of a series of common characteristics.

But before looking at the best and the worst examples of the sites, we'll examine briefly the information that these sites should disclose to be of use to investors and other observers who might want to consult them.

As with other sites, an absolutely key element in any site is ease of navigation. This means first of all a low graphical content to enable those users accessing the site with a relatively low speed modem connection and an average PC not to become frustrated over the time taken for the information at the site to download. Equally important is ease of navigation around the site—whether it is laid out in a logical way with the various main areas of information clearly signposted.

A strong plus point in this direction is for the site to include either a schematic site map laying out exactly what topics are covered where on the site, and/or for the site to be searchable. We have assumed that most sites have an English version available although a few (notably those in Latin America) do not.

When it comes to the content available at the site rather than its organisation, arguably the most important aspect for investors is whether or not a reasonable range of key indicators are present. These include the country's inflation rate, money supply statistics, gross domestic product (GDP) growth, and so on, and they should be freely available at the site and regularly updated month by month.

Another strong plus point is whether the site indicates precisely when in the next few months, in terms of dates and times, key announcements of new data will be made. In the more prominent economies, data like this can be extremely important in determining the shorter-term movements in the market. Many sites have what is usually called an advance release calendar giving these important dates, so forecasters can be prepared.

Sites should usually contain (but sometimes don't) news releases relating to data and other matters. Another important point relates to the availability of publications. The norm is for key economic highlights to be available at sites like this free of charge and for news releases regarding important data to be reasonably freely available. Most sites, however, do levy charges for the regular publications they produce, usually in print and occasionally in CD-ROM form.

A rare few make their publications largely if not exclusively available online free of charge. Finally, many sites allow statistics personnel (rather than simply the webmaster) to be emailed with enquiries. Many sites also have links, often to other statistics organisations or in some instances to business related links in the country concerned.

I have analysed around 60 national statistics organisations on this basis, itemising their characteristics and scoring them on the basis of the system used earlier. This gives two points for easy navigation (light graphics), one point for medium and zero for heavy graphics or obscure layout, plus one point each for the other characteristics mentioned above. This gives a maximum of 10 for a site with light graphics/easy navigation and every other attribute present.

How did the sites fare?

European sites   Looking first at European national statistics organisations (Table 11.1), there are almost 30 such organisations ranging from the

Table 11.1 European national statistics organisations

Organisation	Web address	Advance release dates	Press releases	Key indicators	Publications	Email contact	Country	Score
Federal Statistics Office	www.statistic-bund.de	Yes	Yes	Yes	Yes	Yes	Germany	9
OSZ	www.oestat.gv.at	No	Yes	Yes	Yes	Yes	Austria	6
NSI	www.acad.bg/BulRTD/nsi/	No	No	No	No	No	Bulgaria	1
CroStat	www.dzs.hr	No	No	No	Yes	Yes	Croatia	4
CSU	www.czso.cz	Yes	No	Yes	Yes	Yes	Czech Republic	5
Statistics Denmark	www.dst.dk	Yes	No	Yes	Yes	Yes	Denmark	8
Statistikaamet	www.stat.ee	Yes	Yes	Yes	Yes	Yes	Estonia	10
Statistics Finland	www.stat.fi	Yes	Yes	Yes	Yes	No	Finland	7
ONS	www.ons.gov.uk	No	Yes	Yes	Yes	No	UK	6
HCSO	www.ksh.hu	Yes	Yes	Yes	Yes	No	Hungary	7
CSIO	www.cso.ie	Yes	Yes	Yes	Yes	Yes	Eire	9
Statistics Iceland	www.statice.is	Yes	Yes	Yes	Yes	Yes	Iceland	8
ISTAT	www.istat.it	No	Yes	Yes	Yes	No	Italy	5
CSB	www.csb.lv	Yes	Yes	Yes	Yes	Yes	Latvia	6
Statistics Lithuania	www.std.lt	No	No	No	Yes	Yes	Lithuania	3
STATEC	statec.gouvernement.lu	Yes	No	Yes	Yes	Yes	Luxembourg	5
General Bureau of Statistics	www.cbs.nl	Yes	Yes	Yes	Yes	Yes	Netherlands	10
Statistics Norway	www.ssb.no	Yes	Yes	Yes	Yes	Yes	Norway	9
INE	www.ine.pt	No	Yes	Yes	Yes	Yes	Portugal	6
SUR	www.sigov.si/zsr	No	No	Yes	Yes	Yes	Slovenia	6
Slovak Statistics	www.statistics.sk	Yes	No	Yes	Yes	Yes	Slovakia	7
Statistik Schweitz	www.admin.ch/bfs	Yes	Yes	Yes	Yes	No	Switzerland	5
PSP	www.stat.gov.pl	No	Yes	No	Yes	Yes	Poland	4
SCB	www.scb.se	No	Yes	Yes	Yes	Yes	Sweden	9
COS	www.magnet.mt	No	Yes	Yes	Yes	Yes	Malta	5
SZS	www.szs.sv.gov.yu	No	Yes	Yes	Yes	Yes	Yugoslavia	6
NCS	cns.kappa.ro	No	No	Yes	No	Yes	Romania	3
Goskomstat	www.gks.ru	No	No	Yes	Yes	No	Russia	4

smallest of the Baltic states through to Russia and Germany. Large size does not necessarily equate to a good score, however.

Of the 28 sites, only half have a calendar of advance release dates for key statistics available at the web sites and only 11 have a site map or a search engine on site. Navigation is clearly a problem at some sites. Although there are quite a number of sites with commendably low graphical content and fast response times, some are needlessly convoluted and frustrating to use.

At the time of writing the worst offenders were CroStat, the statistics organisation of Croatia, ISTAT in Italy, the Lithuanian site, STATEC, the

Luxembourg site (which had particularly heavy and unwieldy design), and the Polish and Portuguese sites. It is sometimes hard to discover whether or not the slowness of the site is simply down to the design shortcomings, or to the slowness of the server. In the case of Portugal, however, the site was hard to navigate and much of the key information available only in Portuguese.

All but ten of the sites included news releases as part of the information freely available at the site and encouragingly 24 out of 28 had a free key indicators page or pages. All but two sites had details of publications available from the organisation (the two offenders being Bulgaria and Romania, although the latter did have links to its monthly bulletins). Only a select few sites offered publications either substantially or wholly free: Estonia, Hungary, the Netherlands, Russia, Slovakia, Sweden, Switzerland and Serbia. Some 21 out of 28 sites offered some form of email contact, while 19 had sites with links to other statistics organisations and general sites of interest.

Putting all this together the best sites among European statistics organisations looked at in this reasonably objective way are Statistikaamet in Estonia (www.stat.ee) and the Central Bureau of Statitistics in the Netherlands (www.cbs.nl) with Eire (www.cso.ie), Germany (www.statistik-bund.de) Norway (www.ssb.no) and Sweden (www.scb.se) close behind.

The worst are Bulgaria and Romania, whose sites are pretty devoid of content but which obviously have some scope for improvement as they adjust further towards a market economy. The disappointment is that countries like Italy and the UK score so poorly, while the French and Spanish were at the time of writing impossible to access.

Among the interesting features of the sites were the links in the Statistics Denmark site (www.dst.dk) to econometric models of the Danish economy, with the opportunity of entering into dialogue with the statisticians there and the ability to access research papers. Sites notable for good links include the Finnish site, the German site, the UK's ONS and Italy's ISTAT.

Having said all that, many of the sites are very good and the criticisms are no more than quibbles that may not be particularly important to some investors. For most major European economies a very reasonable amount of free information is available at these sites.

The Americas sites　Of sites in the Americas outside of the USA, I can be much less charitable (see Table 11.2). Statistics Canada (www.statcan.ca) is

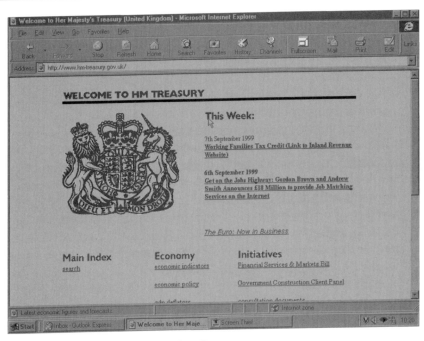

Figure 11.5   HM Treasury's disappointing site

by far the best offering, with most of the required attributes with the somewhat surprising exception (at the time of writing, at least) of a calendar of advance release dates. The problem with the Americas sites, especially those of South American countries, is the disinclination to provide English versions of their sites. Only Brazil, Guatemala, Mexico and Venezuela of the sites surveyed had an English version. Some of the sites also suffer from heavy graphics and poor navigation. Brazil's site is very heavy and not especially focused towards financial statistics.

Asian and Australasian sites   Of the dozen or so Asian and Australasian sites, by far the best is the Philippines (www.nscb.gov.ph) which records a perfect score (see Table 11.3). Only four of the 12 have details of the timing of advance releases, only three offer free publications, but all have key indicators available on site. It is perhaps somewhat surprising that Australia, new Zealand, Singapore and Japan did not really rise much above the mediocre—Australia is on a par with Indonesia in this scoring system,

Table 11.2 The Americas national statistics organisations

Organisation	Web address	Advance release dates	Press releases	Key indica-tors	Publica-tions	Email contact	Country	Score
INDEC	www.indec.mecon.ar	Yes	No	Yes	Yes	Yes	Argentina	5
Statistics Canada	www.statcan.ca	No	Yes	Yes	Yes	Yes	Canada	9
INE	www.ine.gov.bo	No	Yes	Yes	Yes	Yes	Bolivia	6
IBGE	www.ibge.gov.br	No	Yes	No	Yes	No	Brazil	6
DANE	www.dane.gov.co	No	No	Yes	No	No	Colombia	3
INEC	www.inec.gov.ec	Yes	No	Yes	Yes	Yes	Ecuador	7
INE	actualidad.araucania.cl/in	No	No	No	Yes	No	Chile	3
INEI	www.inei.gob.pe	No	Yes	Yes	Yes	Yes	Peru	6
OCEI	www.ocei.gov.ve	No	No	Yes	Yes	Yes	Venezuela	5
INEGI	www.inegi.gob.mx	No	No	Yes	Yes	No	Mexico	4
Guatemala	sever.rds.org.gt	No	No	Yes	Yes	Yes	Guatemala	5
INE	www.ine.gub.uk	No	Yes	Yes	Yes	Yes	Uruguay	6

Table 11.3 The Asian, Middle East and African national statistics organisations

Organisation	Web address	Advance release dates	Press releases	Key indica-tors	Publica-tions	Email contact	Country	Score
Australian Bureau of Sta.	www.statistics.gov.au	No	Yes	Yes	Yes	No	Australia	6
OSR	www.pio.gov.ck	No	Yes	Yes	No	Yes	Cyprus	6
SIS	www.die.gov.tr	Yes	Yes	Yes	Yes	No	Turkey	6
Hong Kong	www.info.gov.hk/censtatd	Yes	Yes	Yes	Yes	Yes	China	5
JSB	www.stat.go.jp	No	Yes	Yes	Yes	No	Japan	7
Statistics New Zealand	www.stats.gov.nz	No	Yes	Yes	Yes	Yes	New Zealand	7
PCBS	www.pcbs.org	No	No	Yes	Yes	Yes	Palestine NA	6
CBS	www.cbs.gov.il	No	Yes	Yes	Yes	Yes	Israel	7
CBJ	www.cbj.gov.jo	No	No	Yes	No	No	Jordan	3
NSCB	www.nscb.gov.ph	Yes	Yes	Yes	Yes	Yes	Philippines	10
BPS	www.bps.go.id	No	Yes	Yes	Yes	Yes	Indonesia	6
DOS	www.statistics.gov.my	Yes	Yes	Yes	Yes	No	Malaysia	4
Statistics Singapore	www.singstat.gov.sg	Yes	Yes	Yes	Yes	Yes	Singapore	7
Statistics S Africa	www.statssa.gov.za	Yes	Yes	Yes	Yes	Yes	S Africa	9
DOS	www.nic.in/stat	No	Yes	Yes	Yes	Yes	India	4
Kazstat	www.asdc.kz/kazstat	No	No	Yes	Yes	Yes	Kazakhstan	3
Azeristat	www.azeri.com/goscomstat	No	No	Yes	Yes	No	Azerbaijan	5
Ministry of Stats	president.gov.by/Ministat/	No	No	Yes	No	Yes	Belarus	4
ONS	www.ons.dz	No	No	Yes	No	Yes	Algeria	3

and barely above Azerbaijan. Singapore (www.singstat.gov.sg), however did offer an alternative to the somewhat predictable links to central banks and other statistics organisations by including links to business directories and other helpful sites.

Asia, Middle East and Africa   The few available sites in Asia, the Middle East and Africa did not on the whole score highly with the exception of Statistics South Africa (www.statssa.gov.za). This site, together with that of Turkey, were the only two in the group with details of future release dates for key statistics, although all sites offered a page of key indicators. The Turkish site (www.die.gov.tr) was generally good in terms of content but let down by exceptionally heavy graphics and poor navigation.

The roll of honour for the best sites overall includes all of those mentioned in the preceding paragraphs with a couple of additions: namely, Canada, Germany, Denmark, Estonia, Eire, Iceland, the Netherlands, Norway, Sweden, the Philippines and South Africa.

Those getting the wooden spoon, albeit perhaps because of lack of funding or some other reason, include Bulgaria, Lithuania, Colombia, Chile, Jordan, Romania, Kazakhstan and Algeria.

What all this does show, however, is that there are few economies, certainly in the developed world, where a diligent investor would be unable to get information about the local economy. In turn the impact that the economic background might have on an investment or on a foreign subsidiary of a company in which an investment had been made can be gauged. Economic statistics are another part of the online investor armoury, to be used for gaining as much knowledge as possible about what makes companies tick.

Economic and Market Analysis

Just as important as the raw statistics is interpretation of economic data. This is true whether it is for working out the economic background to an investment company operating in a particular territory or to assess the climate for successful bond investment. Expert analysts at securities firms, banks, and other organisations devoted to economic research are increasingly making their research available to all comers over the web.

Aside from the investment banking sites mentioned earlier in this chapter, many UK broker web sites have posted market commentary and economic analysis online. Table 11.4 shows the URLs of those UK brokers with comments available online. Around half of the UK brokers with web sites appear to include market and/or economic commentary at their site.

Table 11.4   UK web sites with market commentary and economic analysis

Broker name	Web address	Score
Brewin Dolphin	www.brewindolphin.co.uk	6
Capel Cure Sharp	www.ccm.co.uk	2
Carr Sheppards	www.carr-sheppards.co.uk	3
Charles Schwab Europe	www.schwab-worldwide.com	8
Hill Osborne	www.hillosborne.co.uk	5
Hoodless Brennan	www.hoodlessbrennan.com	5
James Brearley	www.jbrearley.co.uk	6
Killik	www.killik.co.uk	4
Redmayne Bentley	www.redmayne.co.uk	7
Stocktrade	www.stocktrade.co.uk	5
Tilney	www.tilney.ltd.uk	4
Torrie	www.torrie.co.uk	7
Xest	www.xest.com	9

The comments contained in these sites are, however, sometimes restricted only to clients of the firm concerned or else require would-be users to register and part with personal details. In addition many of the comments are of the relatively superficial 'market report' type or else the sort of qualitative economic commentary type, written in the rather eccentric style which UK brokers for some reason adopt.

Rarely do they bear comparison with the sort of rigorous analysis published (and sometimes made available free of charge over the web) by international banking groups and large US-owned investment banks.

As noted also in the previous chapter, a number of unit trust groups also publish similar comments on the economy and the markets. Around 16 of the 40 or so UK-based fund groups with web sites publish information of this type. In general terms the comments are brief and tend to cover a number of world markets. For those specifically interested in bond information, however, it is perhaps worthwhile accessing the web sites of the firms noted specifically for bond market funds, including Fidelity, M&G and others.

Some firms, Threadneedle Asset Management is an example, have a comparatively brief series of weekly or daily comments, but also enable users to download PDF files of a monthly comment normally sent out in printed form.

A Footnote on Market Regulators

In addition to central banks and national statistics organisations, national stock market regulators such as the US market watchdog the SEC (www.sec.gov) and the CFTC (CommodityFutures Trading Commission) (www.cftc.gov), which regulates the futures markets. In the UK the FSA (Financial Services Authority, www.fsa.gov.uk) has a range of information of interest to investors. However, this is not normally particularly germane to those wanting views on the course of the markets, since they concentrate more on explaining the regulatory framework. In the UK, a number of documents earlier contained at the Bank of England site have now moved to the FSA site. In other markets, stock market regulators' sites are often accessible from the relevant exchange site, although here again the information available tends to be of varying use to investors.

The Global Information Revolution

When *The Online Investor* was first published, I was resigned to the fact that writing about such a fast developing medium would mean the book would date quickly, but I was not quite prepared for the speed of the change.

No sooner had the book appeared than the Stock Exchange softened its hardline attitude to making share prices available to investors, allowing the now familiar 20-minute delayed free price display services to be set up on the web. Use of online dealing services has exploded in the USA and Germany and is now developing nicely in the UK and elsewhere. UK and European banks are now moving forward on online banking, until recently at a rather more sedate pace than their broking counterparts.

But the biggest change over the past couple of years has been in the attitude of companies towards the creation of corporate sites. Almost all large companies now see that a corporate web site is an essential item, and smaller companies are rapidly following suit.

The design of these sites sometimes leaves a lot to be desired, but the very best are complete one-stop shops packed with all the information an investor could possibly need to make a decision about investing in a company. And as time goes by they are getting better, as companies learn what investors really want.

This gets over the time-consuming and off-putting logistics of getting hold of company information that private investors previously faced. There has also, in some cases, been a genuine advance in the amount of information that private investors can now access on some companies. News releases are widely available, but some companies also include copies of the slide presentations (sometimes even videos) made at analyst meetings and other information previously only available to the professionals. Some sites allow users to register to receive press releases automatically by email as soon as they are released.

Who knows where this revolution might end up? Greater use of hand-held devices may enable investors to keep in touch with share prices, emailed press releases and other breaking news through palmtop computers or mobile phones, and to use them to deal as well. Nokia for one believes this to be likely, and technologically the trick is not that difficult to accomplish.

But, gadgets and gizmos aside, one very important next step in the revolution is, in my view, spreading the interaction with shareholders and would-be investors a stage further. A minority of companies allow individuals to email comments and questions to investor relations professionals at the company. While there are dangers in companies giving out information that is not in the public domain, many questions that investors have can be answered perfectly easily, and this two-way interaction cements relationships between companies and investors in a very constructive and positive way.

There are some signs that the authorities see this emergence of electronic shareholder democracy as a highly positive development to be encouraged, to which I would add my voice. The technology is already in place, for example, to allow electronic proxy voting and some US companies have structured their conference calls with analysts, following the issuing of results, as web 'events' that can be broadcast to anyone who wishes to tune in. Those not wishing to participate can replay the audio of questions and responses at a later time, to pick up the nuances. Even the idea of managing share issues online is no longer particularly far-fetched, and has already been tried in the USA.

The wealth of information available means that there is no obstacle to learning about US or French or German companies as easily as one might learn about companies operating in the UK, or whichever market the investor happens to reside. As business has become more global, the chances are that some 'foreign' companies will be just as familiar to investors as local ones.

Let me give an example. I have been a devotee of Dell PCs and laptops for some time, and order products from Dell online. I might want to invest in Dell, on the very sound investment principle of 'know what you own, and own what you know'. If so, I can visit the Dell web site and find details of their products, their financial results, recent news releases and plenty of other information to enable me to make a good investment decision. If I wanted to invest in Nokia, or Ericsson, because I felt their mobile phone designs were the best in the market, the same would be true.

The next stage in this process is for brokers to begin offering online dealing accounts that allow access to multiple markets with deals funded from the same money market account and the necessary currency conversion taking place invisibly to the user. The new service from E*Trade UK is pursuing this route, and there is little doubt that other brokers, especially those with an international network, such as Charles Schwab, will follow suit.

Services like this are arguably for the informed and sophisticated investor, and I am not here advocating active online 'day trading' in the latest fashionable stock. For me, investment is a slightly more cerebral process than that. But following the wave of privatisations and demutualisations, there are now 16 million individual shareholders in the UK alone. As they become more comfortable with their status, it is likely that their horizons will expand to investing elsewhere, first in other large UK companies and then perhaps further afield, especially if by then the UK is in the Euro zone.

A significant proportion of these 16 million may be among the near 10 million UK Internet users (who knows, by the time this book is published the figure may be even bigger than this!). If so, through the web—as this book has shown—they have the capability to find information on large US and European companies just as easily as on UK ones, and it is important perhaps that if they wish to invest overseas, they are not discouraged from doing so.

The purpose of wider share ownership is not just an abstract one. Its underlying goal is to allow people to be more self-sufficient and be better provided for financially. If that can be achieved, much as professional investors do, by investors spreading risk by investing internationally, so much the better. There are parallel developments that need to take place, notably greater common ground between accounting standards in major markets—so that the numbers can be easily and correctly interpreted by the average investor—but these are under way.

In the end, the power of the net to expand ordinary investors' horizons and aspirations should not be underestimated. The online investing revolution has much, much further to run.

Internet Basics

The times have probably passed when people viewed the Internet either as a universal panacea or an overhyped waste of time, or were even completely unaware that it existed. But it still has the capacity to create both confusion and fear. Some view it as an expensive luxury, or else as a Pandora's box that will open up their PCs to a flood of scams, viruses and other ills that are best avoided.

As usual, perceptions and reality are some way apart. What is certain is that sooner or later most PC users will come face to face with the Internet. Computers are increasingly being sold in an Internet-ready form, with built-in modems, pre-loaded Internet access software, and a service provider to log into. Upgrade your PC and the issue will become not whether you use the Internet and world wide web, but how soon.

For those for whom this prospect is daunting, it is also worth recording that the past few years have seen this new medium move from being one which required a knowledge of arcane UNIX commands and complex file transfer procedures to get the best out of it, to being a medium where non-geeks can not only use it and take full advantage of what it has to offer, but also create their own web sites using simple desktop publishing software.

Yet there is still confusion about terms and definitions, and to get the best out of the Internet and world wide web we need to understand a little of the net's history, exactly how it works, what precisely is the difference between the Internet and the world wide web, and some of its central concepts. Also important is the Internet's geography and demographics—its users, where they are, and how they use it.

A couple of provisos must be added at this point. The remainder of this appendix will be very familiar to experienced net users and computer buffs. I am aiming, in what follows, to outline how the net works in basic conceptual terms rather than in high-tech jargon.

The second point is that any attempt to describe the structure of the Internet in terms of, say, the number of users, the number of individual world wide web sites, and any other statistics, is likely very quickly to become out of date. Internet use appears currently to be growing at somewhere between 50% and 100% per annum. It is quite conceivable, for instance, for usage to have risen by upwards of, say, 30% simply between the time this manuscript was submitted to the publisher and when the book is published.

With that in mind, let's go back thirty years to some very ancient Internet history.

The Internet's Origins

The basic idea behind the Internet is a simple one. It is that connecting two computers, via a normal commercial telephone line or some other form of electronic linkage, enables information on them to be shared and transferred from one to the other.

You may be familiar with this concept through having participated in a local area network (or LAN)—that is, having your desktop PC at work connected to those of colleagues, enabling memos to be sent electronically, and word processed documents and spreadsheets to be shared, as well as information from outside service providers to be distributed to everyone on the network.

Take this idea one stage further and imagine that two LANs, each with 50 computers connected to them, are linked together. What this now means is that not only can the participants in each LAN connect to each other, but that any one of them can connect to any other computer in the other network, assuming suitable access arrangements have been built into the system.

Now assume that hundreds of LANs are connected together in what is known as a wide area network (WAN). Each of the users in each LAN can contact both each other and also any other user in any other network connected to the larger network.

Multiply this idea several hundred times over and add in millions of individual users connected through their home computers, and you get some idea of the scale of the Internet. Paul Gilster's book, *The New Internet Navigator* (John Wiley & Sons, 1995), suggested at that time that the Internet reached 100 countries, and involved more than 50,000 separate networks. These networks are typically at corporations, educational institutions, or governments.

The Internet, said Gilster, then contained more than five million host computers and more than 30 million active users. Hobbes Internet Timeline, surveying the statistics in July 1999, put the number of host computers at 56 million. And a September 1998 survey put the total number of internet users at 147 million. The USA alone is reckoned to have about 100 million users and the UK around 10 million.

The number of connected networks has grown from the original one in 1969 to around 100 in 1985, to 500 in 1989, to perhaps 4,000 by mid-1991 and probably well over 500,000 by early 1999. The sheer volume of information available is mind-boggling. Let's assume, for simplicity, that each network has 100 computers connected to it and that each computer's hard drive contains 100 separate accessible files. Say for the sake of argument that there are 100,000 networks connected to the net. The implication is that any user could have access to any single one of a billion files.

Any file could, in theory, be downloaded by any user anywhere in the world in a matter of a few minutes or less. A message could be sent from any computer anywhere on the network to any other computer. Files in any format could be sent attached to messages.

It is only comparatively recently that what was a more or less closed network used for the benefit of government, military and academic institutions was opened up to normal home PC users. These potential new users, estimated at perhaps 300 million in number, can now dial in at will—using a modem and a normal telephone line—via an Internet service provider who has the wired-in connection to the net.

It happened like this. The Internet started life as the ARPANET in the late 1960s. The idea was to let academic researchers share information and communicate with each other. The network was at that time funded by the US Advanced Research Projects Agency (ARPA). One objective in designing it was to create a web-like structure so that if any one computer or a series of computers were knocked out (say by an earthquake or a nuclear war), the network could still continue to function. Initially there were four sites, based at US universities, although many other institutions connected to it during the 1970s, once the concept of what the network could accomplish really began to take hold.

In the 1980s ARPANET continued to function, with a military-oriented network hived off from it. Ten years or so ago the US National Science Foundation created a souped-up version of ARPANET using supercomputers and high-speed access. The management of this network was then turned over to a group of universities and eventually it absorbed AR-PANET. By 1990 the more or less exclusively academic nature of the network was beginning to be lost. The enacting of the US High Performance Computing Act, in 1991, also meant that commercial organisations were brought into the loop for the first time. Other networks were also being created during this period, including ones in countries other than the USA.

The ability of these networks to connect with each other stemmed from the US Defence Communications Agency's insistence, back in 1983, that a standard set of computer instructions be used for all communications through ARPANET. This allowed each network that might connect to it to function autonomously, yet also permitted messages and instructions to be passed through 'gateways' into the wider network.

An upgrading of the structure of the network was undertaken between 1990 and 1992, in what amounted to a joint venture between America's National Science Foundation and commercial organisations such as MCI and IBM. When the new Internet 'backbone' began operating in late 1992, it resulted in a 700-fold increases in the traffic capacity of the network. Further increases in capacity have been constructed since then to keep pace with the net's phenomenal growth.

The dramatic increase in capacity in 1992, however, was the seminal event in the history of the Internet. It freed up capacity on the network, hitherto the preserve of the military, government and educational establishment, to enable commercial and private users to get connected.

Why has the Internet caught the imagination of so many users?

One particularly interesting aspect of the Internet is that no one owns or controls it. Because the networks that comprise it are made up of many different organisations, no single body can truly influence or censor the Internet's content. Governments and commercial organisations may club together to upgrade basic communications infrastructure or try to control the organisation of Internet 'addresses' (although even this has been controlled for many years by an organisation independent of government), but each network linked to it is autonomous.

A side-effect of this is that the net can be used for purposes for which it was not originally intended. There has been considerable focus in the press, for example, on the use of the Internet as a channel for pornography, or on its use by paedophiles. There are concerns about its use for fraud and money-laundering, and as a possible conduit for leaking sensitive information, and there are some moves from governments to attempt to censor or control information passed over the Internet. But because of its deliberately flexible web-like nature, attempts at control like this prove difficult to administer, and defining the bounds of good taste and legality may have to be left to ISPs to administer as best they can.

But amid all the criticism of the Internet there is little acknowledgement of its role as a force for promoting democratic ideals and free speech, and in opening up hitherto closed societies to outside influences and uncensored news. It is significant, for example, that Internet access is unavailable in Iraq, North Korea, Mongolia, and Burma.

The Internet's Size

Charting the Internet is like hitting a moving target. Paul Gilster's book, published in 1995, talks of 40,000 networks being connected to it as at mid-1994. At the time this edition of *The Online Investor* was written (in mid 1999), the figure for connected networks is probably well over 500,000. And of the networks joining the Internet, by far the fastest growing segment is represented by those located outside the USA. A few years ago the US alone probably represented slightly more than a 50% share of the total. While the development of Internet use has been fastest by far in the USA, this is almost certainly no longer the case.

Looked at from another direction, from the standpoint of exactly who is using the net, the figures are equally hard to pin down. In September 1998 worldwide user numbers were put at around 147 million. Now the figure could be 200 million or more. What percentage of these are users in the academic sphere (mainly students with free access via a university computer) or those accessing the web on a computer in the workplace is unclear. In the mid 1990s about 67% of users were academic-based and around 20% employees of large companies. Much of this usage was at that time confined to email and other basic services.

But just as the make-up of the number of connected networks has changed, so also has that of net users. Individual users have grown in number by leaps and bounds. The figures contained in the first edition of *The Online Investor* have been convincingly overtaken by events. US usage is now estimated at 100 million, UK user numbers at 10 million, usage in France at five million and in Germany at eight million. There are expected to be around 20 million users in Japan by the end of 1999. Some 40% of Europeans are expected to be connected by 2002, compared to 13% in early 1999. AOL alone expects to have 10 million European users by that date.

As a percentage of population, usage is highest so far in North America and, elsewhere, in Scandinavia, while the UK and Germany appear to be leading the way among the larger countries of the EU. Over recent years, estimates of Internet usage have almost always undershot the eventual figures. In a survey conducted in 1995 some seven million private Internet users were expected in Europe by the end of 1997, whereas all the signs were that this figure had been achieved in the UK alone by late 1998. Forecasts now suggest 320 million world users by 2002, although even this could prove to be an underestimate.

Some sources suggest taking a different view of the way the Internet is structured. This envisages a 'core' Internet group comprising people and computers who offer interactive services, whether they are sites on the world wide web, files available for transfer, or other facilities. On the other side is the consumer Internet. This consists of those who have the ability to connect to the world wide web, download files and make other use of the services provided by the 'core'.

The remainder represents an outer core that lacks a true interactive connection, but who have the ability to send and receive electronic mail and access basic Internet services through it.

In geographic terms, full Internet conductivity is available across North America and much of South America and across Europe and Asia, including China and the former Soviet Union, in Australia, India, Saudi Arabia, South Africa, Egypt, Indonesia. Much of Africa has either no Internet connection, or connectivity only by email. These exceptions apart, the Internet stretches from Alaska to Antarctica, and from Vancouver eastwards to Sakhalin and down to Tasmania, and from Tierra Del Fuego to Greenland and across to Siberia.

A simple point is that the Internet's content, and that of the world wide web (the net's commercial information bank) broadly reflects its user base. Much of the information of interest to online investors currently has a US bias. But, in line with the rapid growth of non-US users, this is changing rapidly. Since the publication of the first edition of *The Online Investor*, though US content has increased in scale and scope, non-US sources of investment information have also increased dramatically. And let's not forget that the web itself is huge. Recent estimates suggest there are more than six million individual domain names registered and some seven million web servers, each capable of hosting many web sites.

How It All Works

There are a number of concepts that are fundamental to understanding how the Internet works. The main ones to be grasped are those of data packets, packet switching and computer communications protocols.

The Internet is sometimes called the information superhighway, a phrase first coined by the US politican Al Gore. The metaphor is a good one, and can be used to explain things more clearly.

Information sent over the net is broken down into small packets of information. Data packets are in effect the vehicles that travel along the Internet road, packet switches are junctions that allow them to take different routes to their destination, and the communications protocols involved are the highway codes that allow each to get to the right destination safely.

A recent report took the use of this metaphor to an even higher degree, describing ISPs as the toll roads that offered access to the Internet, a PC and modem as a car, and a PC with a dedicated line as a truck.

The 'highway code' protocols that allow the Internet to work as it does are known as TCP/IP, an acronym that stands for Transmission Control Protocol/Internet Protocol. In effect, because the Internet was deliberately designed to function without a central controller, each computer connecting to the net must be able to establish contact with any other. Protocols establish a common language by which different computers can communicate, whether they are IBM/Windows based, Apple Mac-based or UNIX-based. These simple logical rules were first written in the 1970s and have stood the test of time.

They specify how the network is to move messages and handle errors. IP is responsible for network addressing, while TCP is designed to ensure that messages are delivered to the right destination. Other networks that form part of the Internet may use different protocols to talk to each other, but once messages pass through to the Internet, the TCP/IP standard kicks in. So a good definition of the Internet is that it is a global link-up of those networks that are capable of running the TCP/IP protocols.

For the ordinary Internet user, however, the switching between networks and protocols is done automatically, without any human intervention needed.

The diffuse nature of the Internet relies on fibre-optic backbones to transmit high volumes of data around the network, particularly in and out of the USA, where most users are currently concentrated. It is supplemented by routers, special computers that decide how the information being transmitted is to reach its destination. The route taken is via a series of hubs, rather like the motorway network, and the information then transfers to smaller local roads to reach its destination.

Imagine I am travelling from my home in NE London to visit my mother-in-law in Lancaster. I travel from my driveway via several side roads to the A12, from there to the M11, from the M11 either via the A14 or the M25 to the A1 or the M1, continuing the journey on the M6 and then transfer to local roads until I reach my destination. There are several different ways in which I can vary the journey. If one road is blocked, or clogged with traffic, I can take a detour in order to save time, perhaps travelling slightly further but arriving sooner.

This is a good way of imagining how data, say the electronic mail message I send from London to a friend in Southern California, might reach its destination. I am not really interested in whether the message is routed via Miami, Minnesota, Los Angeles or Tokyo, as long as it reaches my friend in the quickest possible time.

There is another element to be considered. In an electronic message, anything other than a very brief piece of data is unwieldy. This is why technique has been developed whereby the inherently unwieldy message you send is broken up into small sections, or packets, each with a code attached that determines its eventual destination.

These packets, each with only about 200 bytes of data in them, are then sent on their way, perhaps travelling via different routes to their destination. In the course of their journey they may split further or be combined with other packets. Eventually, though, thanks to the logic in the TCP protocol, they are reassembled in the correct order to be read by the recipient.

There are several advantages to this method. One is that this transmission system automatically adjusts for the different running speed of sender and recipient computer, acting as a buffer between them. A second advantage is that if a packet is lost or destroyed, then the system will pass back an instruction for it to be resent, persisting until the complete message is assembled. Another positive aspect is that packets from many different sources can share the same telecommunications line, which means that the available capacity (known as bandwidth) can be used with a high degree of efficiency. For some time bandwidth has been viewed as scarce but, though still apparent, this scarcity is eventually expected to be removed by increases in capacity and the advent of new technology.

The drawback to the present packet switching regime is that packets travel through the net on a first-come first-served basis. If usage is heavy at a particular time of day, delays may be the result. Many UK Internet users may notice, for example, that their connections are more sluggish than usual in the evening, when US demand is at its peak. It's the equivalent of an electronic traffic jam.

This takes care of TCP. Let's look briefly at how the IP part of the protocols work. The IP protocol is, in effect, a system of uniquely numbered addresses. Over and above this group of numbers, a user may also be identified by an address in normal characters, rather than numbers.

The IP system has another use as well as making sure messages get to the correct address. When sending and receiving electronic mail and participating in newsgroups it is possible to tell something about the other party by examining their email address.

Let's illustrate this by some examples. Most UK Internet users, certainly private individuals, will probably have an email address that ends *.uk*. Mine is peter@ptemple.compulink.co.uk. This also indicates, for instance that my Internet service provider is Compulink Information Exchange (CIX for short), that it is a company, and that it is based in the UK. The word to the right of the '@' sign is a shortened version of my company name Peter Temple Associates, and the word to the left of the '@' sign is my first name. My wife's email address, if she were to receive email via the same system, would be lynn@ptemple.compulink.co.uk. My son's would be david@ptemple.compulink.co.uk. And so on.

Country names generally provide the end of Internet addresses, with the exception of the USA. Hence *.fr* is France, *.de* is Germany (deutsche-land), *.es* is Spain (espana), *.ca* is Canada, and so on.

And while commercial organisations may have the suffix *.com* (if they are of US or international origin) or *.co* (if they are UK) so there are a variety of other suffixes that describe the function of the user—such as *.gov* (government), *.ac* (academic institution), *.org* (other organisation) and so on. In the UK, new Internet addresses have begun to spring up. Some companies now have an address which ends *.plc.uk* or *.ltd.uk* depending on whether they are respectively a public or private limited company.

The Internet and the World Wide Web

Before they sign up, would-be Internet users are sometimes confused by references to the world wide web. The distinction between the web and Internet is sometimes not entirely clear.

The best way to explain it is that the web is a giant interactive library that occupies part of the Internet. But Internet tools such as electronic mail and file transfer function independently of the web. In fact, an Internet user can perfectly easily never visit the web, just as you might never go to your local library. It doesn't stop you finding reading matter.

Having said that the web has exploded in size in the past few years because of its value as a shop window for commercial organisations wishing to tap into the large number of users the Internet brings with it. Internet users are typically viewed as being in socio-economic groups attractive to commercial organisations, or (in the case of student users) likely to be so in the future.

But the web is not only about commercial self-promotion. Governments, universities, and a whole host of other organisations also have a presence there.

So online investors will themselves not only be using the classic functions of the Internet such as electronic mail, newsgroups and bulletin boards (which are really an extension of electronic mail), and file transfer, but also visiting world wide web sites to access the information there. In fact many Internet users will more than likely mainly use the Internet only for web access and using email, and not explore the Internet's other capabilities at all. The web has gone from being a curious new service to being, along with email, the main reason for getting connected.

Although solely text-based pages are sometimes offered as an alternative, the classic use of the web is via full colour text and graphics-based pages. Either way, the concept behind it is that certain highlighted parts of the text (or images) at web sites contain embedded links to other pages of information, either within a particular site, or in a web page on a related subject operated by someone else. By a simple point and click, the link can be activated and the data transferred to enabled the contents of new link to be viewed.

Similarly the new site may contain links back to the original one, but will also contain links to others, totally different from those at the first site visited, and so on. The concept of links that activate the downloading of new data is known as hypertext.

Web sites operate through computers known as servers, which automatically respond to site visitors and route them through the site as they wish. Web sites vary in the functions they perform. They can be a library or reading room, an encyclopaedia or reference book, an amusement arcade, or a shop.

The web servers act as librarians or cashiers depending on the nature of the site. The web is developing fast as a means of transacting business, whether it is buying information, trading shares, or purchasing some other form of goods and services. Certain types of product, such as books and music CDs, software and tickets have proved particularly suited to buying over the web. Web bookshops, e.g. Amazon.com, are able to offer a searchable catalogue many times larger than even the largest bookshop, take credit card payments online through a secure server, and then ship the book to the customer within a couple of days.

The security issues that once inhibited consumers from buying online are now breaking down. A survey in July 1999 found that almost one half of American web users had made at least one purchase online.

Basic Internet Tools and Concepts

We looked in some detail at how to get connected and what benefits your connection might bring in Chapter 2. This section is designed to be read separately and looks at some of the basic features of the Internet and how they can help you function efficiently as an online investor.

Electronic Mail

Electronic mail is arguably the single most important aspect of the Internet for many of its users. It was originally included in the forerunner to the Internet as something of an afterthought. But email subsequently became an indispensable part of the net, as users discovered it was an easy way to exchange ideas quickly with colleagues, friends and collaborators.

Email allows you to:

❏ Send messages to (and receive messages from) one or more people anywhere in the world at negligible cost, provided you know their email address.
❏ Send (and receive) document files (text, spreadsheets and so on) attached to email messages.
❏ Retrieve information through automated electronic mailing lists.
❏ Participate in electronic bulletin boards (these are simply email collected together at a central point and viewed by all members of the group).

These features alone are worth the expense of signing up for an online account. Sending files by email is considerably cheaper than using a fax or the conventional postal system (known derisively as 'snail mail' by net users). Sending conventional letters by email is cheaper than snail mail, even for those going short distances. Above all it offers convenience and, because of the ease with which messages can be composed and sent, it encourages both speedy responses and brevity.

There are also a number of free web-based services such as Hotmail (www.hotmail.com) which function exactly as normal email accounts and enable conventional email to be accessed from any remote computer connected to the web.

File Transfer

One of the outstanding properties of the Internet is the opportunity it offers to download to your computer a variety of publicly available files at various remote computers on the network. The system by which this works is known as file transfer protocol (or FTP).

An online investor might use this to download a particular piece of investment software, which it might currently only be available in the shops in America. Demo programs, shareware, and a variety of other programs can be acquired comparatively simply by this method at little or no cost.

Sometimes software programs are restricted in some way, either with their functions severely hampered or with a time limit to their use. Only when the full cost of the program is paid can the authorised version be downloaded. Nonetheless, even in this case, much of the software is exceptionally good value by UK standards, and the ability to get hold of a demo version without undue fuss is valuable in itself. This topic, and the types of programs available, is discussed in more detail in Chapter 5.

The procedure for downloading varies depending on where the 'target' file resides. If it is in a normal commercial web site then merely clicking on the indicated link will automatically set up a download to a specified directory on your own computer's hard drive. It is a good idea to have a blank directory available to take the download.

This is not the end of the story, however. Often downloadable files come in zipped form, that is to say with their contents compressed to limit the amount of time taken to download them. Once downloaded they must be 'unzipped' by using PKZIP or a similar utility. This small program or its equivalent can be downloaded from several FTP sites and you will probably be signposted to them at your original download site.

Once unzipped a variety of files will be released into the directory. One of these should have a *.exe* or *.ini* suffix. Clicking on this will load the program or initiate its set-up sequence.

If the file you require is not contained at a web site, then the process is a little more complex. The basic procedure is to go the appropriate FTP site, login in as a guest user, interrogate the remote computer using a standard software package, find the file and then download it.

UNIX and FTP Client Software

It may be cheating slightly to include UNIX in this section on Internet tools, since it is much more than that. It has been described as the *lingua franca* of the Internet and, while you may never need to use it at all, equally there may be occasions when you need a smattering of it to get by. This applies even if you happen to be using client software programs that automate procedures such as FTP, because it may be necessary at some point to interrogate the remote computer, although normally the software will automate the commands. An FTP client software program will almost always be supplied by your ISP as part of the signing on package. Alternatively these simple programs can be downloaded easily from the usual software sites like Download.com.

It is probably a good idea to read a general Internet guide to get a good understanding of UNIX commands, but a few basics can be illustrated with an example of file transfer using what is known as 'anonymous login'.

Why anonymous login? Because you are not a normal user of the remote computer you will not have the password access to many parts of the computers' hard drive. Those parts that are, as it were, open to the public must still be accessed using a password. The normal procedure is to type in the word *anonymous*, with the password being your full email address.

To download a file it is necessary to know roughly what it might be called, have some idea of the directory in which it is located, and perhaps (as a foolproof way of identifying it) know roughly what size it is in bytes.

Using your FTP client software it should be possible to arrive at a master list of directories contained on the remote computer.

Let's assume that the file we require is in the directory called *'public'*. We now need to change to that directory and list the files contained in it to find the one we require.

Clicking on the change directory button on the FTP client and specifying the desired directory logs onto that directory. Once that is done it will list the files in the directory. Note that once in a directory part way down the tree, just clicking on the up arrow in the corner of the window will move up a branch on the directory tree.

In UNIX, for instance, typing *cwd public* [enter] followed by *ls* [enter] will again provide us with a list of files and subdirectories in the 'public' area. Clicking on the appropriate button in the FTP client will activate these commands. Let's assume that the file we require is called *xnetsc22.zip* and is roughly 3Mb in size. We locate the file.

Downloading the file is accomplished by typing the UNIX command *'get'* followed by a space and then by the filename. Thus typing *get xnetsc22.zip* [enter] will begin the download process and transfer the file. In an FTP client environment, the procedure is simply to highlight the file and click on the arrow which points towards the home directory. This will then transfer the file to the specified directory in your hard drive.

Once the download has been completed, clicking on the button to close the connection (the equivalent of typing the UNIX command *'logout'*, *'bye'*, or *'quit'*) will exit the remote computer and disconnect the modem.

As with DOS, with which many computer users will be familiar, UNIX has many other commands, but few of them will be required. A useful one is *'pwd'*, which shows the name of the current directory; *'cat'* (for catalogue) followed by the filename displays the file on screen in a scrolling form; and *'help'* is a universal command. The command *'more'* followed by a filename displays the file one page at a time, enabling it to be read. Hitting the spacebar moves to the next page.

I am not really exaggerating by saying that, provided you have a reasonable idea of what the file is called, what directory it is in, and how big it is, the commands already mentioned will be all the UNIX you'll ever need to know. In fact, you may never need to use them since the interface should generally always be possible via the FTP client software which automates the process.

Other Internet Tools

The objective of this appendix is to provide an initial insight into what might be useful from the standpoint of online investing. There are a number of other Internet tools available which have been largely superseded by the growth of the world wide web. An example is Telnet, which allows you to log into a remote computer network and then, once access has been gained, move around it as though one's keyboard were actually attached to a computer on the remote network.

There are occasions when this could be of use, which any up-to-date Internet guide will explain, but this and other similar tools such as Archie (large, typically academic-orientated, computers with hosts of publically available files) and Gopher, a prototype web directory system, tend these days to be used only by aficionados in the academic world.

Is The Internet Right for You?

The previous sections have really only scratched the surface of what can be accomplished using the Internet as both a communications medium and a source of online information. The chapters in the main body of this book will show how the online world can work for you as an investor.

But the contents of this appendix probably cover 90% of techniques the average user will need to learn to get the full benefit from the resources the online world has to offer. I have dwelt only briefly in this edition on the mysteries of using UNIX commands (less so than in the last edition because FTP software now essentially automates these commands). Even if you do have to use them, with a little practice these are not difficult for the average computer user to grasp.

I have not dealt here with the software that is normally supplied when a user first connects to the system, since each ISP uses a different set of programs.

But there is, for instance, no need to use UNIX commands to send email messages, although this is possible if you so wish. A ready-made 'client' email program is normally provided or the default program in any Windows computer can be used. The same is true of many other Internet functions, where software is provided to make telnetting and organising FTP sessions relatively simple.

Bibliography

Gilster, Paul (1995) *The New Internet Navigator*. New York: John Wiley & Sons.

Hagstrom, Robert (1994) *The Warren Buffett Way*. New York: John Wiley & Sons.

Temple, Peter (1996) *Getting Started in Shares*. Chichester: John Wiley & Sons.

List of Abbreviations

ADSL	asymmetric digital subscriber line
AIM	Alternative investment market
AOL	America On Line
ARPA	Advanced Research Projects Agency
ASCII	American Standard Code for Information Interchange
ATM	automated teller machine
AVC	additional voluntary contributions
BBS	bulletin board system
bps	bits per second
CAROL	Company Annual Reports On Line
CBOE	Chicago Board Options Exchange
CBOT	Chicago Board of Trade
CD	compact disc
CD-ROM	compact disk—read only memory
CFTC	Commodity Futures Trading Commission [USA]
CGT	capital gains tax
CIX	Compulink Information Exchange
CME	Chicago Mercantile Exchange
CSV	comma separated values [used for spreadsheet data]
CTA	commodity trading adviser
DJIA	Dow Jones Industrial Average
EBRD	European Bank for Reconstruction and Development
EU	European Union

FAQ	frequently asked questions
FIND	Financial Information Net Directory
FSA	Financial Services Authority
FSBR	Financial Statistics Briefing Room
FT	*Financial Times*
FTP	file transfer protocol
FTSE	Financial Times–Stock Exchange [100 Share Index] ('footsie')
Gb	gigabyte
GDP	gross domestic product
GSM	global system for mobile communications
HKFE	Hong Kong Futures Exchange
HTML	hypertext mark-up language
HTTP	hypertext transfer protocol
IDB	Inter-American Development Bank
IFA	independent financial adviser
iii	Interactive Investor
IMF	International Monetary Fund
IP	Internet Protocol
ISA	individual savings account
ISDN	integrated services digital network
ISP	Internet service provider
KB	kilobyte
KLOFFE	Kuala Lumpur Options and Financial Futures Exchange
LAN	local area network
Mb	megabyte
Mbps	megabytes per second
MHz	megahertz
NASDAQ	National Association of Securities Dealers Automated Quotations
NAV	net asset value
NYSE	New York Stock Exchange
OECD	Organisation for Economic Cooperative Development
OEIC	open ended investment company
OHLCV	open, high, low, close and volume
OLR	offline reader
ONS	Office for National Statistics
PC	personal computer
PDF	portable document file (or format)

PEP	personal equity plan
POP	point of presence
POP3	Post Office Protocol, version 3
PPP	point to point protocol
REFS	Really Essential Financial Statistics
RSP	retail service provider
SEC	Securities & Exchange Commission
SETS	Stock Exchange Electronic Trading System
SFA	Securities and Futures Authority
SIB	Securities and Investments Board
SLPP	serial line Internet protocol
TCP	transmission control protocol
TESSA	tax exempt special savings accounts
UN	United Nations
URL	uniform resource locator
VBI	vertical blanking interval
WAN	wide area network
WSD	Wall Street Directory
WSJ	Wall Street Journal

Glossary

Archie A program that will search for files stored on *FTP* sites across the Internet.

Adobe Acrobat Reader A program that allows you to view, print and download documents as they appear on the screen, even if you don't have the software the document was created in (by using the *PDF* file format).

ASCII American Standard Code for Information Interchange—format understood by all computers. An ASCII file will contain bytes of seven bits. *See also binary.*

backbone The high-capacity part of a network that links other networks.

bandwidth How much data you can send over a communications link. *See also baud.*

baud The unit of measurement for modem speeds. One-baud is one signalling element per second.

binary A format in which a file might be saved. A binary file will contain bytes of eight bits. *See also ASCII.*

bits The smallest piece of information a computer deals with. A collection of bits are a *byte.*

bits per second (bps) The standard measure of *bandwidth.*

bookmark To save the address of Web sites in your *navigator.*

Boolean operators Words such as AND, NOT and OR which you can use to help fine tune a search expression.

browser A program such as Netscape Navigator or Microsoft's Internet Explorer that enables your computer to download and display documents from the *World Wide Web.*

bulletin board system (BBS) A common area on the Internet where anyone can read or write messages. Private BBSs can be set up for group discussions.

buttons Small online advertisements at Web sites.

byte Seven (see *ASCII)* or eight (see *binary) bits.*

CD-ROM drive Similar to a floppy drive, but for a CD-ROM (compact disk read only memory). This is a storage device similar to a music CD that can hold a vast amount of information.

cyberspace The 'universe' of the Internet and World Wide Web.

dialog box A box on screen in which you type more information or make specific choices to enable the program to perform a particular function.

domain suffix Part of the address that specifies your computer's location, the domain suffix will show what sort of organisation the computer is used in. For example, an address that contains the suffix .ac.uk indicates that the computer is within a UK academic environment.

DOS Disk Operating System—a basic program for controlling a PC.

download To transfer data from a distant computer to your own.

email Electronic mail—a message that can be sent to any other computer connected to the Internet—provided you know the recipient's exact email address. Files and documents can be attached to email.

file transfer protocol (FTP) The computer conventions by which files are transferred across the Internet.

freeware Software distributed without charge. Ownership is retained by the developer.

frequently asked questions (FAQs) A file often found in newsgroups or email lists that lists the most common questions asked by newcomers, together with their answers. If you have a question, it is good *netiquette* to check a relevant FAQ file first to see if it has already been answered.

Gopher A menu-driven facility that conveys a wide range of information.

hit A file that has been found as a result of your search using a search tool.

home page The first page of a web site. It is a *hypertext* document used as the starting point for exploring the site.

host computer The computer you contact to enable you to get on the Internet.

HyperText Mark-up Language (HTML) The language used for creating documents accessible on the World Wide Web.

HyperText Transfer Protocol (HTTP) The standard for transferring HTML documents between Web servers. Web site addresses always start with the letters http.

hyperlink A file that is linked via *hypertext.*

hypertext An embedded pointer to related text. By clicking on it the user can go straight to the relevant file.

Internet A collection of computers from all parts of the world that can communicate with each other using telephone lines and modems.

Internet service provider See *service provider.*

ISDN Integrated Services Digital Network. A digital high-speed telephone line that allows transfer of data, audio, and video signals.

Java A programming language often used for creating interactive multimedia effects on the web.

jumping-off point A Web site from which to get pointers to other related sites via *hyperlinks.*

kilobyte 1,024 *bytes.*

lurking Reading what is going on in a newsgroup or mailing list, but not joining in.

megabyte 1,048,576 *bytes.*

meta-search tool A site that searches several search engines simultaneously.

modem A MOdulator/DEModulator. Equipment that translates digital information into analogue information so that it can be passed down the phone lines.

navigator Another name for a *browser.*

net Shortform for the Internet.

netiquette Generally understood rules of good behaviour while online.

newsgroup The bulletin boards for particular topics on the Internet. They are either integral to a service provider such as CompuServe, or open to all. The largest collection of open newsgroups is operated under the auspices of *Usenet.*

offline Doing tasks while not on the phone line. For example, you can write your email messages offline, ready to send when you connect to the Internet. You can download files to read offline at your leisure, to save on phone costs.

offline reader A program that enables you to read and compose email and newsgroup messages while offline.

online Doing things while you are actually connected to the Internet. For instance, you will need to be online to get updates of information.

packet switching The underlying communications methods of the Internet. A packet is a bundle of data that is transmitted across the network.

PDF Portable document format. A file format that preserves the layout, typeface size and pictures in a form that can be viewed and printed with an *Adobe Acrobat Reader.*

point of presence (POP) A local Internet access point set up by a service provider. By connecting to a local POP, you will be paying only local call rates when you are *online.*

POP3 The protocol used for receiving email. It stands for Post Office Protocol, version 3.

portal A *jumping-off point.* Typically a portal site will have some combination of, among other things, a catalogue of web sites, a search engine, news, discussion groups. A portal site may also offer email and other service to entice people to use that site as their main 'point of entry'.

protocol The way two devices on a network communicate with each other.

pull-down menu Menu headings are given along a bar at the top of the screen. When you click on one of these headings, you are given a list of further options

search engine A tool that looks through the contents of the World Wide Web to find specified words or phrases.

server A central computer through which information (e.g. Web pages) are made available to Internet users.

service provider/access provider A commercial organisation charging users a fee (usually monthly) for using its computer to connect to the Net and send and receive email.

shareware Software distributed on a trial basis. At some point you will be required to register and pay for it, for which you will receive technial support and perhaps additional documentation or the next upgrade.

shell account An indirect connection to the Net offering *email, FTP* and a text-based *browser.*

site A particular company's, organisation's or individual's web presence.

smileys Small 'pictures' made up of punctuation to indicate 'emotion' in your email messages.

spamming Posting the same message to many newsgroups.

surfing 'Browsing' through files on the Internet.

TCP/IP stack A section in your computer's hard drive that generates the commands to enable connections to be made to and received from the Net.

teletext TV-based information medium such as the BBC's CEEFAX.

Telnet The Internet protocol for remote access.

toggle button A button you click on to turn a function on, and then click again to turn a function off.

UNIX An operating system that enables many computers to access a main computer at the same time. There are special commands for use with this system.

unzip *See zip.*

URL (uniform resource locator) The address of any resource on the Internet.

Usenet The collective name for the vast number of newsgroups or discussion groups on the Internet.

webmaster The person in charge of administering a world wide web site.

world wide web The generic name given to all hypertext-based documents on the Internet. These documents contain links to other documents.

zip Compress data so that it takes up less space. To read the text again, you need to unzip it. You need a special program to do this.

Useful Internet Addresses

Chapter 1: Why Online Investing

Companies House   www.companies-house.gov.uk
Online company searches

EDGAR   www.sec.gov/edgarhp/htm
Free company data

Hemmington Scott   www.hemscott.com
Free company data

LIFFE   www.liffe.com
London International Futures Exchange

New Online Investor   www.new-online-investor.co.uk
The site of the book

Winsite   www.winsite.com
Downloadable software site

Yahoo! Finance   http://finance.yahoo.co.uk
Quotes, company data and news

Chapter 2: Getting Connected

Georgia Tech 10th Annual Survey   www.cc.gatech.edu/gvu/user_surveys
Internet demographics

Netscape Online   www.netscapeonline.co.uk
AOL's free UK ISP

Chapter 3: Browsing and Searching

Adobe   www.adobe.com
Download Acrobat PDF reader

All-in-one   www.albany.net/allinone/
Multiple search engine access

AltaVista   www.altavista.com
Leading search engine

AOL   www.aol.com
ISP cum content provider

Beaucoup   www.beaucoup.com/engines.html
Multiple search engine access

Bloomberg News Radio   www.bloomberg.com
Hear the tones of Bloomberg

BPAmoco   www.bpamoco.com
Corporate site from UK giant

Britax   www.britax.com
Corporate site from UK minnow

BUBL   www.bubl.ac.uk/link
Links for academics and others

eDirectory   www.edirectory.com
Multiple search engine access

Excite   www.excite.com
'Portal' and search tool combined

FAST   www.alltheweb.com
New comprehensive search tool

Financewise   www.financewise.com
Specialist financial search tool

FIND   www.find.co.uk
UK-oriented financial site directory

Go.com   www.go.com
Disney-fied 'portal'

Hemmington Scott   www.hemscott.com
Free company data

Interactive Investor   www.iii.co.uk
Comprehensive personal finance site

Internet Bookshop   www.bookshop.co.uk
This sort of site could cost £1.5 million to develop

Investorama   www.investorama.com
Investment jumping-off point

Investormap   http://investormap.com
Investment jumping-off point

JJB Sports   www.jjb.co.uk
UK sportswear retailer's site

Lenape Investment Corporation   www.enter.net/-rsauers/
Listing of new finance-related sites

Lycos   www.lycos.com
Search tool

Microsoft   www.microsoft.com
Needs no introduction

Misys   www.misys.co.uk
Corporate site

Moneyworld   www.moneyworld.co.uk
Comprehensive personal finance site

MSN   www.msn.com
Microsoft network site

Netscape   www.netscape.com
From web browser to 'portal'

Northern Light   www.northernlight.com
Superb search tool

Peter Temple Linksite   www.cix.co.uk/~ptemple/linksite/
Find all the sites in this book, and more

PKWare   www.pkware.com
Download that decompression utility

Qualisteam   www.qualisteam.com
Thousands of banks and exchange sites

RealPlayer   www.realnetworks.com
Audio plug-ins

Sage Group   www.sage.com
Site of the UK accounting software giant

Search Engine Showdown   www.notess.com/search/stats/size.html
Search tools compared

The Big Hub   www.thebighub.com
Sleuth's new identity

The Internet Bookshop   www.bookshop.co.uk
UK forerunner of Amazon.com

UK Directory   www.ukdirectory.com
UK search tool

UK Invest   www.ukinvest.com
Freeserve's finance and investing channel

University of Strathclyde   www.dis.strath.ac.uk/business
Sources of business info on the net

Virtual Search Engine   www.dreamscape.com/frankvad/search.htm
Multiple search tool access point

Yahoo!   www.yahoo.co.uk
UK site from the original 'portal'
Finance-specific site   http://finance.yahoo.co.uk

Chapter 4: Online News and Opinion

Australian Financial Review   www.afr.com.au
Good site from Oz business paper

BBC   www.news.bbc.co.uk
News site from the 'Beeb'

Bloomburg   www.bloomburg.com
News site

Chicago Sun-Times   www.suntimes.com
Metro-Chicago daily's site

ClariNet   www.clari.net
Wholesale wire service news

CNN   www.cnn.com
Needs no introduction

CNNfn   www.cnnfn.com
CNN's financial news site

Deja   www.deja.com
Searching Usenet newsgroups

Electronic Share Information   www.esi.co.uk
*E*Trade's UK affiliate*

Electronic Telegraph   www.telegraph.co.uk
The original UK newspaper site, still good

Euromoney   www.euromoney.com
Superb financial news site

Forbes   www.forbes.com
The best of the US magazine sites

Handelsblatt   www.handelsblatt.de
The best German language newspaper site

Interactive Investor   www.iii.co.uk
Comprehensive personal finance site

Liszt   www.liszt.com
Email lists galore

Los Angeles Times   www.latimes.com
News from Tinseltown daily

Market Eye   www.market-eye.co.uk
Prices, news and opinion online

Motley Fool UK   www.fool.co.uk
Savvy UK bulletin board site

News 365   www.news365.com
Market news site of sites

Newslink   www.newslink.org
Links to online newspapers

Newsnow   www.newsnow.co.uk
Aggregated news stories with an IT bias

NewsUnlimited   www.newsunlimited.co.uk
The Guardian's searchable news archive

Press Association   www.pa.press.net
Good all-round news

PR Newswire   www.twoten.press.net
Press releases online

San Jose Mercury News   www.sjmercury.com
The 'Silicon Valley' daily

Sky   www.skynews.co.uk
Murdoch online

South African Financial Mail   www.fm.co.za
Jo'burg business daily

This Is Money   www.thisismoney.co.uk
Associated Newspapers' multi-paper site

Treasury   www.hm-treasury.gov.uk
Great George St's online presence

Yahoo! Finance   http://finance.yahoo.co.uk
Finance-specific search engine

Chapter 5: Share Prices, Company Data and Software Online

CAROL   www.carol.co.uk
Online annual reports

Citifeed   www.citifeed.co.uk
Market data site

DBC   www.dbeuro.com
Charts and data

Download.com   www.download.com
Download that software

ESI   www.esi.co.uk
E*Trades UK affiliate

File Pile   www.filepile.com
Big software site

Filez   www.filez.com
Downloadable programs

Freequotes   www.freequotes.co.uk
Sign up for the ISP to get free 'live' share prices

FT Annual Reports Service   www.icbinc.com
Online ordering of ARs

FTQuicken   www.ftquicken.com
Quicken's personal finance site

Hemscott.net   www.hemscott.net
Hemmington Scott's portal site with free REFs pages

Investorweb   www.financialweb.com
Redesigned financial portal

Investorsoftware   www.investorsoftware.com
Commercial software downloads

Market Eye   www.market-eye.co.uk
Prices, news and opinion online

Mathwiz   www.informatik.com
Financial calculator for download

MoneyXtra   www.moneyextra.com
Microsoft Money's site

MyTrack   www.mytrack.com
Track your shares online

Quote.com   www.my.quote.com
Classic quote site

SEC   www.sec.gov/edgarhp.htm
Edgar—a searchable index of SEC filings

Sharescope   www.sharescope.co.uk
Software producer's site

Shareware.com   www.shareware.com
More software downloads

Synergy Software   www.synergy-software.co.uk
Long-established UK software house

This Is Money   www.thisismoney.co.uk
Newspaper site offering a personalised service

UK Online Investing   www.ukonlineinvesting.com
Links to free research and other resources

Wall Street Directory   www.wsdinc.com
Download site for free and paid-for packages

Winsite   www.winsite.com
Download site

Winstock   www.winstock.co.uk
Home of 'The Analyst' chart software

Xest   www.xest.com
Online dealing from Charles Stanley

Yahoo!   http://finance.yahoo.co.uk
Finance page with a built-in quote server

Chapter 6: Company Information Online

Dow Jones Business Directory   http://bd.dowjones.com
Source of US corporate web sites

Financial Times   www.ft.com
The FT's excellent site

Fortune 500   http://pathfinder.com/fortune/fortune500.index.html
Ditto

FTSE International   www.ftse.com
Links to some 'footsie' company sites

NASDAQ   www.nasdaq.com
Links to NASDAQ-listed sites, prices etc.

Northcote Internet   www.northcote.co.uk
Links to some corporate sites

University of Strathclyde   www.dis.strath.ac.uk/business
Sheila Webber's Business Information Sources on the Internet

Chapter 7: The Online Investor in Action—Building up the Picture

AltaVista   www.altavista.com
Search site

DBC   www.dbceuro.com
Charting of share prices

Deutsche Borse   www.exchange.de
German stock exchange site

Deutsche Telekom   www.dtag.de
The German phone system provider

EDGAR Online   www.edgar-online.com
User friendly filing service operated by SEC

ESF   www.eurosalesfinance.com
Typical small UK company site

European Central Bank   www.ecb.int
So-so site from Frankfurt

Financewise   www.financewise.com
Specialist financial search tool

Forbes   www.forbes.com
One of the best free sources of business information on US companies

FT Annual Report Ordering Service   www.icbinc.com
Ordering annual reports

General Electric   www.ge.com
One of the best US corporate sites

Hemmington Scott   www.hemscott.com
Hemmington Scott's Company Guide

Northern Light   www.northernlight.com
Search tool

Richard Holway   www.holway.com
Site of UK computer company guru

Times   www.the-times.co.uk
News on the net from 'The Thunderer'

UK Factors and Discounters Association   www.factors.org.uk
Typical trade association site

Yahoo! UK Finance   http://finance.yahoo.co.uk
Yahoo!'s UK finance end

Chapter 8: Dealing Online

Datek   www.datek.com
Cheap US online broker

DLJ Direct   www.dljdirect.co.uk
New UK online brokering service

Goy Harris Cartwright   www.ghcl.co.uk
New online dealing service from the UK broker

JB Oxford   www.jboxford.com
US online broker

National Discount Brokers   www.ndb.com
Another US online broker

Schwab Europe   www.schwab-worldwide.com/europe
The broker formerly known as Sharelink

Xest   www.xest.com
Web dealing offshoot of Charles Stanley

Xolia   www.xolia.com
US brokers compared

Chapter 9: Personal Finance Online

AAA Investment Guide   www.wisebuy.co.uk
Background on personal finance topics

Aberdeen Prolific   www.iii.co.uk/aberdeen-prolific
Fund site

AIB Asset Management   www.aibgovett.com
Fund site

Allied Dunbar   www.allieddunbar.co.uk
Fund site

b2   www.b2.com
Barclay's new fangled fund manager

Bank of Scotland   www.bankofscotland.co.uk
Probity online

Bradford & Bingley   www.bradford-bingley.co.uk
Newly demutualised building society

Bristol & West   www.bristol-west.co.uk
Building society site

Citibank   www.citibank.com/uk
The site that never sleeps

Egg   www.egg.com
Online banking from the Pru

Equitable Life   www.equitable.co.uk
Excellent insurance company site

Exeter Fund Managers   www.moneyworld.co.uk/exeter
Fund site

Fidelity   www.fidelity.co.uk/ direct/
Get your ISA here

Financewise   www.financewise.com
Search for financial sites

FIND   www.find.co.uk
Search for UK financial sites

Flemings   www.flemings.lu
UK fund's Luxembourg site

Gartmore   www.iii.co.uk/gartmore
Natwest fund arm

Global Asset Management   www.ukinfo.gam.com
Fund site

Hamilton Direct Bank   www.hdb.co.uk
Online bank

Hill Samuel Asset Management   www.hillsamuel.co.uk
Fund site

Interactive Investor   www.iii.co.uk
Comprehensive PF site

Legal & General   www.landg.com
Insurance company site

Lloyds Bank   www.lloydsbank.co.uk
The site of the black horse

M&G   www.mandg.co.uk
Now with the Pru

Marks and Spencer   www.marks-and-spencer.co.uk/financial-services
High Street meets financial services

Martin Currie   www.martincurrie.com
Scottish fund managers

MoneyeXtra   www.moneyextra.com
Money's own site

Moneynet   www.moneynet.co.uk
Find the best bank loan or mortgage online

Moneyweb   www.moneyweb.co.uk
PF background from former IFA

MoneyWorld   www.moneyworld.co.uk
The UK personal finance site

Murray Johnstone   www.murrayj.com
Glasgow fund managers

Nationwide   www.nationwide.co.uk
Building Society turned bank

Norwich & Peterborough   www.norwichandpeterborough.co.uk
Banking online

Norwich Union   www.norwich-union.co.uk
Site that's part of the Union

Pearl   www.pearl.co.uk
Cover yourself in pearl?

Perpetual   www.perpetual.co.uk
Henley-based fund group

Premier Asset Management   www.premierfunds.co.uk
Fund site

Prudential   www.pru.co.uk
The mighty Pru

Royal Bank of Scotland   www.rbos.co.uk
Bank online with Scots

Sarasin Investment Management   www.sarasin.co.uk
Excellent site from a tech-aware fund group

Save & Prosper   www.prosper.co.uk
Fund site

Screentrade   www.screentrade.co.uk
Insurance quotes online

Singer & Friedlander   www.singer.co.uk
UK funds

Standard Life Investments   www.standardlifeinvestments.co.uk
Banking, investment and insurance online

TrustNet   www.trustnet.co.uk
Superb database of unit and investment trust stats

Woolwich   www.woolwich.co.uk
Building society site

Chapter 10: Futures and Options Online

Allinthemoney   www.allinthemoney.com
Educational material on derivatives

Applied Derivatives Trading   www.adtrading.com
Online options mag

CBOE   www.cboe.com
Chicago's finest online

Charles Schwab   www.schwab-worldwide.com/europe
It's that broker again

Futures and Options resources on the Web   http://w3.ag.uiuc.edu/ACE/ofor/
General site for options info   resource.htm

Futures and OTC World   www.fow.com
The industry mag

LIFFE   www.liffe.com
Liffe, the universe and everything

MBRM   www.mbrm.com
Professional options software

Nigel Webb Software Warp 9   www.warp9.org
Downloadable options pricer

Numa   www.numa.com
Lots of stuff on derivatives

Options Direct   www.options-direct.co.uk
Excellent broker site, with added downloads

OptionSource   www.optionsource.com
Data and software

Underground Software Group   www.tugsg.com
Home of The Covered Option Writer

UnionCAL   www.unioncal.com
UK options broker to the gentry

Wall Street Directory   www.wsdinc.com
Options software to buy online

Chapter 11: Bonds, Statistics and Economic Commentary Online

Alta Plana   http://altaplana.com/gate.html
Excellent general source of stats information

Bloomberg   www.bloomberg.co.uk
Bond prices and news online

Central Bureau of Statistics (Netherlands)   www.cbs.nl
Superb general stats resource

CFTC   www.cftc.gov
The US regulator online

Danish Statistical office   www.dst.dk
Figures for Denmark

Duff & Phelps   www.dcrco.com
Chicago based bond rating agency

Eire CSO   www.cso.ie
Stats of Southern Ireland

EU Europa   www.europa.eu.int
Slow server in Brussels

Federal Reserve   www.bog.frb.fed.us
News releases

Fedstats   www.fedstats.gov
US Federal stats online

Fitch ICBA   www.fitchicba.com
Bond ratings and research online

FSA   www.fsa.gov.uk
UK regulator's site

FSBR   www.whitehouse.gov/fsbr
Links to statistics

Germany's Federal Statistics Office   www.statistik-bund.de
Stats for Deutscheland

INSEE   www.insee.fr
Hard-to-access French statistics

Inter-American Development Bank   www.iadb.org
Interesting supranational site

Intermoney   www.intermoney.com
Pithy commentary on bonds and economics

JP Morgan   www.jpmorgan.com
Bond experts online

Kauders Investment Management   www.gilt.co.uk
Gilts info online

Lombard Street Research   www.lombard-st.co.uk
Excellent economic research site

Mark Bernkopf   www.patriot.net/users/bernkopf
Central banks links on the web

Merrill Lynch   www.askmerrill.com
Online research from The Thundering Herd

Money & Bonds   www.moneyandbonds.com
Bond prices etc., at a price

Moodys   www.moodys.com/economic
Ratings online

Norway Statistical Bureau   www.ssb.no
Norwegian stats

OECD   www.oecd.org
Rich world statistics

Qualisteam   www.qualisteam.com
Banks on the net

Salomon Smith Barney   www.sbil.co.uk
Salomon research

SEC   www.sec.gov
US market regulator

Singapore Statistics   www.singstat.gov.sg
Singapore data online

Singapore University   www.ntu.edu.sg/library/statdata.htm
Excellent general stats source

Standard & Poors   www.ratings.standardpoor.com
More online ratings

Statisikaamet   www.stat.ee
Excellent stats site from Estonia

Statistics Canada   www.statcan.ca
As its name suggests

Statistics South Africa   www.statssa.gov.za
Stats from the Southern Hemisphere

Stat-USA   www.stat-usa.gov
Another US statistics organisation

Sweden's Statistical Office   www.scb.sc
More Scand stats

Federal Reserve   http://bog.frb.usa/releases
Superbly detailed releases from the Fed

Financial Statistics Briefing Room   www.whitehouse.gov/fsbr
Ditto

Office for National Statistics   www.ons.gov.uk
UK stats site—could do better

The Syndicate   www.moneypages.com/syndicate/bonds
Bond background online

US Census Bureau   www.census.gov/main/www/stat.int/html
Excellent statistics links worldwide

World Bank   www.worldbank.org
It had to have a site . . .

World Trade Organisation   www.wto.org
. . . but why did it bother?

Treasury   www.hm-treasury.gov.uk
UK financial mandarins online

Turkey Statistics Department   www.die.gov.tr
Heavy design but interesting content

Yardeni Economic Network   www.yardeni.com
Superb economics site from Dr Ed

Index